Suzy Gershman's

Born to Shop

Italy

The Ultimate Guide for Travelers Who Love to Shop

12th Edition

1807 WILEY 2007 BICENTENNIAL

Wiley Publishing, Inc.

For Egon von Furstenberg and Maria Teresa Berdondini, who gave me so much of Italy and so much of themselves, and who changed my life forever, with love and thanks.

Published by:

Wiley Publishing, Inc.
111 River St.
Hoboken, NJ 07030-5774

ISBN: 978-0-470-14666-8

Editor: Leslie Shen
Production Editor: Suzanna R. Thompson
Cartographer: Andrew Murphy
Photo Editor: Richard Fox
Anniversary Logo Design: Richard Pacifico
Production by Wiley Indianapolis Composition Services

For information on our other products and services or to obtain technical support, please contact our Customer Care Department within the U.S. at 800/762-2974, outside the U.S. at 317/572-3993 or fax 317/572-4002.

Wiley also publishes its books in a variety of electronic formats. Some content that appears in print may not be available in electronic formats.

Manufactured in the United States of America

5 4 3 2 1

CONTENTS

1	The Best of Italy in an Instant	1
2	Details	11
3	Italian Style	54
4	Rome	63
5	Beyond Rome: Naples & the Amalfi Coast	103
6	Florence	123
7	Venice	179
8	Milan	223
9	The Riviera	292
10	Hidden Italy	308
	Index	331

MAP LIST

Rome & Its Shopping Neighborhoods	70
Via dei Coronari	87
Naples	105
Florence	127
Venice Orientation	185
Central Venice	187
Milan	229
Navigli	249
Bologna	311
Verona	325

Although every effort has been made to ensure the accuracy of prices appearing in this book, please keep in mind that with inflation and a fluctuating rate of exchange, prices will vary. In this edition, prices are quoted in U.S. dollars ($) and euros (€). Dollar estimates have been made at the exchange rate of 1€ = $1.30.

ABOUT THE AUTHORS

Suzy Gershman is a journalist, author, and global-shopping goddess who has worked in the fashion and fiber industry for more than 25 years. Her essays on retailing have been used by the Harvard School of Business; her reportage on travel and retail has appeared in *Travel + Leisure, Travel Holiday, Travel Weekly,* and most of the major women's magazines. She is translated into French for Condé Nast's *Air France Madame* magazine and writes a shopping column about cruise destinations for *Porthole Magazine.* Suzy is also the author of *C'est La Vie* (Penguin Paperback), the story of her first year as a widow living in Paris. In March 2008, Wiley will publish her guide to world shopping, *Where to Buy the Best of Everything: The Outspoken Guide for World Travelers & Online Shoppers.* She recently sold her flat in Paris and now divides her time between San Antonio, Texas (her childhood home); a small house in Provence; and the airport.

Suzy also gives shopping tours. Visit www.suzygershman.com or write to suzy@suzygershman.com for details.

Sarah Lahey has worked as news director for Born to Shop for 3 years and will become editorial director in the near future. Her responsibilities include researching for revisions, writing additional listings, and telling Suzy that she isn't really fat. Sarah shows and sells English smalls at several northern California antiques fairs and also sells on eBay. She lives with her husband and two dogs, Bentley and Beckham, and travels extensively to research and rewrite Born to Shop editions.

Jennifer McCormick is a paralegal in Los Angeles and works as editor and destination expert for a content provider. She also reports for Born to Shop and carries an expensive handbag.

Aaron Gershman is a singer-songwriter who lives and sings in Los Angeles; he is also a contributing editor for Born to Shop.

TO START WITH

This is a disturbing confession, but here goes: I have most of my money in euros and I use the French—that is, European—banking system because I have been a French resident for the last 7 years. That understood, I still find that prices in Europe are high and a trip to Italy these days is enough to make you pull out your hair and scream, "*Mamma mia!*"

Don't pull out too much hair, though, because we did find a wonderful deal on the best shampoo in the world. More on that later.

This book has always been different from other titles in the series because Italy has so many primary shopping cities. This edition is packed with even more destinations—with luck, someday we'll expand to two books with even more details. I feel like more and more people are interested in driving around, in renting a summer home, and maybe even in purchasing a second or retirement home. I strongly believe that getting out of the tourist towns and into the hidden parts will save you money and delight you and your family.

The fall of the dollar has made me especially sensitive to prices. Besides, with prices as high as they are, I think that more and more people are interested in outlets and local sources, which tend to be out of the major cities. I found Florence so filled with tourists (and it wasn't even "in season") that I can't imagine anyone thinking this would be fun.

I hope some of my extra side trips will inspire you to reach out past the big cities and to slow down, smell the slow food, and buy a little olive oil. There are more factory outlets in this edition, and there's also more information about arranging for someone to drive you into the countryside if you do not want to drive yourself.

In order to make this book as accurate, up to date, and fresh as possible, I did a lot of driving around Italy and leaned on many friends, Italian and American-Italian. These pages, and my heart, are totally indebted to Logan Bentley (as always), Maria Teresa Berdondini, and Sarah Lahey. Special thanks to Karen Preston and the guys at Leading Hotels of the World in New York, who helped me organize most of my stays. I would also like to thank the general managers and the entire front-desk team at the various Baglioni hotels, who assisted me with everything from insider information to special Born to Shop rates and map printouts to help me on my way. Frederico Pollenti guided the way and everyone helped out.

My dog, Toffee, who went on this research trip, wants you to know that Italy is great, but if he has to pick one place to stay forever, he's left his heart at the Villa d'Este—where he was allowed to scamper up and down the wide and glorious halls to his personal delight.

Chapter One

THE BEST OF ITALY IN AN INSTANT

Italy has more style per square mile than you can shake a *formaggio* at, especially in the northern regions. The south has more *limoncello,* that delectable lemon liqueur that makes me tipsy after one thimbleful. Wherever your travels take you, I know you'll find a lot to buy and a lot more to enjoy.

Things are expensive, though. Yup, even that glass of limoncello is dear. (I paid $20 for a Bellini at Harry's Bar!) Prices have gone up, while meanwhile the dollar has gone to a new low against the euro. Thankfully, there's still plenty to buy—and even a few bargains to be had.

If you're in a hurry, you may want to breeze through what I consider some of the highlights of the whole country, crammed into these pages up front, so when you stop by these places, you can worship and shop and feel like you've indulged in a tiny taste of Italy.

By no means is my list comprehensive; it will take years for me to perfect it, so bear with me while I shop, shop, shop.

The Best Store in Italy

10 CORSO COMO
10 Corso Como, Milan.

No, that's not a typo; the store's name is its address. And it's even added on a three-room hotel called, you guessed it, Three Rooms.

There's much more written about this store in the Milan chapter (see chapter 8), but suffice it to say that this is a bazaar, a magic act created by one of Italy's most famous fashion editors and stylists who turned to retail and hasn't looked back.

The store is well bought, but for people who shop a lot, there are no surprises in terms of merchandise. What's yummy is the way it's laid out and presented and served on your platter. You can gawk and enjoy and not buy a thing, but don't miss it. Note the cafe (speaking of served on a platter), the furniture in the garden, and the upstairs bookstore. ✆ **02/2900-2674.** www.10corsocomo.com.

The Second-Best Store in Italy

VENETIA STUDIUM
Multiple locations in Venice.

Fortuny-inspired pleated silks made into wraps, bags, flowers, tassels, and treasures . . . a wonderland of fairy tales and dreams in colors that will make you swoon. There are several shops in Venice and one in London (go figure). Studium sells clothes and Fortuny chandeliers as well. ✆ **041/522-9281** or 041/522-9859. www.venetiastudium.com.

The Best Grand-Scale Shopping City

MILAN
Milan may not be adorable or overwhelmingly charming or flashy, but the shopping is divine. One reason is that Milan offers high-quality goods in many different price ranges. The city has excellent alternative retail—street markets, jobbers who sell discounted designer clothing, and more—all of which help you to make do with less. Less is always more, as Mother used to say.

The Best Small Shopping City

DERUTA
Italy is filled with tiny cities, devoted to craftspeople and artists, where shopping has been elevated to an art form. But the best

Suzy's Five Best Buys in Italy

- Yohji Yamamoto blazer, from outlet store, $300.
- Ferragamo bronze suede slip-on mocs, from outlet store, $200.
- Armani men's sports coat for my beloved, from outlet store, $165.
- Tablecloth from Lisa Corti, Florence, $90.
- Crystal drop earrings from Astolfo, Venice, $60.

of them all is the city of Deruta, in Umbria, where every store sells hand-painted faience (a style of ceramics). Deruta is about 2 hours from Florence.

The Best Port City for a Quick Spree

VENICE
Venice is not included on every Mediterranean cruise, but if you can get here, even if only for a day, do—it is magic. The shopping isn't bad either.

The Best Factory Outlet: North

FACTORY STORE (GIORGIO ARMANI)
Vertemate.

There are Armani outlets dotted all over Italy, but this one is the best. It's a tad hard to find, situated near Bregnano (which is between Milan and Como), and once you get there the building is marked only with the words FACTORY STORE (seriously), but once inside you are talking clothes for men, women, and children, plus lingerie and home style and accessories—all at very affordable prices. ✆ **031/887-373.**

The Best Factory Outlet: South

THE MALL
Via Europa 8, Leccio.

About 45 minutes outside Florence and not far from the Prada outlet, you get an outlet mall with the unfortunate name of The Mall. But it's got big-name designer outlets such as Gucci, Pucci, Burberry, Yohji, Ferragamo, and Tod's—to name just a few. ✆ **055/865-7775.** www.outlet-the-mall.com.

The Best Outlet Malls

Eeeny, meeny, miney, moe . . . I'm going with **Barberino Designer Outlet** (✆ **055/842-161;** www.mcarthurglen.it) because it knocked my socks off. Also, it's not far north of Florence—it's actually midway between Florence and Bologna—so you are well situated for all sorts of bargains in a number of different outlets and malls.

As runner-up, I have to name **Serravalle Designer Outlet** (✆ **0143/609-000;** www.mcarthurglen.it), the mother of all Italian outlets. This large village-style mall is between Milan and Genoa.

Sarah's Five Best Buys in Italy

- Frette Euro-size pillow shams, from the Piazza VIII Agosto market in Bologna, $13.
- Gold sparkly ballet slippers, from the Centrale train station in Milan, $25.
- Tod's suede driving mocs, from The Mall outlet village outside Florence, $150.
- Silk-and-velvet flower pins, from Venetia Studium, Venice, $30 each.
- 36-inch Murano glass and crystal necklace, from Murano, $100.

The Best Airport Shopping

LEONARDO DA VINCI INTERNATIONAL AIRPORT
Rome.

It's a virtual shopping mall, with all major designers represented. Furthermore, a guide to its shops, which lists prices, is made available once a year. Use it to comparison-shop. Not everything is a bargain, but you'll have a great time finding out which items are well priced.

The Best Sales

FENDI
Via Borgognona 39, Rome.

You haven't lived until you've wandered into the Fendi store in Rome at sale time—twice a year, January and July. There are mounds of goodies (some of them a few seasons old) selling at a fraction of their regular price. Affordable luxury goods!

While Fendi sales are good at all Fendi shops, the best sale is in this Rome location. From a design perspective, it is the most fun-to-look-at shop in the Spanish Steps luxury shopping district; to get a sale and an eyeful of glamour at one time is indeed to see the face of bliss. ✆ **06/696-661.** www.fendi.com.

The Best Department Store

LA RINASCENTE
Piazza del Duomo, Milan.

In response to competition, La Rinascente has redone its image and redone its interior. The store is a lot like an American department store and may not impress you at first. But wait until you experience the details—that's where its greatness lies. The store offers non-Italian-passport holders a flat 10% discount on health, beauty, and makeup treatments on the first floor. And there's a tax-free office upstairs, as well as a travel agency, hair salon, and full-service bank. The cafe overlooks the

Duomo and will drench you with magic and memories. ✆ 02/88-521. www.rinascente.it.

The Best Historic Shopping Experience

ANTICO SETIFICIO FIORENTINO
Via Bartolini 4, Florence.

You will step back in time when you enter this 18th-century silk factory that was renovated by the Pucci family. It still produces damasks, silks, and cottons on looms that have hummed for hundreds of years. ✆ 055/213-861. www.setificio fiorentino.it.

The Best Street Market

MERCATO DI VIALE PAPINIANO (SAN AGOSTINO MARKET)
Tuesday and Saturday on Viale Papiniano, Milan.

Fun? It just doesn't get much better than this! Two days a week, you have a chance to enjoy this fabulous street market, which sells fruits and vegetables in one part and designer goods in the other. Arrange your visit to Milan so that you're in town for one of the market days!

The Best Weekly Market (Runner-Up to Best Street Market)

SIENA MARKET
Wednesday in Siena.

I have been to a fair number of markets in my life, and celebrated market day in a large number of cities all over the world, so when I say this is one of the best, I really mean it.

It helps if the sky is blue, the sun is shining, the temperature is not too high, and the crowds aren't too bad. Yeah, sure. If you come by car, it also helps if you can find a parking space.

But any way you slice it, this is a market for locals, filled to overflowing with everything from shoes to tractors. It takes up a half-moon area at the top of town and is thoughtfully organized by category of goods, with foodstuffs to one side and dry goods on the other. Sometimes you find name-brand closeouts for low prices. But you go for the glory, not the shoes.

The Best Affordable Clothes

OVIESSE
Multiple locations in cities all over Italy.

Owned by the department store Coin, Oviesse is the Italian fashion version of Target, with clothes and accessories for all members of the family. There's a good plus-size department for women, too. On the last visit, I bought one of my best outfits of the summer here: beige drawstring linen trousers with a linen blazer—$100 for the two pieces. www.oviesse.it.

The Best Hotel Gift Shop: North

VILLA D'ESTE
Via Regina 40, Cernobbio (near Como).

It's rare for a gift shop to so perfectly sum up both the clients and their aspirations, but the shops at Villa d'Este do that, with their own branded merchandise as well as a store of men's and women's clothing from nearby mills such as Lora Piana. © **031/3481.** www.villadeste.it.

The Best Hotel Gift Shop: South

EMPORIO LE SIRENUSE
Via Colombo 30, Positano.

Emporio Le Sirenuse, across from the hotel of the same name, is attuned to both sophistication and a relaxed lifestyle, offering handpicked resort wear as well as home style. This is where I first fell in love with Lisa Corti's colorful fabrics. There is also a catalog and online business. © **089/812-2026.** www.emporiosirenuse.com.

The Best Gifts for $10 or Less

- **Designer pasta in fashion colors:** Find it in all sorts of brand names, in all Italian cities, in grocery stores, *enotecas* (wine/food shops), and TTs (tourist traps); $6 to $10 a package.
- **Regional pasta:** As an alternative to designer pasta, look for regional specialties of pastas. Barilla, which is the largest maker of pasta in Italy, creates specific "designs" for specific markets. In Venice, I bought Casarecce, a style only available there. Go figure. For less than $2, I look like a genius to a foodie.
- **Chocolate postcards:** I wouldn't try mailing these as I suspect they will crumble, but they are darn cute gifties. Caffarel, a mass maker of chocolates, does a series of postcards called "Italy's Treasures" that depict famous historic sites. I found a selection of "cards" representing five different cities, all for sale in the main Milan train station.
- **Bellini mix:** Sold in delis, wine shops, and street market stalls, this peach purée mixes with Champagne or Proscecco to make classic Bellini cocktails. Available in two sizes, the small 20cl bottle costs $8 (less than half the price of a Bellini at Harry's Bar) and makes four cocktails.
- **Limoncello liqueur:** Sold most readily in southern Italy below Florence and in most supermarkets and airports, this is a wonderful souvenir. It's like lemon vodka with a pucker; serve chilled.
- **Milk-frothing machine:** This battery-operated job looks like a small wand and makes the milk in your cappuccino stand up and smile. I found the old-fashioned ones in a market in Rome for $10, and in an appliance store in Florence for $15. Then I found a new, modern, and well-designed one for $18 in Siena. Seek and ye shall froth.
- **Soap:** Try Weekend Soap from the Farmaceutica di Santa Maria Novella stores in Florence and Rome. The 9€ ($12) package consists of three bars of soap, one each for Friday, Saturday, and Sunday.

  Or pick up any of Rancé's soaps sold from its free-standing store in Rome at Piazza Navona. Rancé sounds French because the firm was started in France 100 years ago, but it's now Italian (although it does specialize in Marseille process soaps).

You can also buy Italian soaps in grocery stores or at any *erborista* (herbalist).

- **Lush gifties:** Yes, Lush is a British firm famous for its bath and beauty products, and yes, there are now Lush stores in the U.S., but the Italian Lush products are made with local ingredients, so you can buy limoncello soap or shampoo. There are branch locations all over Italy, often in mainstream tourist areas.
- **Cardinal's socks:** Sold only in Rome, at about 8€ ($10) a pair. Fine cotton knits; they come only in red. Of course.

The Greatest Gift of Love

This was just too important to me to let common sense take over, so I bought three tall bottles of **olive oil** for Aaron and Jenny. Not any three, mind you, but samples of the Ligurian, Umbrian, and Tuscan oils so they could taste the difference.

Then I had to wrap each bottle in masking tape and then bubble wrap and then bag each in plastic and then wrap each in clothes that could be washed, just in case. I won't mention how much room they took up in the suitcase or what they weighed.

No greater love hath a foodie mother for her son who likes to cook.

Buyer Beware

When giving extravagant gifts of love, be sure that the recipient recognizes the value of the gift. We spent almost $100 on a small bottle of balsamic vinegar for a business contact and I swear, despite the fact that he's Italian and should know better, his weak "thank you" seemed to say that he didn't know the grocery-store stuff from the blue-blooded stuff. A gift only works when the recipient appreciates it.

The Best Extravagant Gifts

- **Important art glass:** Venice or Murano. Expect to pay $500 for a hefty vase. Shipping will be $50 to $100 more.
- **Jewelry from any of the new Venetian bead maidens:** Look for something in the $100-to-$200 range. Also consider jeweled or beaded sandals for the Cleopatra in your sole.
- **Gucci dog collar:** Hmm, Gucci anything. Gucci outlet, anyone? It's outside Florence.
- **Suede mocs in an oddball but divine color:** I bought a chrome-yellow pair a few years ago and this year got lime green. The odder the color, the better they go with everything. Try to buy at an outlet for $125 to $150 unless you are forced to go the distance and pay $300 at regular retail.
- **Etro paisleys:** Silk or cashmere; in all Etro stores, in most major cities . . . but then, maybe you can find them at the Etro outlet in beautiful downtown Milano.

Chapter Two

DETAILS

WELCOME TO ITALY

I'm not sure when you were last in Italy, but my heavens, *madonna mia,* have things gotten expensive. That doesn't mean I didn't find $20 shoes, $5 gifts, and designer clothes to drool for; it just means I suffered some sticker shock before I realized I had to really dig to find things I wanted that I could also afford.

Italian prices have gone up, up, and then up again so that locals complain about their cost of living and the government complains that it can't afford the maintenance on the landmarks. Seriously, folks. There's the possibility that the Italian national monuments will be leased out or perhaps sold to private firms. So along with the Rose Bowl and the Orange Bowl being sponsored events and corporate stadiums, you might have the Enron Leaning Tower of Pisa . . . or maybe the Pizza Hut Leaning Tower of Pisa. I kind of like that one.

When lire were converted into euros, the official exchange rate was essentially two to one, but prices are now so high that things cost in euros what they cost in lire. That means prices are perceived as being twice as high. Not prices for tourists, mind you, but prices for everything and everyone, even the government.

Gas costs $7 a gallon. Need I say more?

Thank heavens spaghetti is still cheap, so even with high prices, careful shoppers will rejoice. Bring on the cheap shoes!

Lo Shopping

It's possible the Italians invented modern shopping—maybe not trade, but certainly aspects of the current art form of shopping, such as browsing and finding the newest new thing, everywhere from markets to malls. Some of it was borrowed from the Chinese when Marco Polo brought magic from China to the Old World, but Marco's fine eye and curious shopping skills only created the foundation and set the pace for generations to come. There have been lots of other influences, especially lately.

Meanwhile, the French are making a big contribution to Italian style. French designers have, for years, produced their clothing in Italy. Everyone knows that Karl Lagerfeld (a German Frenchman at that) has designed the Fendi furs for decades. Now the French are getting into an Italian mood with some serious spin—for starters, French architect-cum-designer Philippe Starck has created a New Age lion for the gates of Venice and moved there. Sephora, the French-born beauty supermarket that's now international in scope, has a huge store in the Rome train station and other locations dotted all over Italy. And these days one of the best ways to get to Italy is on a low-cost flight from France. In fact, in this edition I will prove that your trip to Italy actually begins in France. Read on.

Italian Contrasts

As you shop in Italy, you can appreciate views of hills as old as the ages, peeling palazzi with tile roofs and handmade wrought-iron gates and window grills, masterful antiques, and then whammo!—smack in the middle of it all, tables perched precariously on bent triangles, clothes in medieval colors, shoes and bags in styles you've never thought of, and a pride of craftsmanship in absolutely everything.

At the same time, in today's Italy you'll find that flea markets and antiques fairs are bigger than ever, and that Italians have taken seriously to resale and to outlet shopping—several new outlets and outlet malls have opened recently.

Most shocking, you'll soon discover that even though the Italian border hasn't moved, many Italians are going to stores and spas in Slovenia and Croatia. Dubrovnik is just a boat ride away. In fact, Croatia is the newest link to the eastern Riviera. Everyone is getting creative in order to have fun, eat well, and shop a little.

GETTING THERE

From the U.S.

You'll find the best fares for direct flights from the U.S. to Italy if you latch on to a new gate or a promotional rate, or even the launch of a code share . . . so watch local papers closely.

It may even pay to make a domestic hop to a nearby city if direct flights to Italy have just begun to be offered from there. Ask your travel agent.

You can always go via New York; explore other options if you are looking for a price break. Note that deregulation of intra-European flights has brought on all sorts of new choices and that many low-cost European carriers specialize in getting folks to Italy.

You might also want to remember that Italians still have a tendency to declare a strike—or even threaten a strike—every time someone gets PMS. Backup plans (and planes) are a good idea; also stay away from those carriers that are more prone to strikes than others. Always check your trains before you go to the station. Strikes are usually posted in the *International Herald Tribune*.

Alitalia (www.alitalia.com), the Italian national carrier, has various flights and connections from the U.S. to Italy but doesn't play by the same promotional rules as U.S. carriers. It is also being denationalized and trying to fend off the low-cost carriers, so watch for competitive prices.

I usually fly **Delta Air Lines** (www.delta.com), partly because I can go into Milan and come out of Rome without much ado. Delta also has code shares with several other airlines—thus allowing me to use Paris as a hub (traveling onward with Air France). For this edition, we used Nice as our entry point to Italy (it's a great trick—see p. 17).

Note that Delta is one of those airlines that did away with regular first class and instead installed Business First, which is much more first class at a business-class price than any other business-class seat on other airlines. If value is related to the size of your seat, and you tend to splurge on business class or upgrade travel, this is the way to go.

American Airlines (www.aa.com) has service from Chicago to Milan and from New York to Rome. Note that American still has three classes of service.

United Airlines (www.united.com) offers daily nonstops to Rome from Dulles in Washington, D.C.

US Airways (www.usairways.com) has service from Philly to Rome. In fact, most carriers, in conjunction with their code-share partners, have a way to get you to Italy with minimum stress.

From London & Continental Europe

Low-cost airlines have made a huge dent in the Italian tourism business, especially flights from the United Kingdom. Sometimes **British Airways** (www.ba.com), **Air France** (www.airfrance.com), and **Alitalia** (www.alitalia.com) get so annoyed at these discounters that they go to war with low, low fares.

BA recently advertised promotional one-way fares from Gatwick to Pisa at £39—for an American traveler, that's about $80. The price includes all taxes and fees and therefore represents a nice bargain.

There are also train and plane wars, since the rail companies want to make sure those who fly the low-cost carriers know there are other alternatives, especially for short hops. A recent promotion for **SNCF** (www.voyages-sncf.com), the French

Best Deals

- Book online. Or at least check it out. Look at regular carriers as well as brokers for discount tickets. I was amazed (maybe because I am unsophisticated in these things) to learn that many airlines have two different sites with different kinds of deals. So if you check out alitaliausa.com, you get deals created just for the American market; there's another site (in another language) for other deals.
- Compare deals on the airlines' sites to the discount offerings—although many airlines say their sites offer the best deals, for the research for this book I found regular sites offering summer fares from JFK to Rome for $2,000+ while the discount websites had fares ranging from $780 to $1,036. All of the discounted flights were on well-known carriers; many required a change of planes in London, but to save that much money, I'd willingly change planes on the moon. I found good fares on travelocity.com, expedia.com, and cheapflights.com.
- Book off season. Off-season travel always offers better value.
- Look at packages and promotional rates that have inclusive perks. Breakfast these days is very expensive, so if you can get air, hotel, and breakfast combined in one deal, you may score savings.
- Book specialty tours that include everything and are prepaid in dollars. The way the dollar is going, you don't want any nasty surprises or escalating costs. If the dollar goes back to its previously strong position, buy Italy.
- Use up your miles. You can usually get the awards you want by booking 9 months in advance (which for most carriers is when they open bookings).
- Consider low-cost carriers. Some of them (such as Eurofly) have long-haul service from the U.S., while others have service from European cities. It may pay to fly one carrier into London and then connect to your low-cost carrier of choice. Just be sure you match airports and luggage weight requirements, as many low-cost carriers allow less weight and are strict on these rules.

national train system, offered second-class TGV (fast train) tickets from Paris to Milan or Turin for 25€ ($33), or first-class seats for 70€ ($91); you could also book an overnight berth on a slower train for 35€ ($46).

Trenitalia (www.trenitalia.com), the Italian national rail company, had the same promotion; look for "Smart Price" bargains on the website.

Many of the low-cost airlines have gone out of business or merged with others, so I can't promise this will be around when you are ready to travel, but you might want to look into **Volare** (www.volareweb.com), an Italian airline that serves Paris from the Beauvais airport and flies to Milan's Malpensa, Venice's Marco Polo, and also to Bari. When it has promotional deals, one leg on a round-trip ticket can cost as little as 1€ ($1.30) . . . with a 3€ ($3.90) supplement for security.

Sometimes you'll save money by flying into a European city and getting a low-cost flight from there. Do make sure you know which airport you are using, however—many low-cost airlines use alternative airports. This can be especially important when you think you are flying to Venice, since the regular airport (Marco Polo) is slightly out of town and the alternative airport is significantly out of town.

Some thoughts: **Air One** (www.flyairone.it) is a division of Lufthansa and offers flights beginning at $75. **Air Berlin** (www.airberlin.com) flies to Milan from many German cities (not just Berlin). From Paris, take **Vueling** (www.vueling.com) to Milan's Malpensa, Venice, Pisa, Naples, or Rome. **Ryanair** (www.ryanair.com) flies from London's Stansted to Turin, Milan, Treviso, Trieste, Genoa, Pisa, Ancona, and Rome, with additional service from Brussels and Frankfurt to a handful of Italian cities. Meanwhile, **easyJet** (www.easyjet.com) flies from London's Gatwick to assorted cities including Palermo. **BMI** (www.flybmi.com) prides itself on what it calls its "cheap flight" program.

Meridiana (www.meridiana.it) is an Italian carrier with small planes that serve a remarkable number of cities. Its online "shopping calendar" feature leads you to the best of the fares—for example, Catania (Sicily) to Florence for 45€ ($59). It's terrific for intra-Italian flights.

If you don't know where some of the aforementioned cities are, look at a map. Also check to see if new destinations or airports are available.

Another option is crossing the channel and connecting to sleeper trains, which are usually routed through Paris. At certain times of the year, British Airways does a promotion that offers a free layover in London to passengers with ongoing outbound flights. These fares are dramatically priced and should be considered, even if you hadn't at first thought about adding on a British stopover.

Secret Cities

If you are coming from another European country via train, try combining your U.S.-bought train passes. A complete Eurailpass may be a wasted value, especially if you are just visiting two countries (say, France and Italy). Nowadays, however, there are so many different types of rail passes that it pays to figure out which kind is best for you.

If you are flying between connecting European cities, price your tickets carefully. I needed to go to Rome and priced the airfare both from Zurich and from Nice, and found Nice offered me a $500 savings. If I'd had the Swissair pass program, it would have been less money, but since I didn't, I could just call my travel agent and pray. French prayers were answered.

For Americans, the various air-pass systems offered by different carriers can be a lifesaver—surely a fare saver. But they do have restrictions and must be bought in the U.S. before you depart.

Keep in mind: The city of Nice (in France) is only 229 miles from Milan and a little more than a 1-hour drive from the Italian border. If you are a Delta customer, as I am, note that you can travel to Italy by flying to Nice, Milan, or Rome. If you are driving around northern Italy, or combining the two Rivieras (Italian and French), this is even better—as you'll be in Torino in no time at all.

To depart from Italy through Nice, you can take the train from Milan to Nice, or even from Venice to Nice (this is an overnight journey and saves on a hotel room), or you can fly (a 1-hr. flight).

Also note that since Nice is the turnaround point on the train lines, you may want to simply hop on the overnight train to Rome, or points south. This involves a transfer from the Nice airport to the Nice train station, which can be done by bus or taxi.

As a historical note, Nice—along with the part of France that lies between it and the current border—has for centuries gone back and forth between France and Italy. Monaco, which is now covered in this guide, prints information in three languages: English, French, and Italian. The Grimaldis have been considered Italian princes and French as well.

Specialty Shopping Tours

I've just started doing an annual Italian Born to Shop tour—go to www.suzygershman.com for details on the next trip. The last one included Florence and Milan, with a side trip to outlets and a few insider treats.

Two companies offer trips to various Euro cities that include airfare, hotel, and an antiques dealer to help you—try **Antiques Abroad Ltd.** (© 704-332-5577; www.antiqueslimited.com) or **Through the Looking Glass** (© 800-640-2269; www.throughthelookingglass.com). Both companies have Italian antiques shopping packages for about $2,500; their expert goes with you and helps with shipping and shopping.

Some hotels offer special shopping packages. For instance, Milan's Principe di Savoia has an Outlet Weekend Package that includes a trip across the border into Switzerland for the FoxTown outlet mall. For more on FoxTown, see p. 45.

GETTING AROUND IN ITALY

By Plane

Most intra-European flights are outrageously expensive. However, as European skies deregulate, new local services are popping up. There are now air wars over business travelers flying between Rome and Milan, a 20-minute trip. **Alitalia** flies this corridor, of course, but so do some upstarts, and now **Lufthansa** has gotten into the action by going into partnership with **Air One.** Also check out **Meridiana,** mentioned above. Check with your travel agent for details.

Note that prices may vary based on the time of day. Usually, flights between 11am and 3pm are 40% cheaper than early-morning and late-afternoon flights.

Alitalia also has advance-purchase deals: If you buy your tickets 7 days in advance, you get a 40% discount; 14 days, 50%; and 21 days, 55% off. Not bad.

By Train

I just can't imagine driving around Italy when you can take a train to the big cities and then rent a car to explore the countryside for a day or two.

Or stay in cities where you don't even need a car.

This edition was researched mostly on road trips, but for Venice and Rome, I left the car parked in other cities and hopped on the train.

While train fares from city to city are not expensive (especially in second class), your best buy is an Italian rail pass, which can be purchased through a travel agent or **Rail Europe** in the U.S. before you leave. Call ✆ **800/361-RAIL** or (also toll-free) 888/382-7245, or go to www.raileurope.com. You can not only book online but also compare products and get promotional offers.

The price of the rail pass, which comes in a variety of flavors, depends on many factors, including the class you choose and the number of days you actually want to travel within a given 2-month period. The kids—ages 22 and 23 for this research trip—bought passes for those ages 12 to 26, which offer second-class travel at a low rate.

On my first trips to Italy, I purchased first-class passes; thereafter, I switched to second class. I usually pay about $200 for a 5-day second-class pass, and it's good for unlimited travel on all trains, including the luxury Eurostar, the faster IC (Inter-City) trains, and the *rapido*.

I have also used the three-country Eurailpass and splurged on first-class seats. I flew into Milan and out of Nice, and used the Eurailpass to connect to Venice, Geneva, and Monte Carlo before returning to Nice. I got five train rides for about $300, which I thought was a fabulous bargain.

On my most recent trip, we were doing short hops at short notice and just asked for the schedule at our hotels and then went to the train station. In most cases, a first-class seat was $10 to $15 more than a second-class seat. There was no charge for Toffee, my long-haired dachshund (on French trains he is required to have a dog ticket).

Reservations Required

If you have a first-class ticket and a reservation, which are two completely different things (and are even purchased separately), you will not have to worry about finding a seat on a crowded train—which can be hairy, especially if you are schlepping luggage with you.

Having a rail pass does not mean you have a specific reservation—so plan ahead and book one if you will need it. Note that reservations in Italy are one of the items that have gone sky-high, price-wise. They cost 8€ ($10) each, which for me was enough of a reason to not book one and take my chances instead.

There are extra *supplemento* charges for some trains, and reservations are required—even with the rail pass—for others. I suggested that Aaron and Jenny save the cost of reservations, but they ended up paying a fine (32€/$42 each) when they got onboard. *Mea culpa!*

Curious You

Do note that some trains are called **Eurostar Italia.** These trains do not go through the Chunnel, but they are new, fast, and deluxe. And expensive. They even come with a cute little boxed snack. Such trains are marked "ES" on the schedule or the big board in the station.

By Car

If you want to drive around Italy, reserve your car in the U.S. before departure, using a prepaid plan. It will be half the price you'd be charged in Italy—even if you reserve through an American rental agency, such as **Avis** (© **800/331-1084;** www.avis.com) or **Hertz** (© **800/654-3001;** www.hertz.com). The Italian division of Thrifty, **Thrifty By Car** (© **800/847-4389;** www.thrifty.com), has beefed up promotions with fair daily rates and special 2-day weekend rates.

Fly-drive packages may offer the best prices; check to see if your airline has a fly-drive affiliation with a particular car-rental agency.

The best rental deal I've ever used came from **Kemwel** (© **800/678-0678;** www.kemwel.com); our car rental in Italy went smoothly . . . and inexpensively. Its rentals have a 3-day rate (the minimum), so a four-door Ford Fiesta (automatic transmission with air-conditioning) goes for about $365.

I have not used this source personally so I cannot vouch for it, but I was very impressed with the offerings at **Rental Car Group** (© **866/735-1715;** www.rentalcargroup.com). Prices are quoted in euros (for a 1-week period), so do the math realistically. I priced a car in Florence at 179€ ($233) for a week. One of the good things about this site is that it has comparisons to brand-name rental services, so you can see that Thrifty also has a car for 179€ ($233) and Alamo for 204€ ($265).

When you are renting a car, consider how many people will be with you and how much luggage you will be hauling, since European cars tend to be smaller. Do not accept free upgrades to larger models unless you really need the space. The smaller the car, the less gas you will use, and the easier it will be to get into parking spots and to maneuver medieval streets and alleys.

Let me also remind you that because of the crime rate in Italy, car rentals there are far more expensive than in other European countries, and various insurance plans are mandatory. You have no choice.

Furthermore, American Express and credit- and bank-card firms that offer car insurance automatically with your membership have now waived coverage in Italy. *Do not assume you are covered by your credit card.*

U.S. vs. Euro Rentals

European rental rates are usually more expensive than those offered in the U.S. for use in Europe, although a package plan will always be less expensive than a daily rate. Avis in Italy offers a 3-day winter promotional package for 147€ ($191) and a 7-day package for 312€ ($406)—these include unlimited mileage—so if you can read Italian, go online to www.avis autonoleggio.it.

Shopper's trick: If you are already in Italy and want a car at the last minute, you can reserve by making a long-distance call to the U.S. and paying by phone. You'll receive a faxed prepaid voucher with U.S. prices.

Driving Around

I bought the Michelin spiral-bound map book to Italy (18€/$23) for a proposed driving trip. This book also has a handy mileage chart, so you can plan just how far you want to drive.

I have lived in France for about 8 years and drive happily there. But I must tell you that driving in Italy is not for the fainthearted. Aside from my personal problems with heights and curvy roads, I came to hate Italian drivers who really will

I Have Gas

The cost of gas in Europe is four times what you are paying in the U.S.; you will also pay high fees for the use of highways. Gas in Italy is slightly less expensive than in France, so if you are driving to or from France, gauge accordingly

Both highways and gas stations do take credit cards, but automatic tellers at toll booths and in gas stations only accept CB, the European version of Visa. If you have a U.S.-issued Visa card, it will work in Italy, but probably not in these situations.

come right up to your bumper and flash their lights at you. I have even been tapped on the bumper.

I have driven all of the major *autostrada* in Italy, and although they are nice roads, they are not as nice as French highways nor as well maintained. They are just as expensive, however.

Car & Driver

If you can afford it or you want to splurge, a car and driver are a wonderful way to do a day trip or to connect to other parts of Italy. I certainly wouldn't want to be driving the Amalfi Pass on my own. And sometimes I have so much luggage that a trek through a train station can be a nightmare.

However, make sure your driving company knows where it's going. I recently used a service to drive me to Como and to outlets along the way . . . and not only did the driver not know where anything was, but he didn't speak English, refused to call the factories for directions, and wouldn't cross the border into Switzerland to get to FoxTown. *Urrrrrgggh.*

To avoid problems like this, consider taking a train to your destination city and then hiring a local taxi driver for a flat rate.

SLEEPING IN ITALY

While there is specific hotel information in each of the following city chapters, for those who like to make all or most of their reservations with one hotel chain or one phone call, there are a few firms that can help you out. Ask each if it has promotional deals.

BAGLIONI HOTELS This is a small chain, still owned by a real family and offering up four- and five-star hotels in major cities. The top of the line is the one in Milan (the Carlton, a member of Leading Hotels of the World), but my fave is the nugget in Florence, the Bernini Palace. Baglioni is a member of the Sterling Hotels & Resorts booking group. There is no toll-free reservations number in the U.S. www.baglionihotels.com.

BOSCOLO HOTELS This chain has over a dozen properties in Italy. Some are normal four-star hotels that are good finds; a few are to-die-for places worthy of a spread in *Architectural Digest*. ✆ **888/626-7265** in the U.S. www.boscolohotels.com.

HILTON Exhibiting a recent burst of energy, Hilton now has several new hotels dotted across Italy. In some cases, the hotels are not in the downtown area—such as the one in Florence. In Venice, the hotel is located on an island near San Marco. ✆ **800/HILTONS** in the U.S. www.hilton.com.

INTER-CONTINENTAL This chain is changing its image and renovating many properties. While its showcase hotels are in Hong Kong, London, and Paris, there is a gorgeous hotel in Rome (the Inter-Continental de la Ville Roma) with a great location right at the top of the Spanish Steps; it has just had some major renovations and boasts more terraces and gardens than any other hotel in Rome. ✆ **800/327-0200** in the U.S. www.intercontinental.com.

JOLLY HOTELS Jolly is a leading four-star chain in Italy, with hotels in other European cities and some spas, too. Many of the hotels are modern and, from the outside, may look like they're stuck in the 1960s—but on the inside they're great. Some are re-habbed grande dames. Check the special weekend promotions—you can luck into a very good hotel for 63€ ($82) per night per person. Trust me on this; Jolly is a great find and lets you make all your Italian bookings with one chain. © **800/247-1277** in the U.S. www.jollyhotels.com.

LEADING HOTELS OF THE WORLD Leading Hotels of the World also represents Leading Small Hotels of the World, with a wide selection of the fanciest accommodations anywhere—sometimes multiple choices in the same city (three hotels in Florence, three in Milan, and five in Rome). © **800/223-6800** in the U.S. www.lhw.com.

Note that most of the hotels have their own websites as well. Also check out **www.luxury-alliance.com**, which is the combined website for Leading Hotels and Relais & Châteaux.

RELAIS & CHÂTEAUX With some 30 properties all over Italy, Relais & Châteaux guarantees that you'll rest in a luxury property and eat awfully well to boot. © **800/735-2478** in the U.S. www.relaischateaux.com.

SINA HOTELS It's a sina (sorry) if you overlook this Italian chain of luxury hotels, with four- and five-star properties in all the key Italian cities. It offers promotional deals in most destinations as well as some packages that include meals, late checkout, and more. There is no toll-free reservations number in the U.S. www.sinahotels.com.

SOFITEL Part of France's Accor Group, Sofitel has hotels in Venice, Bologna, Rome, Florence, and Sardinia. The company's weekend promotional deal takes 30% off the room rate and includes complimentary breakfast in most of its European hotels. In winter, there's sometimes a dollar/euro-at-parity promotion, requiring a 3-night minimum stay (use the code USD by phone or the code USDOF online). © **800/763-4835** in the U.S. www.sofitel.com.

WESTIN Westin ended up with some of the old CIGA hotels through Starwood, so it does have several luxury hotels in key cities and can take care of your needs with one swift phone call. ✆ **888/625-5144** in the U.S. www.westin.com.

For Starwood's **Luxury Collection** hotels and resorts, call ✆ **800/325-3589** or go to www.starwood.com/luxury.

Sleeping Promotions

When business is slow, promotional rates get better. Airlines do 'em, hotels do 'em, and even credit card companies will play ball. Check with the travel service division of all the cards you hold to find what's on offer; also go to hotel and airline websites—very often there are special deals offered only online. Most chains such as Jolly (www.jollyhotels.com) have deals, either with partners or just to sell rooms in odd seasons or on weekends.

Don't be shy about calling a hotel directly and asking for a deal. Just don't be rude or pushy. Sometimes a nice fax to the hotel's general manager can get you a good rate plus added perks. Write something to the effect of "I love your hotel, have stayed there for years, but prices are too high now; can you cut a deal for me?"

Home Suite Home

If you'd rather rent an apartment or even a villa, there are several services that will assist you. For something very high-end, tour masters **Abercrombie & Kent** (✆ **800-323-7308;** www.abercrombiekent.com) has a rental division, but a castle may well cost you $30,000 a week. **The Best in Italy** (www.thebestinitaly.com) handles properties that begin at around $10,000 a week. If your budget is far below that, try **Custom Italy** (www.customitaly.com), where prices begin around $4,000 per week. **Villas International** (✆ **800/221-2260;** www.villasintl.com) has properties all over Europe, so you can compare prices and locations. Also consider trading houses (try www.intervac.com) or renting an apartment through craigslist.com.

Buyer beware: Avoid agencies and rental offices based in the U.K. or that offer prices in pounds, since with current

Electronically Yours

Here are some unusual websites you may want to check out before you begin your Italian adventures:

- **The Vatican** (www.vatican.va): Dial a prayer.
- **Italian Government Tourist Board** (www.italiantourism.com and www.enit.it): Use these sites to find a hotel, look up train schedules, or research arts events.
- **Design Centro Italia** (www.italydesign.com): This California firm can help you price Italian furniture and design, which may actually be cheaper in the U.S.
- **Made in Italy Online** (www.made-in-italy.com): Logan Bentley's site has info on wine and food, travel, and shopping. You can also arrange Roman shopping tours with Barbara Lessona.
- **Faith Heller Willinger** (www.faithwillinger.com): Browse all sorts of food, restaurant, and recipe info. She also does cooking classes in her home.
- **Tuscany by Tuscans** (www.tuscanybytuscans.it): This is Maria Teresa Berdondini's site—she arranges shopping and cooking tours and tastings. I book my car and driver through her. I book everything through her.

exchange rates, you will pay more than if you rent in euros or get a guaranteed dollar rate.

PROFESSIONAL HELP

If you are looking for guidance in making travel plans, there are a few organizations that specialize in showing you the insider's Italy. The good ones are usually regional. They charge, by the day or half-day, but sometimes you have to spend money to save money. Try contacting these people, whom I know, trust, and have in most cases worked with:

- **In Tuscany:** Maria Teresa Berdondini, Tuscany by Tuscans, Villa L. Galvani 13B, 51016 Montecatini Terme, Italy (©/fax **0572/704-67**; www.tuscanybytuscans.it; tuscany@ italway.it)
- **In Rome:** Barbara Lessona (© **348/450-3655**; info@personal shoppersinitaly.com)
- **In Rome & Florence:** Elisa Rossi, With Style, Via Monte Santo 2, 00195 Rome, Italy (© **06/481-9091**)

PHONE HOME

Please remember:

- International calls made from the U.S. to Europe are far less expensive than those made from Europe to the U.S. If you are in Italy and want to talk to the U.S., call home and ask family or friends to call you back.
- An international call from Italy to the U.S. on your cellphone may be less expensive than calling from a hotel—especially if you have a cellphone with an international calling plan.
- Phone cards can be the cheapest solution, if you don't mind making calls from a public phone. I buy a SIPS card at any *tabacchi* (tobacco shop) in Italy and use it at pay phones.
- Considering how inexpensive a phone card can be (I just bought 800 min. to the U.S. for $6.50), you may be willing to pay local charges from your hotel room. Ask at the front desk—sometimes local calls are free.
- USA Direct is a marvelous gimmick and is often a lifesaver, but it doesn't necessarily give the best rate possible. If you prefer to use your American long-distance carrier, the access codes for the major carriers in Italy are: **USA Direct** (AT&T), © **800-172-444**; **MCI Direct,** © **172-1022**; and **Sprint,** © **800-825-8745**. Each carrier charges a flat fee for providing this service; it will appear on your monthly phone bill.

Phone Codes

For calling Italy from abroad, the **country code** is **39.** The access codes (area codes) for the major cities are: **Florence,** 055; **Milan,** 02; **Venice,** 041; **Rome,** 06; and **Naples,** 081. For example, to call Rome from the U.S., you would dial 011 + 39 + 06 (the access code for Rome) + the number. All calls, both local and long distance, include the "0" (zero).

Plugging In

If you are using your laptop to connect to the Internet, work with your hotel's front desk or business center. I have had great difficulty with the difference between digital (European) lines and analog lines (which AOL uses).

The more modern your hotel, the better your chances of getting connected. Four Seasons hotels have 110-volt electricity and direct dataports in all rooms. Baglioni hotels offer free Wi-Fi in all of their rooms throughout Italy.

Hotels that are not Internet-equipped in guest rooms may still have a business center or an e-mail center where you can buy time online.

SHOPPING HOURS

Shops open at 9 or 9:30am and usually close at 1:30pm for lunch. They reopen at 3 or 3:30pm (or even 4pm) and stay open until 7:30pm.

Some stores close on Saturday from 1 to 4pm. Stores are open on Saturday afternoons in winter but are closed on Saturday afternoons in summer.

Some stores do whatever they please.

The notion of staying open all day is catching on in big cities, but not the countryside. You never find shops open all day in the south, where it is too hot to think in the afternoon, let alone shop.

Stores that do not close for lunch usually write their hours as "nonstop." In all cities, major department stores stay open at lunchtime . . . unless it's Monday, which has its own rules—see below.

Surviving Monday

Monday mornings are a total write-off for most retail shopping in Italy. With the rare exception, most stores open at 3:30pm on Monday.

But wait, that's why God invented factories. Because factories are open on Monday mornings, most factory stores are also open. Not all, just most. Call and ask, or have your hotel's concierge call for you. Grocery stores are usually open as well, but mom-and-pop minimarts may not be.

Sunday Shopping

Laws have changed, and most of Italy's big cities have some Sunday shopping now; often big department stores are open even if mom-and-pop stores are not. If you want to shop on a Sunday in a town that has no regular retail, try a flea market.

- Venice is wide, wide, wide open on Sunday, as is nearby Verona.
- Milan is far more dead on Sunday than other communities, but you can get lucky—at certain times of the year, things are popping on Sunday. During fashion weeks, stores in Montenapo district often open on Sunday; they also have specific Sundays when they open beginning in October and going on until Christmas. Some stores in the Navigli area are also open on Sunday. The regular Sunday stores are **10 Corso Como** and **Virgin Megastore.** Sunday hours are most often from noon to 5pm. But wait, in Milan I am seeing a trend of more and more designer stores opening late Sunday afternoon, from 3:30 to 7pm.
- Florence has a lot of street action on Sundays; department stores and chains are usually open.
- Rome has special Sundays when stores stay open.

Exceptional Hours

SUMMER HOURS Summers in Italy have two problems: It can be too hot to shop, and stores can be closed. Summer hours begin in the middle of July for many retail businesses; August is a total loss from a shopping point of view because it is the official summer vacation season, especially in northern Italy.

Sophisticated people wouldn't be caught dead in Milan in August; shoppers, beware. Most shops in Milan and many in Rome close between August 1 and September 1; almost all upscale shops in Naples are closed the first 3 weeks in August. Shockingly, some stores close for a longer time.

When stores are open in August, they close at lunch on Saturday and do not reopen until 3:30 or 4pm on Monday.

In southern climates, especially in summer, expect stores to close from 1 until 5pm, during the heat of the day, but to be open until late in the evening.

HOLIDAYS The period between Christmas and New Year's Day can be tricky. Stores will close early a few days before a major holiday and use any excuse to stay closed during a holiday. Sales begin in the first week of January (usually after Epiphany), but store hours are erratic before then. But then, the entire first half of January can be erratic (see below). Note that there are weekend candy markets around the Duomo in the weeks before Lent.

Also keep track of local holidays, since shops will be closed. (When you check into a hotel, always ask the concierge if there are any holidays approaching and how they will affect the banks and stores!) Cities celebrate religious holidays with differing amounts of piety. Shops that are closed in Rome may be open in Milan. (For instance, Dec 8 is a big holiday in some towns, a medium holiday in others.) All stores are closed on August 15, a major religious holiday (one of the feasts of the Virgin).

EARLY JANUARY The first week to 10 days of January are slow to slower—all factories are closed until after Epiphany, as are many stores. Others decide to close for inventory. Do not assume that shopping life returns to normal on the first day of business after New Year's Day.

NIGHT HOURS Stores usually close between 7:30 and 8pm. Should you need an all-night pharmacy, there is usually one at the train station in a large city.

Sale Shopping

Each city in Italy has the right to decide when the twice-a-year—in January and July—official sales will begin. It varies from city to city by as much as a week. Good luck.

SCAMS

There are plenty of locals who are ready to take advantage of tourists and especially consider Americans as fair game. Most try small-time shopping scams, but they are annoying nonetheless, and can be expensive if you get taken.

Scams exist in stores, on the streets, and in taxis (especially when you don't know your way around). Reputable shops (and hotels) are usually safe. But even in classy establishments, be careful when you talk to strangers. I've met some wonderful people in hotels and on airplanes around the world, but there is a rather well-known scam in which the con artist pretends to be just the kind of person you'd like to know and then—whammo—takes you for a ride.

Remember:

- Merchandise, especially name merchandise, selling at a price that is too good to be true is usually too fake to be true. I don't care how fancy the store. I don't care how good the sob story about why they are taking a loss.
- If a person volunteers to go shopping with you, to steer you to some real "finds," to help you find some long-lost family members of yours, or whatever—don't trust him or her! There are more tourist scams of this nature in Italy than any place else, except maybe Hong Kong.

- No matter how well dressed the person is, no matter how friendly the person is, no matter how helpful and endearing—the answer is still "No." If such a person is following you or becomes a real nuisance, call the police, duck into a prestigious hotel and ask the concierge for help, or walk right into the American embassy.
- Likewise, if a person volunteers to take your money and buy an item for you cheaper than you could get it because you are an "Ugly American," forget it. If you want the concierge of a reputable hotel to handle some shopping for you and you know the hotel well enough to trust the concierge, by all means, do so. (Don't forget to tip for such a favor.) Otherwise, you are taking a risk.
- Always check your purchases while they are being packed by the store, and when you return to your hotel, unwrap them to make sure you got what you thought you were getting. Mistakes occur, but occasionally someone will switch merchandise on you. Return to the shop the next day if an error has been made. Bring your sales slip. If you anticipate a language problem, have the concierge call the shop for you and explain the situation, and then have him tell the shop when you will be in for the proper merchandise.
- Don't forget the old newspaper scam. A street person (or two or three) spots you with an attractive shopping bag. He or she is reading or holding a newspaper as he passes you on a crowded street—or worse, on a bridge. The newspaper passes over your shopping bag while the thief's hand goes into your bag for the goodies. The person reading the newspaper may or may not be the thief—this scam is worked by mothers with three or four children in tow.
- Watch out for the old subway trick. You know the one, where some "boys" pick a fight among themselves between subway stops, and your pocket is picked, and they are out the door before you know what has happened.
- There is a variation of this one that I call the "Ice-Cream Trick." Someone bumps into you and knocks his ice-cream

cone all over you. He's very apologetic and helps clean you up. He also cleans you out.

- And then there's the old *O sole Mio* scam. You are involved in a transaction being conducted in Italian, which you barely speak. If you question the mathematics, the vendor rolls his eyes, waves his arms, and screams at you. You feel like an idiot and leave, not wanting to cause a scene. You have just been cheated out of $50 in correct change. (This actually happened to me.)
- My favorite (this also happened to me): You give the taxi an address that is slightly off the beaten track. He pulls up to a door and says something to the effect of "here you go." You say "no" because you know this isn't it. He insists on getting out of the cab, going to the front door, and verifying the fact that this is not the place you want. Meanwhile, the meter is running . . . and running.

It's a Crime

I don't want to put a damper on your shopping spree before you even start out, but I do feel compelled to point out that the hard times in Italy have brought more and more criminal elements to the front. They are in front of, and behind, your handbag. And your rental car.

I was accosted not once but several times by thieving bands in Milan. Two incidents occurred on different days, but in full daylight, in the area immediately surrounding the Duomo. In one case, it was a Saturday, and I was surrounded by a throng of shoppers. When I screamed out, none of the other shoppers even gazed in my direction.

Keep handbags close to your body and under your coat or sweater. Don't put valuables in a backpack or fanny pack that is beyond your watchful eye. Don't sling shopping bags across a shoulder and away from your body so that their contents can be lifted from the rear. Leave nothing in your rental car, and be careful where you park it. Last time I rented a car in Italy, I was told which cities, such as Naples, were considered unsafe for parking a car on the street or in an unattended lot. If you're given a similar warning, heed it.

SENDING IT HOME

Shipping anything from Italy begins before you get there. If you are smart, or serious, you will do some homework before you leave and have your shipping arrangements partly made before you even arrive. You'll complete the transaction once you arrive in Italy with a pre-selected and guaranteed broker.

Contact a shipper in your hometown, or in New York, London, or your chosen port of entry for your goods, and work with them to make sure all your shipping days are pleasant ones. The shipper should be able to act as your agent—the buying game will be much less tense once you have someone to take care of you.

Find out if you need a customhouse broker to meet your goods and clear them, or if the shipping agent does this, and if so, is it included in the shipping cost, or is there an additional fee? Likewise, make sure you pay for adequate insurance and do not assume that it is included in the freight price.

Small items should be shipped via FedEx, DHL, or another courier service you know and trust. Italy does have a service called "express mail," but don't trust it.

Before I totally pooh-pooh the Italian mail system, I want you to know that all the postcards I've ever sent from Italy have been delivered home and abroad, sometimes in less than a week. I've also noticed that concierges have charged differing rates for a simple postcard stamp. Actual postal rates are posted at the post office. I have mailed items in jiffy bags from large city post offices, and the gifts have indeed arrived—but always mark an item sent to the U.S. as "unsolicited gift, under $50."

THE MOSCOW RULE OF SHOPPING

The Moscow Rule of Shopping is one of my most basic shopping rules and has nothing to do with shopping in Moscow, so please pay attention. Now: Average shoppers, in pursuit of the ideal bargain, do not buy an item they want when they first see it, because they're not convinced that they won't find it elsewhere for less money. They want to see everything available, then return for the purchase of choice. This is a rather normal thought process. However, if you live in Russia, for instance, you know that you must buy something the minute you see it, because if you hesitate, it will be gone. Hence this international law: the Moscow Rule of Shopping.

When you are on a trip, you probably will not have the time to compare prices and then return to a certain shop. You will never be able to backtrack to a city, and even if you can, the item might be gone by the time you get back anyway. What to do? The same thing they do in Moscow: Buy it when you see it, understanding that you may never see it again. But since you are not shopping in Moscow and you *may* see it again, weigh these questions carefully before you go ahead:

- Is this a touristy type of item that I am bound to find all over town?
- Is this an item I can't live without, even if I am overpaying?
- Is this a reputable shop, and can I trust what they tell me about the availability of such items?
- Is the quality of this particular item so spectacular that it is unlikely it could be matched at this price?

If you have a good reason to buy it when you see it, do so.

Now hear my tale of warning. I bought a pair of trousers at Marina Rinaldi in Rome that turned out to be great for me. They were also available in navy in Rome, but by the time I realized I couldn't live without them, it was Sunday and I couldn't go back to the store. When I got to Florence, I went to the Marina Rinaldi store, wearing the trousers, and asked for them in navy. The saleswoman swore they weren't from Marina Rinaldi. Then she suggested that they came from Marina Rinaldi in the U.S., a different kettle of pants. When I told her they came from Rome, she simply shrugged.

Lesson learned: Buy it when you see it, and don't expect the same brand to have the same stock.

Caveat: The Moscow Rule of Shopping breaks down if you are an antiques or bric-a-brac shopper or if you are shopping in a factory outlet. You never know if you will find another such item, or if it will be in the same condition, or if the price will be higher or lower. It's very hard to price collectibles and bargains, so consider doing a lot of shopping for an item before you buy anything.

ITALIAN CITY PLANNING

If you are going to a variety of Italian cities, you're probably wondering which one offers the best price, the best selection, and the best value. There are no firm rules—the Moscow Rule of Shopping really applies—but I do have a couple of loose rules to guide you.

The City of Origin Axiom An item usually is least expensive in the city where it's made or where the firm's headquarters are located. That's because the trucking and distribution costs are lower. Following this rule, **Pratesi** linens should be bought at the factory store in Pistoia; **Fendi** goodies should come from the mother store in Rome; and **Etro** should come from the factory near Como (or, at least, the outlet store in Milan).

The Milan Rule of Supply & Demand If you don't know the city of origin for an item, or want to be safe, use the Milan Rule of Supply and Demand. Because Milan is the center of the fashion and furnishings businesses, it should have the best selection of big-name merchandise. If you're shopping in only one city or creating a schedule that allows only a 1-day spree, Milan is the city for you.

Milan is far more industrial than the other big cities. Its entire psychology is one of moving and selling goods and services. Furthermore, while in Milan you have the opportunity to shop at factories that are just outside of town, or at flea markets that sell leftovers from factories (you mean those ties didn't just fall off a truck?), or you can luck into very good sales that are created to move merchandise.

The Roman Holiday Rule of Shopping If all you want are designer merchandise and a good time, forget about the rest of Italy and just do Rome. You won't get the faience, the souvenirs, or the gilt-wood trays, but you will find all the big names in one easy-to-shop neighborhood.

Venice and Florence are crammed with visitors, especially in the spring and summer months, and the shopkeepers will know you are a tourist. Prices in Venice are high to begin with and soar in peak season. Florence has changed dramatically in the last couple of years: The merchandise in the streets and stalls has gotten junkier and junkier, but prices for clothing are often lower than in nearby cities because of the turnover.

If you're going on a cruise of Italy, please note that chapter 5 in this book has information on shopping in various Italian port cities. Unless you have a pre- or post-cruise layover in Rome or Venice, you will not have the opportunity to do much traditional Italian-designer shopping.

The Coca-Cola Price Index To find out how prices fare in any destination, ask for the price of a Coca-Cola. Just so you know, the price of a single can of Coke in a grocery store is .56€ (70¢). A six-pack is about 2.46€ ($3.20). The average Coke on the street costs 2€ ($2.60); it is expensive if it costs 3€ ($3.90), and it is a crime if it costs 7.50€ ($9.75). Shop accordingly.

SHOPPING FOR FAKES

In years gone by, some of the best buys in Italy were on fake designer leather goods and scarves. These items are harder to find now, and once found, are often so inferior to the real thing that the game is no fun to play at all. Although there is that pesky little rumor that Prada makes its own fakes.

Markets no longer sell anything that resembles a reasonable copy; the Senegalese teams that prowl the streets of Venice with their blankets and bags have branched out into other cities and have fairly decent copies. But knowing what to pay is a frightening question. To test the waters, I inquired about a "Bottega" bag and was quoted 125€ ($163). I said no thanks and walked away, figuring the bag would sell to the average tourist at 75€ to 100€ ($98–$130). Imagine my shock when the vendor followed me down the street, lowering the price at each step and finally begging me to take the bag at 20€ ($26).

The bigger question is, why buy a fake when you can have the real thing through an outlet store or at a sale? Fendi key chains were going for 12€ ($16) at the sale in Rome. I mean, *really* . . . get real, buy real.

IN THE BAG

Shopping bags are freely given out at boutiques and department stores when you make a purchase. Not so in grocery stores. Either bring your own or expect to pay about .50€ (65¢) per plastic sack. Europe is going green, and the idea is to save trees and reduce plastic pollutants.

If you score at a sale in a designer shop, you can ask for gift wrap and a designer bag, but you may not get them. Pucci gave me tons of attention and free wrap; Fendi settled on tissue and Fendi bags—no wrap or ribbon for marked-down merch. Best of all was Armani, where all I bought was a blush, but they gave me a canvas tote bag.

In some cases, the bags and wrapping are considered part of the experience and are quite extravagant. Tod's gave me a felt bag for the shoes, a fancy shopping bag, and two catalog books that I didn't ask for, want, or need. It was a horrible shame to throw away everything but the shoes.

BAR NONE

This is not strictly a shopping secret but is nonetheless a strategy: Next time you belly up to the bar, consider how much money you've just saved. That's right—eating at the bar (while standing) is a money-saving tactic.

If you see a bar you'd like to wander into for a coffee or a snack, remember that all bars in Italy have two systems: Either you order at the bar and stand at the bar, or you order at the bar or a table and sit down. To eat at a table will cost just about double the price of a meal at the bar. It is considered rude to order at the bar, pay at the bar, and then wander to a chair with your snack and sit down.

TO MARKET, TO MARKET

Market versus Flea Market

Each village—or community within a large city—has a specific market day. Markets may be oriented toward fresh foods and veggies or toward dry goods. Some sell both in two different parts of the same street. New merchandise, even designer items that fell off a truck, may be sold at market. There are good markets for this sort of thing in Florence and in Milan, so see those chapters for specific details.

A flea market sells only antiques and used merchandise. In most cities, the flea market is held in the historic center of town, but there are exceptions. In very large cities, such as Milan and Rome, there may be several different flea markets on a variety of different dates. If I am planning my route according to flea markets, I only go to those with 100+ vendors. Actually, I like 400 vendors better. See below.

Rules of the Marketplace

One of the difficulties of shopping in Italy is deciding which markets to visit and which to pass up. Italy is crawling with good markets, for food and for fleas. There are dozens of them, and it's impossible to get to them all unless you spend a month doing little else. Maybe a year . . . or two.

Remember:

- Dress simply; the richer you look, the higher the price. If you have an engagement ring or one of those wedding bands that spells out "Rich American" in pavé diamonds, leave it in the hotel safe. Do not carry a $1,000 designer handbag.
- Check with your hotel's concierge about the neighborhood where the market is located. It may not be considered safe to go there alone, or after dark. Beware Rome. Beware the Ides of March.
- Have a lot of change with you. It's difficult to bargain and then offer a large bill and ask for change. As a bargaining point, be able to say you have only so much cash on hand.
- You do not need to speak any specific language to make a good deal. Bargaining is an international language of emotion, hand signs, facial expressions, and so on. If you feel like you are being taken, walk away.
- Branded merchandise sold on the street may be hot or counterfeit. If the deal seems an exceptionally fine one, suspect fraud.
- Go early if you expect the best selection. Go late if you want to make the best deals, price-wise.
- Never trust anyone (except a qualified shipping agent) to mail anything for you.
- In Florence and Rome, most market areas are so famous that they have no specific street address. Usually it's enough to give the cabbie the name of the market; ask your concierge if you need more in the way of directions. Usually buses service market areas as well. Expect markets to be closed on Monday morning.

Flea Markets of Note

I've rarely met a flea market I didn't like, but some are worth planning your travel dates around just so you find yourself in the right place at the right time. Consider some of these:

CITY	NO. OF VENDORS	DATE	PHONE
Arezzo	450+	first Sun of month	05/7537-7993
Lucca	250	first Sat–Sun of month	05/8344-2155
Milano	400	last Sun of month	02/8940-9971
Naples	300	varies	08/122-9613
Nizza	350	third Sun of month	01/4172-0507
Padova	160	third Sun of month	04/9820-5881
Piazzola	700	last Sun of month	329/237-2475
Roma Pza Verdi	160	third Sun of month	06/907-7312
Torino	200	second Sun of month	01/1436-9741

OUTLET SHOPPING

Italian factories have had outlet shops for their employees or the local community for years; these addresses used to be secrets. Not anymore. They say the second-most-visited sight in Florence, after the Uffizzi, is the Prada outlet store.

Outlet Literature

Outlets are so popular with locals and visitors alike that there are now locally published guides to them. I often use a book called *Lo Scopriaoccasioni (Bargain Hunting in Italy)*, written in Italian, which is a listing of over 3,000 outlets, according to the cover. This book costs about $25 and is in its 10th edition, just released as we go to press.

Note, however:

- There is another edition of the same book *(Designer Bargains in Italy)* that costs as much, is in English, and isn't revised as often or as comprehensive. Beware. I consider this book a waste of money.
- Check the copyright page before you buy. For obvious reasons, you want the most up-to-date edition possible.
- Finally, may I say that I don't agree with a number of the listings (of the ones I've checked out, which is a small portion of the total). Call ahead if you are driving out of your way or solely trusting this book. And ask your hotel's concierge to give you a Michelin printout of the driving route.

There is another book that I would recommend to civilians over the big bible because it costs only 5€ ($6.50), it's a small size, and it's more easily used (though it's also in Italian). *Guida Dove Agli Spacci,* from Rizzoli, is available in most bookstores. Note, however, that it, too, lists some incorrect information that could make a big difference in travel plans. For example, the book says that the Armani outlet near Como is closed on Mondays. This is not true. I called and I visited on a Monday. The driving directions may also be vague (as are most directions in Italy).

Outlet Malls

There are a number of new, American-style, factory-outlet villages that are, frankly, amazing. The outlet malls are in the middle of nowhere but not far from big cities. We went to 10 outlet malls on our most recent drive across Italy—and these were all chosen because they were right off major highways between cities we were going to visit anyway.

Only the visit to The Mall and the Prada outlet (which are near each other) or drives to seek specific stores within actual factories (such as Pratesi) forced us to take a road just to get to the shopping.

Do understand that these malls were created primarily for the local market, so you'll see names and brands you can get at home for less money. On the other hand, these same brands may have styles or colors not available in the U.S.

Choosing an outlet mall will depend on where you are, what mode of transportation you have, and how motivated you are. Below is a list of the big malls in easy-to-get-to locations; some have shuttle-bus service or tours or can be reached by public transportation.

If you are driving, have good directions. There are no billboards on the highway to alert you to the malls, as you would see in the U.S. And once you take the proper exit, you may be hard-pressed to see the small (usually brown) signs that may only say OUTLET. At least parking is free and plentiful.

Outlet malls are open on Sundays. Note that Monday hours may be unusual.

- South of Rome, there's the **Castel Romano Designer Outlet,** owned by McArthur Glen (www.mcarthurglen.it). This mall is built like an antique Roman village. See p. 99 for more. ***Warning:*** Do not get this mall mixed up with the mall named **Castel Guelfo Outlet City,** which I find rather small and disappointing.
- **Barberino Designer Outlet** is the new guy in town from McArthur Glen (www.mcarthurglen.it), accessible from both Florence and Bologna. It's a stunning mall, designed in the village format with a nice sprawl that makes you want to move in. You'll find a Prada outlet and many other designer names here. Note that the hours are irregular; see p. 165 for details.
- **The Mall** (www.outlet-the-mall.com) is certainly the most visited of all the outlet malls in Italy, and it's conveniently located near the Prada outlet outside Florence. Tenants include big names like Burberry, Gucci, Pucci, and Yohji. See p. 166 for details.
- **Serravalle Designer Outlet** (www.mcarthurglen.it), also with a fake village atmosphere in the style most Americans

adore, is between Genoa and Milan and usually listed under Milan shopping resources (p. 277). If you're headed to Turin, you can also get here without particularly going out of your way. It's probably the largest outlet mall in Italy, the oldest, and the best known. It has every store—and designer brand—you can imagine.

- If you're driving from Milan (or Como) toward Venice, you can easily pop into **Franciacorta Outlet Village** (www.franciacortaoutlet.it), which isn't the best outlet mall in Italy, but it does have a number of interesting shops; see p. 277 for details. If you stay off the highway to the next town, you can shop at the hypermarche Auchan, which to me is a great treat.
- **FoxTown** (www.foxtown.ch), one of the older outlet malls, is technically in Switzerland—it's 5km (3 miles) from the Italian border and right near Como. Because it's in Switzerland, and Switzerland does not use the euro, you must change money to CHF (Swiss Francs)—which may or may not be worth it to you. Prices in Switzerland tend to be high (even on bargains), but as we go to press, the dollar is in better shape against the Swiss Franc than the euro, so your money will go further. See p. 291 for more.
- Between Milan and Bologna, there's **Fidenza Village** (www.fidenzavillage.com); it, too, is in the village format. It's not as large as most of the other malls, but it has the benefit of being around the corner from the Big Cheese (see p. 321 for details on both). The mall is pleasant, has a good restaurant, and provides a fun break on your drive.

Stock It to Me

Italy has a system of jobbers (usually called *stochistas*) and also of free-standing outlet stores, often in the heart of a big city and easily on the tourist path. Some are as fancy as regular boutiques. Wait until you shop at the Max Mara and Etro outlets in Milan—you won't believe they're outlets until you see the price tags. Information on these stores is included in the destination chapters of this book.

About Max Mara

Since we're all interested in the Max Mara line—and its subsidiaries—this is a good time to let you in on the secret: Its outlet stores are named **DF/Diffusione Tessile.** To add to the confusion, there are special labels put into the clothes. Even the Marina Rinaldi (plus-size) clothes bear this unusual label. However, if you ask a salesperson, she will readily admit that the stock is from MM and even help you discern which lines are which.

According to their card, there are 11 outlets dotted around Italy. Some DF outlets are free-standing—like the one in the center of Milan that's in a shopping arcade near San Babila—and some are in outlet malls. The very best one I have been to was in the Barberino Designer Outlet mall.

You can also register—in stores only—for e-mail or text-message service that will advise you of sales and new shipments.

Mills & Thrills

Outlets can offer truly great bargains—if they are the real thing. Sometimes outlet villages are so upscale that their prices are actually closer to regular retail. And sometimes the merchandise sold at such outlets was made specifically for sale at outlets; true stock is almost always from a previous season. Even if the store says it's an outlet, pay attention to what's on offer.

There is a small business in hustling big-city locals through warehouses in industrial suburbs that sell fakes . . . or are just normal businesses that market themselves as outlets.

Know your stuff, know your regular retail prices, and know a few other rules of the road:

- Most outlets in factories close for lunch.
- Sales help in out-of-the-way communities may not speak English. It's not a bad idea to bring an Italian-English dictionary with you.

- Be sure you have a size conversion chart, or know the sizes you want in the continental sizing system.
- Many mills are open Monday morning but close in the afternoon; others are closed the entire day. Remember the Monday rule of shopping—anything goes. Call first.
- Mills are never open on Sunday; not all are open on Saturday. Most outlet malls are open on Sunday, however. In fact, in outlet malls, stores are usually open 7 days a week, although there may be modifications to the hours on Sundays and Mondays. Welcome to the new Italy.
- Few mills will take credit cards, although Pratesi does. Outlets will accept credit cards.
- If you have chosen a day trip with specific outlets and/or mills in mind, do yourself (and me) a favor—call first. Actually, have your hotel's concierge call in case your Italian isn't as good as his. Get hours, credit card information, and directions. If you're driving, print out a map search with directions; specify that you want the directions in English if that is important to you. If not, know right and left in Italian.

EUROS & U

Italy, like most of continental Europe, adopted the euro (€) and has successfully switched from lire. Surely they did it for you, to make shopping all of Europe so much easier.

The bad news is that as we go to press, the euro has gained enormous strength against the U.S. dollar, so that the high prices will seem even higher to you.

ATMs "R" Us

The single best way to exchange money is to simply withdraw it from a wall—via an ATM. Bring along your bank card: All Italian cities have banks with ATMs.

There are two caveats here:

- There are a few different types of bank machines that look similar but offer different functions—only a bank machine/ATM (usually marked *bancomat*) will give you a good rate. Those machines that exchange your dollars for foreign currency will cheat you, so don't be fooled.
- There is usually a fee of $2.50 to $5 for using an international ATM, but you do get a good rate of exchange. However, if your bank charges a high fee, you don't want to keep going to the wall for 100€; you want to do it all at once. Ask your bank at home about its international fees; some do allow free withdrawals worldwide.

ATMs are usually located alongside a bank, so that you need not enter the building. If you need cash for a big purchase in a specific store, ask the sales clerk where the nearest ATM is located. Very often a small store will give you a sizable discount if you pay cash and are willing to forego your VAT refund. Of course, they do this because they have another set of books that Brussels knows nothing about, but what else is new?

Currency Exchange

The best way to change dollars to euros is through an ATM. If you want a human transaction, bear in mind that while hotels give a less favorable rate of exchange than banks, they don't charge a fee to guests, are convenient, and rarely make you wait. Your time may be worth the difference.

TIPPING

With the arrival of the euro, tipping becomes an even murkier matter because it's a lot more expensive to be a good sport . . . and the low dollar doesn't make it any better. Do not tip in U.S. dollars.

- **For bellhops:** Figure 1€ per suitcase at a moderate hotel and 2€ per suitcase at a luxury hotel. Or give 5€ for a group of suitcases and totes.
- **For the doorman:** Tip 1€ for calling a taxi.
- **For the concierge:** If the concierge has been helpful, leave 10€ to 20€ depending on *how* helpful. I give the biggest tips to the guys who print out directions for me.
- **For taxi drivers:** Round up the taxi bill, but don't tip if you feel you were cheated. Do tip for extra help—like if he gets you a trolley for your baggage.

TAXING MATTERS

One of the reasons that prices are so high in Italy (and all of Europe) is that tax is already added to the final price tag. As a visitor, however, you may be entitled to a refund.

Italian Tax Refunds

Let's start at the beginning so you understand the system, and then I'll explain the tricky parts. The big picture is that on big-ticket items (roughly speaking, over $200), you can get a 12% rebate.

If you do not carry an E.U. passport, if you reside outside the E.U., and if you will be departing within 3 months of your purchase, you can qualify for a tax refund if you spend 154.94€ ($201) in the same day in the same store.

You must show your purchases when you leave the E.U. in order to get your refund. You must also have the paperwork processed at that time. Expect long lines during the summer season.

Refunds 101: The Easy Part

You only claim the refund when you depart the E.U.—this means the E.U., not Italy. So if you are driving from Italy into France, you are still in the E.U. and can't claim the refund until you leave the E.U. for the U.S. If you go into Croatia, a non-E.U. country, you get the paperwork stamped at the Italian border, before you enter Croatia.

When you depart from an E.U. airport for a non-E.U. country, remember the following:

- Go see the Customs officer at the airport *before* you check your luggage.
- Mail the papers from the airport if you want a credit card refund.
- If you want an immediate refund in cash, find the cash-refund desk. Look for the desk bearing a red, white, and green logo and the sign TAX FREE FOR TOURISTS.

Refund Me, You Fool

Please note that there are several ways for you to receive a refund. This is where it begins to get complicated.

There's the tax-free check, which you can cash or deposit at any bank; or a voucher, which can only be redeemed in currency. The voucher can be tricky because you will lose money on the conversion and have no chance to get a credit card refund. Whenever possible, have the refund applied to your credit card so you won't pay two exchange rates.

The new cash-in-town methods still mean that you have to show the goods at Customs when you depart the E.U. (an imprint is made for the tax refund, and if they don't get the paperwork back, you are charged the difference).

If you are leaving Italy via train or car, there are refund desks at the borders. Remember that you only do tax-free declarations at your final point of exit from the E.U.

Also note that the euro zone has expanded in the last year, so you may not be familiar with the borders. This is not a Polish joke. Know when to apply for the refund and when to wait.

The company that runs most of the refund business is called **Global Refund** (© 0081-355-416-718 toll-free in Italy; www.globalrefund.com).

Detaxe Scam

Many designer shops say to you, after you inquire as to the price of a high-ticket item, "but you get a 15% discount from the tax." The implication is that the item will automatically be about 20% less . . . and this fact is meant to tip your judgment in favor of the sale.

There's just one problem. You don't get the full 15% back; you usually get 12% because there are various fees involved.

RETURNING TO THE U.S.

Airport Duty-Free Shops

While intra-European duty-free shopping has been outlawed, this does not affect travelers leaving the E.U. through Italy. The Rome airport is virtually one giant shopping mall once you pass through Immigration. While there are tons of stores, the savings are not a sure bet. Perfume and cosmetics may be cheaper at the duty-free you left behind in the U.S. or London, or through the in-flight magazine. Not every shop in an airport retail area is duty-free. Ask!

You may get a flat 15% discount off regular Italian retail on Trussardi, Enrico Coveri, and Ferragamo shoes as well as many other things. The catch here is that the Italian retail price might be so inflated that the discount is meaningless.

Don't forget that whatever you buy at the duty-free shop must be declared when you return to the U.S. Unless you eat it on the plane. And never forget that duty-free shopping no longer ends when you leave the airport. All airlines now have duty-free shopping on the plane. The price list should be inside the in-flight magazine.

Security Laws & Liquids

If you buy a liquid—booze, perfume, olive oil, anything—at the duty-free shop in the airport upon departure, here's the only way you can keep those goods and get them to your home in the U.S.

After you have cleared U.S. Customs at your port of entry, repack your luggage before you re-check it. Insert all liquids, as you will not be able to travel any further with them as carry-ons. Cushion small bottles of perfume in clothing. Booze should be wrapped in lots of plastic bags. If you are planning on making a purchase, it doesn't hurt to have some bubble wrap and tape in your handbag (but no scissors!). *Note:* You've got to really want that bottle to go through all this.

U.S. Customs & Duties

- You are currently allowed to bring in $800 worth of duty-free merchandise per person. Each member of the family is entitled to the deduction; this includes infants.
- You pay a flat 10% duty on the next $1,000 worth of merchandise. It's worth doing—we're talking about the very small sum of $100 and being legal.
- Duties thereafter are based on the type of product. They vary tremendously per item, so ask storekeepers about U.S. duties. They will know, especially in specialty stores. Note that the duty on leather goods is only 8%.
- The head of the family can make a joint declaration for all family members and should take responsibility for answering any questions that the Customs officers may ask. Have receipts ready, and make sure they match the information on the landing card. If you tell a little lie, you'll be labeled as a fibber, and they'll tear your luggage apart.
- You count into your $800 per person everything you obtain while abroad—this includes toothpaste (if you bring the unfinished tube back with you), items bought in duty-free shops, gifts for others, the items that other people asked you to bring home for them, and—get this—even alterations to clothing.
- Have the Customs registration slips for things you already own in your wallet or someplace easily accessible. If you

wear a Cartier watch, you should be able to produce the registration slip. If you cannot prove that you took a foreign-made item out of the country with you, you may be forced to pay duty on it.

- The unsolicited gifts you mailed from abroad do not count in the $800-per-person rate. If the value of the gift is more than $50, you pay duty when the package comes into the U.S. Remember, only one unsolicited gift per person.
- Do not attempt to bring in any illegal foodstuffs—dairy products, meats, fruits, or vegetables (coffee is okay). Generally speaking, if it's alive, it's *verboten*. Dried mushrooms happen to be okay. Aged cheese is, too.
- Antiques must be at least 100 years old to be duty-free. Provenance papers will help (so will permission to actually export the antiquity, since it could be an item of national cultural significance). Any bona-fide work of art is duty-free whether it was painted 50 years ago or just yesterday.
- Thinking of "running" one of those new Italian handbags? Forget it. New handbags shout to Customs officers.

FINAL PHILOSOPHICAL NOTE

To paraphrase my fellow Texan Lance Armstrong, please remember that your trip to Italy is not about the handbag. I had this realization while I was online at AOL the other day and clicked on "Deal of the Day," which offered many Italian designer handbags from the biggest brands at half the price. On eBay, there are other sources that sell these brands for lower than U.S. retail.

We travel to see another world and taste another lifestyle. If you get a good deal, that's extra luck.

Chapter Three

ITALIAN STYLE

TOGA, TOGA, TOGA

Italian style goes back, well, centuries—even before there was an Italy. It was the city-state system back then, and even up until the mid-1800s part of what we today know as Italy was in France. What you're talking about when you think of chic is indeed half French. But not the sheets.

I sympathize with the politicos who say that modern Italy is actually two countries—north and south—and I see it in the fashions and the trends. But with a low dollar, you need not worry your pretty little head over politics—it's what's worth buying that is the real question. The answer lies within your own closet and your own lifestyle. Don't buy anything that makes sense in Italy but does not translate to your own world. At these prices, you want classics that will last 20 years.

Northern Fashion

Fashionistas in Milan are known to wear black—as they usually do in New York. To save themselves from going nuts with boredom, their black clothes have to have a style detail that makes them unique. This, then, is the epitome of northern Italian style—hard-edged and clever details. Often the fresh approach revolves around technology and fabrics. New fabrics make the price of the garment go up.

In complete contrast to this style is another style that is worn by real people, not fashion victims—it looks like English country style and is prevalent as far south as Florence. While Italy now sells clothes from all over the world, you will find that certain brands—be they Italian or global—have not ventured into the southern regions, even as far down as Florence—which is north where the south is concerned. Likewise, if you are looking to buy killer style, don't waste much time outside of Milan.

Buying Boutique Lines

If you crave the designer name, but don't want to blow too much money, consider one of the lesser lines by the designer—most of the designers have at least one range of clothing or accessories that's more mass-market.

The tricky part? Big-name designers have boutique lines that may not have their names on them. You'll often find these lesser lines in department stores like La Rinascente or even in the airport duty-free shops. In some cases, these lines end up with their own stores—such as Armani Jeans, Emporio Armani, D&G (from Dolce & Gabbana), and so on. Check out the T Store on Via del Corso in Rome to see what's new at Trussardi.

If you see a name you don't know, ask about it. The Flexa line happens to be the young style division of Fratelli Rossetti. Marina Rinaldi is the large-size version of Max Mara. A. Testoni is rather traditional, but the Duckling line is anything but. Malizia is a lower-priced lingerie line from La Perla, which has its own advertising so that people don't know the brands are actually competitive.

DICTIONARY OF TASTE & DESIGN

Note: Most of the brands and concepts listed below are Italian, but a few are French or British or global in one way or another. The brand may not be well known in the U.S., but you'll have an opportunity to discover it in Italy.

Almaplena Newly popular chain of accessories stores, somewhat glam, with great prices. www.almaplena.it.

Anna Molinari The name you'll remember is not Anna's, but that of her label—Blumarine—which has been making waves for about a decade. There are now a few Blumarine boutiques. The lesser line is called Blugirl: very sultry and sexy. www.blumarine.com.

Benetton Benetton can only be described as a phenomenon. It hangs in there and continues to reinvent, if not the wheel, then the sweater and perhaps the future. Check out some of the Benetton superstores in Italian capital cities; they even have play areas for kids. www.benetton.com.

Bottega Veneta Tomas Maier has his own shop in Miami, but what he is doing for BV is incredibly chic and inventive. There's still plenty of woven leather (in throw pillows!) and thousand-dollar handbags, but you'll also find shoes and clothes and cashmeres. www.bottegaveneta.com.

Brioni A name and a brand synonymous with men's style and elegance. James Bond (the Pierce Brosnan version, anyway) wore Brioni suits. There are stores—and stores that sell the brand—all over the world, but the Milan shop is the temple for service, and the Rome store is the original flagship. The factories are in Penne. www.brioni.it.

Bulgari Perhaps you know them for their gems or watches (lucky you), but now they've branched out into hotels (there's one in Milan) and jewel-toned makeup. www.bulgari.com.

Chocolate Although most people don't associate Italian taste with chocolate, some of the world's most famous chocolate brands do come from Italy. See Nutella below. Perugina, the best-known mass-market brand, sells not only chocolate candy but also chocolate cooking supplies; I buy its tiny chocolate chips at the grocery store.

Coccinelle This mass-market firm makes jazzy handbags at affordable prices; there are free-standing stores in most large Italian cities. Not considered a status range, but who cares? www.coccinelle.com.

I Love Pocket Coffee

Ferrero (the maker of Nutella and other goodies) has the answer you're looking for to satisfy your caffeine addiction. Pocket Coffees are small, individually wrapped chocolate candies with real liquid espresso inside.

These chocolates come in boxes of five and cost about a euro each; they can be found in most grocery stores. Aaron wants to point out that these candies are for extreme coffee enthusiasts only! Apparently the bitterness of the coffee combined with the dark chocolate is not for the faint of heart.

One piece of advice: Put the whole chocolate into your mouth at once, lest you get espresso squirting from your lips and dripping on your new *camiseta*.

—*JKM*

Coffee The best-known brands make coffee for all kinds of coffee machines, not just espresso. My favorite is what I call "magic coffee"—a plastic self-heating container with the brand name of Caldo Caldo. If you want to bring home a bag of coffee or two, try any supermarket; the biggest brands are Segafredo, Illy, and Lavazza. Note that the grind is different for espresso. If you get hooked, fret not—Illy has a home delivery program in the U.S. (© **877-ILLY-DIR**; www.illyusa.com/casa).

Diego Della Valle The man who created Tod's and Hogan (shoes); he's also responsible for Acqua di Parma fragrance.

Diesel This has nothing to do with cars or trains but might inflame the engine of any teen or tween—clothing and jeans that are pricey, tight, and very hot. Stores can be found all over the world but especially in all major Italian cities; see Diesel Style Lab, too. www.diesel.com.

Dolce & Gabbana They are bad boys with reputations on the cutting edge of fashion, and highly influenced by their southern Italian roots. They make clothes, they have a men's store complete with barber and bar, and now they've opened a restaurant in Milan named Gold, which you need much of in order to be a loyal customer. www.dolcegabbana.it.

Emilio Pucci Being dead doesn't mean much when you have a brand name in Italy or children who can carry on the business. Count Pucci's children sold to LVMH so that the Pucci brand could be revived and expanded. New shops and styles are popping up, and the public is Pucci-crazed all over again. www.emiliopucci.com.

Etro The Etro family has been in the paisley business with some of Italy's most famous mills in the Lake Como area for centuries. The fashions for men and women are so chic and whimsical, you could swoon. www.etro.com.

Fabriano It's a paper-goods firm with excellent graphic design and format. Free-standing stores are opening in all major Italian cities. Look for fabulous gift items for less than $10. www.fabrianoboutique.com.

Fendi Fendi is a sisterhood of five women who run various aspects of the family business, which includes leather goods, ready-to-wear, and furs; now their children are in the business. If you just want to gawk, check out the brand-new Palazzo Fendi in Rome, its "global store." There is also a new home-style line. www.fendi.com.

FNAC The French multimedia chain is expanding in Italy—it's good for books, CDs, small electronics, and supplies. www.fnac.it.

Frette This company specializes in Italian bed and table linens, with both consumer and professional (that is, hotel) lines. The brand actually began in the French Alps and then moved into Italy in the late 19th century. It has rejuvenated its look and expanded into home collections (and stores) in recent years. www.frette.com.

Gianfranco Ferré Ferré, a former architect, made creations that were identifiable by their construction and architectural lines. The flagship store in Milan is gorgeous and, of course, stunning from an architectural point of view. Ferré has just opened a spa in Milan. www.gianfrancoferre.com.

Giorgio Armani Giorgio Armani has been called one of the top five designers in the world; if you listen to *garmento* whispers, you can hear the clucking of wonder as to what will happen to his empire when he moves to the great minimalism in the sky. Meanwhile, the line and the business just keep growing. He has opened headquarters in a renovated chocolate factory in Milan and has also begun making (and selling) chocolates. www.giorgioarmani.com.

Gucci The new post–Tom Ford Gucci means a whole new look—if you haven't been keeping up, you should check it out. Besides shoes and leather goods, there's clothing, scarves, jewelry, and yes, pet supplies. www.gucci.com.

Jil Sander This German line was sold to Italians and just re-bought by Frau Sander herself. Watch this space. www.jilsander.de.

Kiton It's the trade name for Ciro Paone, Neapolitan men's tailor . . . although he himself is not the tailor. In fact, there are over 200 tailors working for this menswear brand. www.kiton.it.

Krizia No, Krizia isn't the designer's name—it's the name of a character from Plato. The designer behind it all is Mariuccia Mandelli, who has several licensees and creates many Krizia lines, including fragrances. Imaginative, with a good sense of humor, Mandelli still manages to produce drop-dead elegant clothes that rich women wear. www.krizia.net.

Laura Biagiotti Although she shows couture and ready-to-wear, Biagiotti is best known for her cashmere knits. And her new passion: golf. Many of her styles are loose (they make stunning maternity dresses!) and fit nicely on women with imperfect figures. Her cashmeres are expensive but sought-after. www.laurabiagiotti.it.

Les Copains Despite the Frenchified name, this firm is an Italian sportswear company, something on the order of an American bridge designer. The line is now designed by two young men from southern Italy. It's this southern slant that makes the line hot, they claim. www.lescopains.it.

Loro Piana Although most people associate this name with cashmere, the truth is the factories produce technologically advanced wools for men's suiting and other fabrics of all kinds. Their cashmere is considered unique because it is Italian, not foreign. They also use their fascination for technology in outerwear products and make Storm System as well as cashmere sweaters that are water-repellent. www.loropiana.com.

Luciano Barbera A brand so fancy that most people have never heard of it, this men's haberdashery line is carried at Bergdorf Goodman and Neiman Marcus in the U.S. The clothes are created in the family mills near Biella. Expect to pay over $1,000 for a cashmere sweater. In Italy, there is also a women's line and a golf line. www.lucianobarbera.it.

Lush A British brand, but it's been slightly re-created for the Italian market. It features bath and beauty products with locally made ingredients, so you get things like limoncello soap and shampoo here. These stores are popping up all over the world, but none of the branches have the Italian mode except those in Italy. www.lush.com.

Marni Based in Forte dei Marmi, the Palm Beach of Florence, the Marni family (actually named Castiglioni) has become well known in the U.S. only recently, partly because of the backing of a handful of New York specialty stores. Marni does a cross between whimsy and silly. It makes clothes that people talk about, not the average bland garments—that's for sure. www.marni.com.

Missoni A family venture, the Missoni firm is famous for its use of knits and colors. Prices are high. The architecture of the Milan shop is worth seeing—it's an incredible example of new Italian style. Missoni bed linens are sold in T&J Vestor boutiques around Europe (including Italy). Not to be outdone by the Bulgari family, the Missonis are now in the hotel business—with SAS Radisson. www.missoni.com.

Miu Miu Childhood nickname of Miuccia Prada and name of the designer bridge line with three stores in Italy: in Milan, Florence, and Capri. www.miumiu.com.

Moschino If you have a sense of humor and believe that fashion should be fun, you'll love the work inspired by bad boy Moschino, who was what the French call a *créateur* (a big-name designer who doesn't create couture). www.moschino.com.

Nutella The chocolate/hazelnut spread made by Ferrero is one of Italy's best inventions. You can get it in the U.S., but while you're in Italy you can't (and shouldn't) avoid it. It's best on crepes, fruit, and bread—I've put the stuff on just about everything. If you can find it, Nutella-flavored gelato is a truly legendary experience. Few gelato shops carry it, though many will have a chocolate/hazelnut flavor called *giandujia;* still, the real Nutella flavor is the best stuff.

Patrizia Pepe This line from Prato (north of Florence) has become so successful, there are now free-standing stores in the best shopping areas of all major Italian cities. It's a bridge line, somewhat hip without being totally over-the-top. *Note:* Sarah discovered the sizes run very, very small—at least two sizes smaller than marked. www.patriziapepe.com.

Pratesi It's the family name of the small Italian bedding firm (founded in 1904) on whose sheets most of the crowned heads of Europe were conceived; it even makes sheets for the Pope. There are stores in Boston, New York, and Beverly Hills as well as in major Italian cities. These sheets are considered the most luxurious in Italy. www.pratesi.com.

Roberta di Camerino The Venetian handbag makers who offered cult luxury products in the 1970s are now re-issuing some designs that are hard to find and considered very "in." Vintage versions are also popular. Look for the free-standing store in Venice. www.robertadicamerino.com.

Roberto Cavalli A longtime legendary talent in Italy, Cavalli made it onto the global scene somewhat recently when his wild jeans were spotted on movie stars and rock musicians. Then he segued into sexy chic with the lingerie look. Now he even makes lingerie. His clothes were featured on *Sex and the City,* and people on the street say he is the "new" Versace. www.robertocavalli.com.

Salvatore Ferragamo Ferragamo's most famous for the shoes, then the silks, then the clothes, and now the hotel. The stores give away a free booklet on how to tie a silk scarf—just ask for it. The flagship is in Florence. Note that large sizes are often more readily available in the U.S. www.ferragamo.com.

Sephora The French chain of beauty-product supermarkets. The Italian branches are often in real-people districts and not tourist areas. Try the one in Rome's central train station (downstairs). www.sephora.com.

Shoes Italian leather goods—shoes, gloves, and handbags—have been world famous for centuries. For a fun spree, drive the area between Padua and Venice, where zillions of shoe factories dot the back roads. The most famous factory is Caovilla, where most designer shoes are made.

Valentino The famous designer Valentino, known for his work in beige, is legally named Valentino Garavani. In some countries (for example, Japan), licensed goods are registered under this name. These are not necessarily the man's own designs, however. If you want true Valentino merchandise, you must buy it in Italy. www.valentino.com.

Vintage Clothing Wearing vintage clothes seems to be the trend that just won't end. That's fine with me, since I like clothes with a history . . . just not underwear with a history. Vintage in Italy seems to be a northern thing; Milan is the capital of the look (try **Spazio 29** and **Lo Specchio di Alice,** both on Porta Ticinese).

Chapter Four

ROME

WELCOME TO ROME

I don't know how to be coy about this, so I will just blurt it out: I think the best shopping you can do in Rome is the wander-around-and-enjoy-what-you-find kind of shopping. In short, this is not the best place for a deal, or for much more than wandering and window-shopping, unless you get lucky. There is something magical about the fountains, the street fashions, and the scene that makes you want to buy just enough to feel like you are part of it.

Rome has always had a great-designer, upscale-shopping neighborhood, but the current low dollar has brought new high prices, and the arrival of eBay has brought new opportunities to shop without travel.

Therefore, you want to get spiritual. You don't have to be in a church or Vatican City to get spiritual—just wander the little streets and alleys, munch on ice cream, look through store windows, and pop into the places that really interest you. Another pair of shoes? Sure, why not! Spaghetti at that touristy joint on the Via Veneto, eaten outside while the world passes by? Why not!

Rome is mostly for selection, or for the big brands at discount stores, or for really cheapie fun clothes that will be over in a season but will give you no end of pleasure until then. Part

About Oviesse

I mention Oviesse in the Rome chapter because this is where the store that I first went to is located and because I have spent a lot of time shopping this brand and visiting stores in every Italian city. That I jumped in at a Rome store and was wowed by the designs, prices, and large sizes has a lot to do with my love affair with this brand.

While UPIM remains a dime store/general store and sometimes has nice clothes or lingerie, Oviesse has a far more fashion-forward look. It sells clothing for men, women, and children, with an emphasis on a range of sizes for women. There are plus sizes and petites, junior styles, and everyday styles. There are also accessories and some shoes and even pieces of luggage, which you will need if you buy as much as I did.

The average price of a total outfit at Oviesse is under 70€ ($91); a linen dress costs about 32€ ($42). Are you running with me, team? The styles are the latest fashions, so you can be chic and glam for small amounts of bread. And the large-size fashions are so good-looking that you can continue to eat bread—or pizza.

About the size system: Tags usually have two sizes printed on them—one is the Italian size (these tend to run small, so you probably wear a larger-than-average numbered size—don't freak) and the other is the continental size, usually marked with a D (for Deutschland—Germany) or CH (for Switzerland).

The stores in Rome are not in tourist shopping districts—stores in other Italian cities are, but not in Rome. There are eight branches in Rome, including the one at Viale Trastevere 62/64 (✆ **06/5833-3633**; www.oviesse.it). You can get to a store via the Metro; just ask your hotel's concierge to find the closest location to you and provide the exact directions.

The selection varies, but if you are on a budget, this is going to be your favorite store in Italy.

of the glory that is Rome is that while there are heaps of designer shops, there are also heaps of everything else, too. Even the magazine stands are fabulous to drool over.

If you visit in summer, you'll also note that Rome does southern Italian style, which is much more geared toward resort wear than what is shown up north. Milan thinks summer is a Jackie O A-line skimmer in linen with a single, simple rope of shell beads and a pair of leather sandals. Rome thinks in terms of bright colors, gold, pewter, metallics, beads, embroidery, cleavage, high heels, and lotsa jewelry.

Me? I am amused by Roman fashion, I long to be able to afford that Milanese linen dress (it was about $1,000), and I take great delight in shopping at Oviesse, which may be the best tip I can share with you right now.

ARRIVING IN ROME

By Plane

Thankfully, you can fly into Rome's airport from anyplace in the world. Just allow yourself plenty of time before you are actually in the stores and shopping.

The airport (Leonardo da Vinci) is quite a bit out of town, and a taxi will easily set you back 50€ to 70€ ($65–$91). A private car and driver costs about the same as a taxi, by the way (or a little more, but usually not much). As a result, many people book a car and driver to meet them or ask their hotel to provide this service. When I stay at the Hotel Exedra in Rome, I ask them to pick me up—their airport service is 65€ ($85).

I also use one of the many shuttle services from the airport, which generally cost 50€ to 60€ ($65–$78).

If you can manage your luggage on your own, you may want to take the shuttle train (Leonardo Express) from the airport right to the central train station (Termini) in beautiful downtown Rome. It costs about 10€ ($13) and is a total breeze.

If you arrive in Rome's airport from another E.U. country, there are no formalities. The color of your luggage tag is coded so that you don't even go through Immigration or Customs. You suddenly end up in the luggage-retrieval area, watching fashion shows and car videos on large-screen TV monitors while waiting for your bags.

Trolleys are free. There's both a *cambio,* for changing money, and a bank machine (better rates than the *cambio*), although the lines can be long. Still, since you have to wait for your bags to arrive, you may as well stock up on cash and be ready for the spree to come.

You can connect to the train from within the arrivals terminal (it is well marked), but you must forfeit your trolley to use the escalator, so again, make sure you can handle your luggage on your own or with your travel companion.

If you are headed to the taxi line, be aware that you may be assaulted by taxi drivers: gypsy drivers who may even have official taxis with medallions and may convince you that they are legit. Watch out!

There is an official taxi stand, but you must find it, which I happened to have had trouble doing over a period of many years (slow learner). If you end up on the curb wondering what to do—look right and then walk right, and you will find the taxi stand. I promise.

By Train

All rail tracks do indeed lead to Rome, be it intra-Italian trains or any of the fancy intra-European trains, including Eurostar (Italian Eurostar, not the Chunnel version). Termini—the main station in Rome—has been spiffed up and is looking far better than you may remember it. The fact that it has a giant **Nike** shop in the front and a huge **UPIM** with fancy vaulted ceilings to one side helps. A series of electronic kiosks for e-tickets should give you a hint that this is the *new* Italy.

As you emerge from the main train station, you'll see taxis everywhere; you may even be approached by some drivers who offer their services. Again, there is an official taxi stand with a very long line right in front of the train station. You may wonder why you don't just hop into one of the waiting cabs, defying the queue. Why does everyone stand in line for up to 20 minutes? Because they don't want to overpay, be cheated, or come to blows with aggressive taxi drivers. I was offered rides to a friend's house for 40€ ($52) and 50€ ($65); the legitimate cab fare was 8€ ($10). When I didn't accept the hustlers' offers, they were very insulting in a variety of languages.

Tip: A good reason to stay at the Hotel Exedra: If you can't get a taxi or the lines are loathsome, you can borrow a trolley from the train station and walk to the hotel.

By Ship

If by chance you are coming to Rome via ship, the port is Civitavecchia (say "cheat-a-*veck*-ee-ahhhh"); it lies along the coast north and west of Rome. It can take up to 2 hours to get into downtown Rome from here, although 1 hour is the no-traffic estimate. If you are going directly from your ship to the Rome airport, it will take 1 hour on a superhighway, and you will not actually go into Rome at all. *(Arrivederci, Roma.)*

And one final ship-to-shore report: On Saturdays during summer, most stores close for the day at 1:30pm. This isn't really a problem for you, however, because you'll arrive in port at 7am and make it to Rome by 9:30am, when the stores open. You then have the whole morning to shop.

Go to lunch at 1:30pm, when the stores close, and slowly eat a glorious Roman midday feast. Head back to the ship around 4pm and arrive in time for cocktails. Or stop off in Tarquinia, a sneeze away from the port, with its cutie-pie retail and—I thought you'd never ask—a few pottery shops.

There is a train station at the port, but you have to get from the boat to the train in order to connect (you can walk, but it can be a hike, depending on your ship's berth). And, as part of the 2000 Jubilee, there was a major renovation and improvement of the port area. They even added on some shopping venues.

GETTING AROUND

The city of Rome is divided into 33 zones, working in circular rounds, much like the *arrondissements* of Paris. The oldest part of the city is 1, *Centro Storico*. I have instead divided Rome into my own areas or neighborhoods (see "Shopping Neighborhoods," later in this chapter).

(Technically speaking, Vatican City is a different city from Rome; that's why it has its own guards, its own postal service, and its own euro coins.)

While in Rome, walk as much as possible. Okay, so it's too hot to walk that much, and the city's too spread out. So, the best time investment you can make is to organize your days so that you *can* do lots of walking; this keeps you out of crazy Roman traffic and on the streets where you can count the fountains.

By Taxi

Roman taxi drivers are known to be difficult, especially to tourists, especially to Americans who can't speak Italian, and most especially to women traveling without men. Be prepared to occasionally argue with the driver; be aware of when you should pay a supplement (for extra baggage and for rides after 9pm and on Sun and holidays). I continue to have unpleasant situations with drivers, enough so that I think the difference between Italy and France can be summed up in the way you are treated by taxi drivers. But enough about me.

Legitimate taxis carry a shield with a number. Cars for hire are black with a shield. Taking any other car can be dangerous.

By Metro

The Metropolitana, or Metro for short, is nice and gets you to most tourist attractions, but it does not blanket the city. You may find the walk from your hotel to the nearest stop (look for the big red M sign) worthy of a taxi in itself. When booking a hotel, I now make certain there is a Metro stop nearby.

To ride the Metro, have change to put into the ticket machine, or look around for a machine that produces change. You must get your ticket from one of the machines; there is no booth selling tickets. (The newsstand will not give you change without a purchase.) Because the Metro is not too involved, it is easy to ride and safe. A Metrobus card, which costs about 4€ ($5.20) per day, allows unlimited use of both the Metro and buses. It's sold in train stations and at newsstands.

Toffee's tip: Dogs can go on the Metropolitana and buses if they are held in their master's arms.

By Bus

I love to take the bus in Rome, although many people will tell you that they're slow and not dependable, especially in the rain. But buses are air-conditioned, give you a nice view of this gorgeous city, and get you easily to the main attractions.

To find out which bus to take, buy a bus map at a newsstand, ask your concierge, or read the sign at the bus stop that lists all the stops on that route. Also, check inside the telephone book in your hotel room, which may have a bus and Metro map.

I once took the right bus in the wrong direction—a typical mistake for those who don't speak the language or know their way around the city very well—but I had a great time and saw a lot of sights.

Rome has many bus islands that act as little stations where buses congregate. There's one such island in front of the Vittorio Emanuele monument in the old city, and another called San Silvestro, which is in the heart of the shopping district at the base of the Via Veneto and halfway to the Spanish Steps.

The bus system in Rome is similar to those in other Italian cities: You must purchase your ticket at a tobacco stand or newsstand ahead of time (the bus driver does not sell tickets or take money); you enter from the rear and cancel your own ticket in the box; and you exit from the center of the bus. Instructions in English and Italian are inside the bus. Tickets are good for 75 minutes, so if you are quick like a bunny, you can get on and off a few times. At 1€ ($1.30) per ride, a single

Rome & Its Shopping Neighborhoods

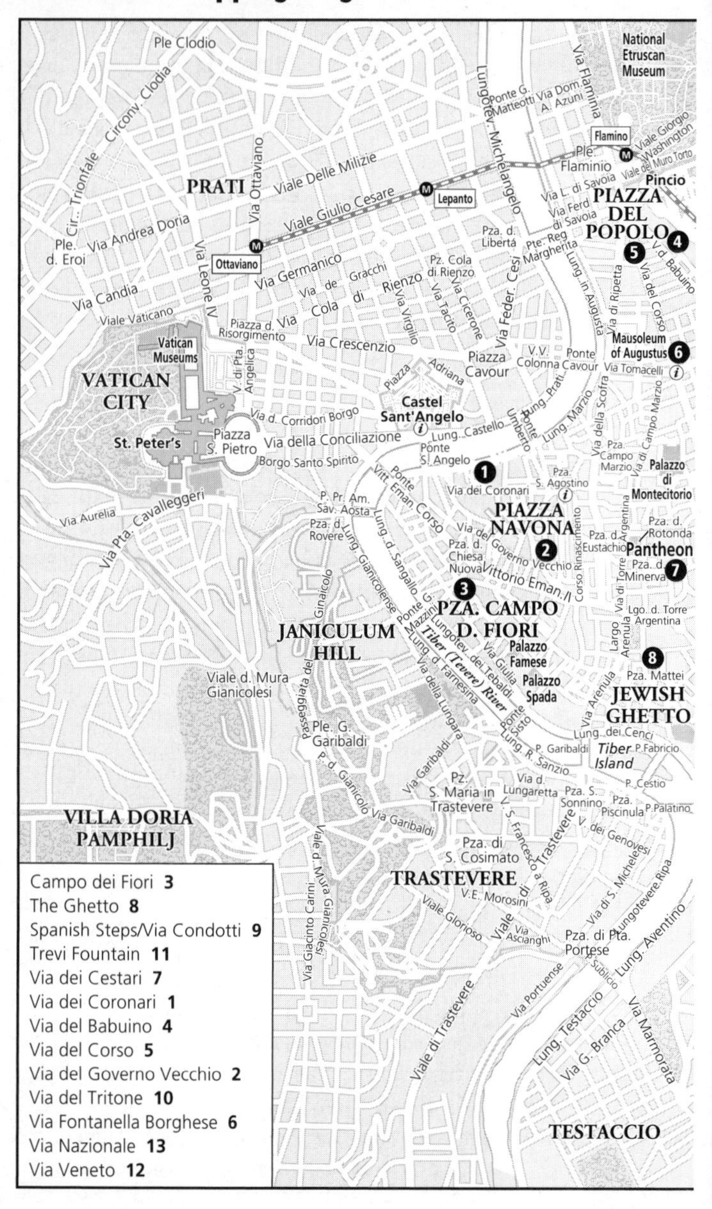

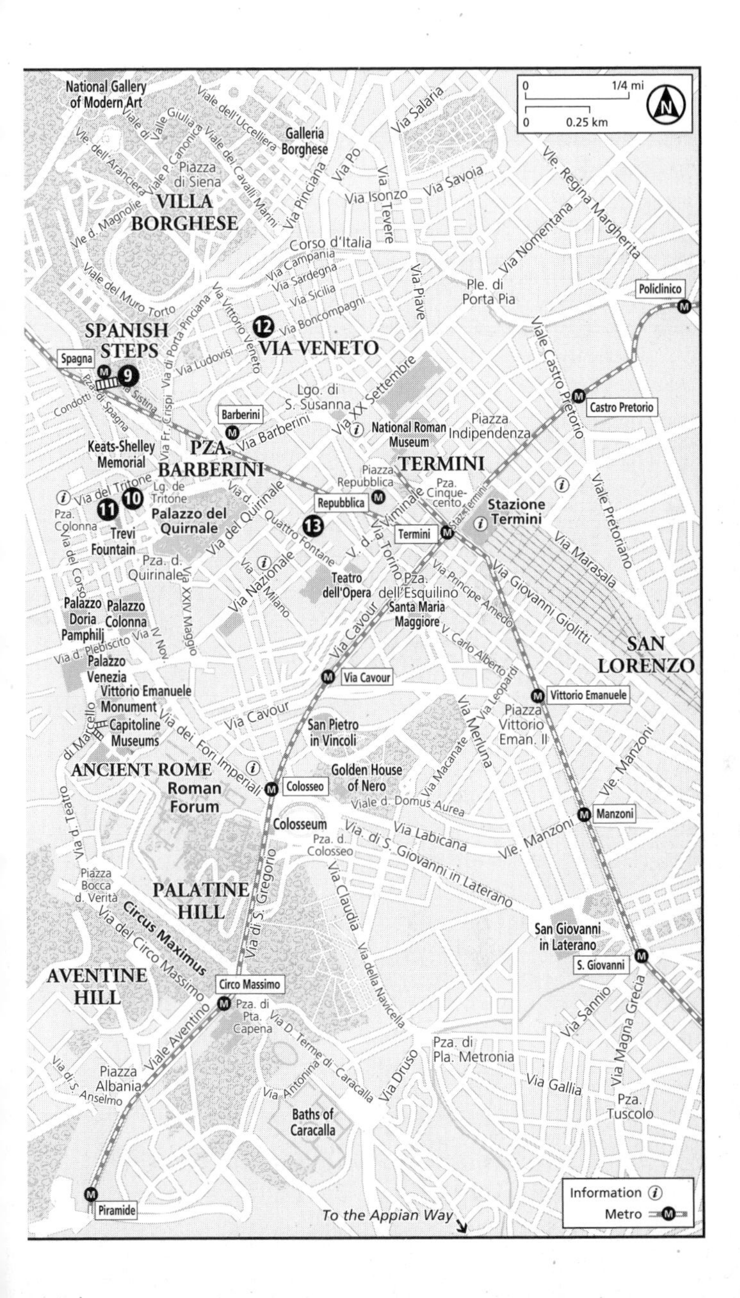
National Gallery of Modern Art
Galleria Borghese
VILLA BORGHESE
Piazza di Siena
SPANISH STEPS
Spagna
VIA VENETO
Barberini
PZA. BARBERINI
Keats-Shelley Memorial
Trevi Fountain
Palazzo del Quirinale
Pza. d. Quirinale
Palazzo Doria Pamphilj
Palazzo Colonna
Palazzo Venezia
Vittorio Emanuele Monument
Capitoline Museums
ANCIENT ROME
Roman Forum
Colosseo
Colosseum
PALATINE HILL
Circus Maximus
AVENTINE HILL
Circo Massimo
Piramide
Baths of Caracalla
To the Appian Way
TERMINI
National Roman Museum
Repubblica
Termini
Stazione Termini
Teatro dell'Opera
Santa Maria Maggiore
Via Cavour
San Pietro in Vincoli
Golden House of Nero
Vittorio Emanuele
Piazza Vittorio Eman. II
Manzoni
San Giovanni in Laterano
S. Giovanni
SAN LORENZO
Castro Pretorio
Policlinico
Ple. di Porta Pia
Piazza Indipendenza
Via Veneto
Via Nomentana
Via Salaria
Corso d'Italia
Via XX Settembre
Via Nazionale
Via dei Fori Imperiali
Via Giovanni Giolitti
Via di S. Giovanni in Laterano
Via Labicana
Pza. di Pla. Metronia
Pza. Tuscolo
Piazza Albania
Piazza Bocca d. Verità
0 1/4 mi
0 0.25 km
N
Information
Metro

About Addresses

Addresses seem to bounce around from street to street; some alternate in a sensible way and some make no sense at all. Frequently, all the stores in a block have the same street number and are designated by letters. It's not unusual for a store to be listed according to its piazza or its street corner.

ticket on the bus is still the deal of the century—you get to sightsee and go to a part of town where you can walk around, all for a low price.

My favorite bus is the no. 80, which you can get at the beginning of the line at the bus island at San Silvestro. You can take this bus directly to a very good **Oviesse** store and enjoy air-conditioning, with door-to-door service.

SLEEPING IN ROME

Luxury Hotel Chains

Note that the U.S.-based hotel chains have made a comfortable dent in the Roman scene; they often offer deals (in dollars, no less) that are too good to be true.

INTER-CONTINENTAL DE LA VILLE ROMA
Via Sistina 67–69 (Metro: Spagna).

The Inter-Continental de la Ville Roma has the best location of any of the U.S. chains for shopping—right at the top of the Spanish Steps—as well as some rather good deals. It has just undergone a major renovation and added a spa. The hotel is divinely swank, as well as service-oriented.

Last time I checked, there was a special rate of 199€ ($259), breakfast included. © **800/327-0200** in the U.S. Local phone © 06/67-331. www.intercontinental.com.

Regina Hotel Baglioni

Via Vittorio Veneto 72 (Metro: Veneto).

Situated right on what I call Hotel Row, this choice is well located for everywhere you want to be and equally well located for the Metro and bus, so you can get around town without taxis. One of Baglioni's 14 properties, this one is breathtakingly swank and yet still intimate.

The building is a small palace that has been renovated in modern style—I could barely swallow breakfast because I was gaping at the wonderful combination of rococo decor with raspberry walls and gray silk velvet upholstery. The hotel also has one of the Baglioni branches of Brunello, a restaurant of North African style with good food and mesmerizing music.

The rooms are old-style, grande-dame, and fancy-schmancy, with modern furnishings and new amenities. There are various promotions depending on the season, but figure $500 a night for a grand deluxe room for two with full breakfast buffet. That includes free Wi-Fi, too. ✆ **06/421-111.** www.baglionihotels.com.

Rome Cavalieri Hilton

Via A. Cadlolo 101 (no nearby Metro, but hotel has free shuttle-bus service).

We all know to trust the Hilton brand, but few of us know that this is one of the most famous, and different, Hilton hotels in the system. Yes, it is out of the downtown area—but the benefits overcome that disadvantage.

The hotel has a fabulous rooftop restaurant, La Pergola. But it gets better: Always famous for its swimming pool and park-like grounds, this Hilton now has a spa. Not just any old spa, as is the rage among all hotels, but a spa of such grand proportions that it was possibly created to make Cleopatra roll over in her grave. This spa has become so important in the local landscape that zillions of celebs now stay here. (Lest you forget, summer in Rome is so hot that you can rarely shop for more than half a day, and it's great to have a pool and a spa to repair to.)

Last time I called Hilton, there was a deal that had to be booked in the U.S., for 150€ ($195) per night. I don't need to tell you that this is about the least-expensive five-star room you can get in Rome. © **800/HILTONS** in the U.S. Local phone © 06/3509-2031. www.cavalieri-hilton.it.

Design Hotels

Sometimes you want a hotel because of its design features alone. The following are all in good locations and offer a little something extra to stare at.

ALEPH

Via di San Basilio 15 (Metro: Barberini).

My heartthrob Adam Tihany designed this cozy, artsy boutique hotel for those who want luxury on the sly. It's got a spa, a Moroccan-style restaurant, and a location nestled far from the Spanish Steps and Via Veneto. This hotel is so hot that it has been photographed for various design magazines, guidebooks, and books on Roman style. Don't miss it, even if you just come by for a drink. Rates are about $300 a night. © **888/626-7265** in the U.S. Local phone © 06/422-901. www.aleph.boscolo hotels.com.

EXEDRA

Piazza della Repubblica 47 (Metro: Repubblica).

You may want to stay here, or you may just want to have a look out of curiosity. The hotel is built over ruins that you can see through glass floors on the lower level (head for the business center). Rates begin at 300€ ($390); I found a room online for 250€ ($325). © **888/626-7265** in the U.S. Local phone © 06/489-381. www.exedra.boscolohotels.com.

PORTRAIT SUITES
Via Bocca di Leone 23 (Metro: Spagna).

Ferragamo has brought its hotel chain to Rome and opened doors—and beds—above the men's store, right on the Via Condotti. There are only 14 units, which is in keeping with the new trend in luxe hotels—small, chic, and yet cozy. Rooms begin at $400. © **06/6938-0742.** www.lungarnohotels.com.

Four-Star Finds

HOTEL PIRANESI
Via del Babuino 196 (Metro: Spagna).

We owe this find to Maria Teresa. The Piranesi is directly across from the Hotel de Russie, one of Rome's grandest addresses. It's at the Popolo end of town, so there are taxis waiting, and you are right on what I call Baboon Street, which is shopping HQ and leads right to the Spanish Steps. In short, few locations are better. This hotel is a gem—trust me.

Rates vary with the season; you may find something good online. A double lists at 320€ ($416) in peak season and 255€ ($332) in winter. © **06/328-041.** www.hotelpiranesi.com.

VILLA LAETITIA
Lungotevere delle Armi 22 (Metro: Lepanto).

This is a bit out-of-the-way, which gives you more of a feel for actually living in Rome. It is also classified as a residence, so there's a kitchenette in each room. There are only 15 rooms, so it's arty and cozy and a great find. But there's more: The residence is owned by one of the Fendi sisters, and the decor includes sketches by Karl Lagerfeld. There is even a Karl Suite. Rates begin at $250 and include Wi-Fi. © **06/322-6776.** www.villalaetitia.com.

SNACK & SHOP

LA CARBONARA

Piazza Campo dei Fiori 23 (no nearby Metro).

This is one of the few places in Rome where it is as pleasant to eat inside as outside, where your experience is as special in winter as in spring. Located right on the Campo dei Fiori, this seems to be the nicest of the surrounding cafes. The interior is done in a rustic country style, with some tables overlooking the piazza. The daily fruit and flower market adds to the charm of the location and makes this restaurant a must. It is one of the few restaurants in the area that is open on Sunday (although it's closed on Tues). Note that the flower market is closed on Sundays. For reservations, call © **06/686-4783.**

MCDONALD'S

Piazza di Spagna, near the Spanish Steps (Metro: Spagna).

Stop laughing. I love this McDonald's, and not just because my son does. The architecture (it's in a fake villa) is astounding, the location is sublime, it's a good place to rest between stores, and the food is inexpensive for Rome. You can get the usual burgers and McNuggets, or load up at the salad bar, which has tomatoes and mozzarella. You have to see this place—the crowd it gets is amazing. Logan, my Roman insider source, says to sit downstairs where it's less noisy; you can also buy Baci (the chocolates), and there's even an ice-cream counter.

NINO

Via Borgognona 11 (Metro: Spagna).

My favorite restaurant in Rome, Nino is a small bistro with dark wood walls, located right in the heart of the Spanish Steps shopping area. It attracts a nice, fashionable crowd without being chichi. Prices are moderate by Rome standards, which to me is incredibly inexpensive, especially for this location and style. My last lunch at Nino, an admittedly simple affair consisting of bottled water, one Coca-Cola, spaghetti, and a coffee, was 20€ ($26). Tip included.

The waiters are friendly; I often eat here solo and feel comfortable doing so. If you get here early (by local standards) for lunch, you don't need a reservation. Closed Sunday. © **06/679-5676.**

Ristorante Girarrosto Toscano
Via Campania 29 (Metro: Veneto).

This country-style place is at the top of the Via Veneto (across the street from the Jolly Hotel, around the corner from the Westin Excelsior). Sit down and feast on the antipasti, for which there is a flat charge per person no matter how much you eat. After you've had more than you thought possible, they bring dinner. The cooking style is Florentine; the wine is chianti (although there are plenty of others); the atmosphere is adorable (covered in tiles and charm); the crowd is well-heeled (although there are some tourists); and the prices are moderate. Make a reservation, especially after 8pm, as the place does fill up. Closed Wednesday. © **06/482-1899.**

THE SHOPPING SCENE

Shopping is something you do in Rome while you are doing Rome—or in between meals. Aside from a frontal attack on Via Condotti and the fancy stores in that area, you will find shopping opportunities as you explore Rome, not vice versa.

Roman style is still a little bit old couture, but Roman fashion mostly reflects Rome's geographic location, which is philosophically—and fashion-wise—the south of Italy. As such, Rome is rather like the Beverly Hills of Italy, and the clothes for sale here have a glitz and gleam to them that you won't find up north. Even the Milanese, who have moved on down here, don't wear black.

Colors are hot in Rome. Women are not flat-chested in Rome. Skirts are shorter in Rome. Nailheads, studs, bugle beads, and sequins with, yes, truly, little bits of fur or feathers—faux and/or real—can be found sewn to clothing and . . . hmm . . . even shoes and tote bags.

The globalization of money and designer franchises means that Italian designers sell their lines all over their own country, most certainly in Rome, and in just about every other country as well. The line may be most fully shown in stores in Milan, but you can find an excellent selection of these designer clothes in Rome. In a few cases, the Rome store will be better than the Milan store.

The Best Buys in Rome

Rome doesn't have any cheap best buys, unless you shop at UPIM or Oviesse. Oops, I lied. You *can* get lucky.

Designer Fashions You won't find too many designer bargains unless you hit a sale, but if you do, things can really go your way. If you are bargain conscious, the best deals in Rome are at a few outlet shops (see "Outlets," later in this chapter) or at the airport, which has a gigantic duty-free shopping area. If you are status conscious, the best buys are due to the fact that Rome has a selection of styles in any given designer brand that goes beyond those of other cities in the world.

Note that items imported to Italy for sale at the airport duty-free shops (English sweaters, for example) are 19% cheaper than they are in a regular Italian store, but they are still outrageously expensive. Buy Italian when in Italy; forget everything else. Also note that, even though it may look like one, not every store in the Rome airport is a duty-free shop.

Handbags Although I usually buy my handbags in Hong Kong and have long ago sworn off $1,000 handbags, I found a store in Rome that not only tickled my fancy (I bought three bags), but also seems to be very popular with visitors. In my week in Rome on my last research trip, every woman I passed in the Spanish Steps shopping district seemed to have a glossy shopping bag from **Francesco Rogani** (Via Condotti 17; © **06/678-7737**) on her arm. See p. 96 for the lowdown.

Home Style From Tad to Lisa Corti, the hot Mediterranean colors and the mix of imported looks with Italian chic have arrived. This is mondo home style, from Asia to the subcontinent and beyond, shaken up with the Italian touch. Lisa Corti is sold at Saks Fifth Avenue, but the Italy prices—even in euros—are better than the U.S. prices. If you can't stand the colors, back into beige or monotones in bed linens from Frette or Pratesi.

Ties I got caught up in the number of status ties for sale in various shops in Rome. Prices are lower than in the U.S. and the U.K. In fact, prices can be so low you may giggle. The average price of a power tie in New York, without New York state sales tax, is $125 to $165. The same ties in Rome cost half that. I kid you knot.

The Five Best Stores in Rome

FORUM TERMINI
Rome central train station (Metro: Termini).

Perhaps you can never take the love of a mall out of the American heart. This is truly an American-style mall located underneath the main train station, but it has French and Italian stores—and places to eat—and is great fun. There's a shop devoted to merchandise for race-car drivers and wannabes. There's a Sephora (the beauty supermarket). There's a real supermarket. Aboveground, on the main level, there's a tease of what's below—a Nike shop, a Benetton, a bookstore, and even UPIM. If you haven't seen the brand Bottega Verde, this is a place to check it out—sort of the local version of the Body Shop. Note the barrel-vaulted ceilings, the ocher colors, and the attempt at a lush-hush historic Roman feel.

LISA CORTI HOME TEXTILE EMPORIUM
Via di Pallacorda 14 (Metro: Spagna).

I am a huge Lisa Corti fan, so I send you here with delight. It's right near the Piazza Fontanella Borghese, not too far from the Spanish Steps. The Lisa Corti collection includes home style, tabletop, and home fashions. Look for the merchandise in any Saks Fifth Avenue catalog, and then compare prices in person. © **06/6819-3216.** www.lisacorti.com.

LUNA & L'ALTRA
Via del Governo Vecchio 105 (no nearby Metro).

This store isn't much bigger than a walk-in closet, but it carries an international cadre of funky-chic names, such as Issey Miyake and Dries Van Noten, and puts it all together in a look that is comfortable and fabulous. © **06/6880-4995.**

SOLE
Via Gregoriana 34 (Metro: Spagna).

This isn't technically a store; it's an atelier and should be visited only by serious shoppers who call ahead for an appointment. The studio is on the top floor of a residential building near the top of the Spanish Steps. If you love creative clothes and an artistic look, you'll find it worth the walk.

Sole is the child of Soledad Twombly, an artist and the daughter-in-law of the famous artist Sy Twombly. Her husband, Alessandro, is also a well-known artist. Her studio features clothes, along with shoes, jewelry, sweaters, knits, and all the pieces you need for a complete look. She does only two seasons; the fabrics all work together, so you can add on pieces and change around the outfits.

Prices are dear, but lower than in stores when you buy directly from the designer. You can order by your size or have items made to your measurements. © **06/6992-4512.** www.soledad twombly.com.

TAD
Via del Babuino 155a (Metro: Spagna).

It's home style by the mile, even though it's not that hard-line Italian look. In fact, the look is somewhat international in scope, with imports galore and items from India with beads and handpainting and glitter and tassels. If you like Anthropologie stores in the U.S., you will love Tad in Rome. Ask for the address of the stock shop that was around the corner when I visited; it may have moved. There's a cafe, too. © **06/3269-5131.** www.taditaly.com.

Shopping Hours

Hours in Rome are the same as in all of Italy, but Sundays are really loosening up. In fact, the department store **La Rinascente** is open on Sunday from noon to 5pm. Wonders never cease. Furthermore, there's a new mall, **Piazza Colonna,** which is not only open on Sundays, but is even open until 10pm. Note that stores that open for Sunday shopping may close for lunch and then reopen from 4 to 7pm.

For normal retail days (Tues–Fri), shops open at 9:30am and close at 1 or 1:30pm for lunch. They reopen at 3:30pm in winter and at 4pm in summer. In summer, stores stay open until 8pm. Because Romans (as do all Europeans) dine late, many people are out shopping until midnight. Do not let any hotel concierge or signpost lead you to believe that stores in Rome open at 9am—even if it says so on the door. This is Rome, remember?

If you don't like to give up shopping for lunch, the department stores and mass merchandisers stay open during these hours, and a growing number of high-end merchants are following suit. Fendi is open through lunch, as are many other stores on Via Borgognona and in the Spanish Steps area.

The odd days are Monday, Saturday, and Sunday. Some stores are closed Monday morning; in summer, they are often closed Saturday afternoon as well. But that's not a rule. On my last Monday in Rome, I found that mass-market stores and chains were open by 10am that day. Designer shops open at 3:30pm on Monday.

Finally, watch out for those August closures—some stores call it curtains totally. Only madmen go to Rome in August. The sales are in July.

Special-Event Retailing

If you happen to be in Rome anytime between December 15 and January 6, get yourself (and your kids) over to the Piazza Navona, where there is an annual Christmas fair. Stalls surrounding the large square offer food, candies, and crafts. You can buy tree ornaments and crèches. ***Warning:*** Much of the Hong Kong–made merchandise is less expensive in the U.S. Stick to locally crafted items at the fair, and you won't get ripped off.

Because Easter in Rome is also a big deal, there are more vendors in Vatican City at that time.

Personal Needs

You will find neither grocery stores nor real-people department stores in the middle of the usual tourist shopping haunts, although there are branches of **La Rinascente** and **UPIM** just near San Silvestro, close to the main tourist areas, such as the Trevi Fountain and the Spanish Steps.

The city has dozens of all-night pharmacies, including one at the airport. The pharmacy at the Termini train station is open until 11:30pm daily. The station also has a fabulous mall that can meet most needs; its stores are open on Sundays.

Rome is more spread out than some other cities you may visit; you might need to take a walk around your hotel to find a local minimart for buying water, snack foods, and all those things that cost too much from your minibar.

Ask your concierge where to find the nearest pharmacy or grocery store. Condoms are sold from machines in public places, as well as at pharmacies and grocery stores.

SHOPPING NEIGHBORHOODS

Spanish Steps/Via Condotti No matter what season of the year, the Spanish Steps are so gorgeous that you can't help but be drawn to them. They are particularly magical because they lead to all the best big-name stores. Don't forget that there's an **American Express** office at the Steps, so when you run out of money on a shopping spree, you can get more without missing a beat, and then get right back to spending it.

The Via Condotti is the leading shopping street of the high-rent Spanish Steps neighborhood—but it is not the only game in town, or even on the block. The area between the Spanish Steps and the Via del Corso is a grid system of streets, all packed with designer shops. Via Condotti has the most famous big names and is the equivalent of Rodeo Drive, but you'll miss a lot of great stuff if you don't do the side streets.

Note: There is one street that leads away from the Spanish Steps, the Via del Babuino (yes, it's the baboon street), which appears to be an equal spoke from the Steps but actually has a very different neighborhood feel to it; so, I have separated it from the rest (see below).

If you have only a few hours to shop in Rome and you are seriously interested in designer fashion, your assignment, should you accept it or not, is to shop the Spanish Steps/Condotti area and to get to some—or all—of the Via del Babuino and a block or two of the Via del Corso down at the Condotti end.

Via Fontanella Borghese Right now, this area is still coming into its own as an extension of the Via Condotti on the other side of the Via del Corso. This street is quiet, unvisited by tourists, and home to several new branches of big-name designer shops, such as the recently built **Palazzo Fendi,** which just about takes up a city block. By all means, stop by the palazzo, which is like an art gallery of creativity. Even the handles on the front door are works of art. You'll also find the new **Lisa Corti** store in this same quiet area.

Via del Babuino Remember when I told you that Spanish Steps/Condotti had another part to it that was the same but different? Well, this is it. It's one of the antiques neighborhoods of Rome, and boasts some snazzy designer shops, too. It's a fun neighborhood, especially if you're looking for furniture, paintings, or the hottest items in Europe these days: Art Deco tabletop accessories. I take it back—this is more than a fun neighborhood. This is a must-do that you should combine with a secondary back street, **Via Maguta,** that has art galleries and more and more stores. The new **Pratesi** store in Rome is back here. The pedestrian-only medieval alley will take your breath away.

Via Veneto I know every American in Rome has heard of the Via Veneto, if only from the movies. While I invariably stay at a hotel in this area, the shopping here is nothing to write home about or to go out of your way to visit. The large bookstalls on the street corners are handy for a vast selection of magazines (all languages), postcards, videos (yes, even dirty movies), and paperback bestsellers in English. There are some shoe shops and several glitzy cafes, too. It's a pleasant street to wander, but not exceptional. If you are staying in the area, you will probably enjoy the side streets more.

Via Nazionale This is a very long street, but its best parts are between Repubblica and Termini, where there are a slew of fashion shops for young women plus a few big names. More and more are opening here, and you can now find **Max Mara, Frette,** and a few others. Watch this space.

Trevi & Tritone From the Spanish Steps, you can walk to the Trevi Fountain and segue into several real-people Rome neighborhoods. Of course you'll want to throw three coins in the fountain, and then have an ice cream.

The shopping is touristy, but the atmosphere is real. Be sure to hit **Via del Tritone,** which is on the way to or from Trevi; both sides of the street have good offerings. You will also find that this niche of shopping and ice-cream heaven is located right near the San Silvestro bus terminal, so you can travel onward to other shopping destinations from here.

Via del Tritone This big, real-people shopping street connects the Via del Corso and Spanish Steps areas to the Via Veneto and Piazza Barberini areas; it is also an extension of the Trevi neighborhood. At the top is the **Piazza Barberini,** with the Bernini Bristol Hotel and a Metro stop. If you need to go online,

easyInternetcafé (Via Barberini 2/16), one of the best in Rome, is right here next to the cinema, and it's open 24/7.

Downhill, the street dead-ends into Via del Corso, where you have a lot of regular shops with more moderate prices than the big-name designer stores 3 blocks away. A large **La Rinascente** department store is on the corner.

Via del Corso Via del Corso is a very long street; the part that you will be most interested in begins where Via del Tritone intersects it and extends all the way to Piazza del Popolo. Both sides of the street are lined with stores; many are branches of famous names, such as **Frette** and even **Benetton,** and many are stores that I just like for local color. A lot of the retailers in this stretch are devoted to younger shoppers, teens, tweens, and 20-somethings.

The really hot part of Via del Corso is right below the Spanish Steps, in the area from Via Condotti to Piazza del Popolo, where you'll find all the fancy designer shops, a zillion teen shops (rock music blaring), and the cheapie fashion stores.

Via dei Cestari If you're looking for a unique shopping experience, a unique gift, or just something special and different after you visit the Pantheon (bad gift stalls), check out the Via dei Cestari, which is filled with ecclesiastical shops selling ribbons, robes, socks, and all sorts of fascinating supplies. Start at **De Ritis** (no. 48) and check out the surrounding stores. Many also sell chalices and religious souvenirs.

Via dei Coronari You say you like to stroll down medieval streets and look at antiques shops? Hmm. Well, have I got a street for you. This particular street takes you back to a previous century and has the best antiques stores in Rome. Located right around the corner from the Piazza Navona, the Via dei Coronari is very small; study your map first.

Walk down one side of the street and back up the other, an area of maybe 2 or 3 blocks. Some shops are extremely fancy salons with priceless pieces; others are a little funkier. Almost all of the dealers take credit cards. If your Italian isn't too sharp, those who don't speak English may speak French. The shop numbers will go to the middle 200s before you've seen it all; there are possibly 100 dealers here.

The dealers are very community minded and have their own block association that has various parties and promotions for the public. They've organized a few nights in May when the stores stay open late, plus a party in October, also for late-night strolling and shopping (officially called the local **Antiques Fair**). Candles and torches light the way.

For a super place to grab a bite in the midst of the antiques stores, try **Osteria dell'Antiquario** (Piazzetta di San Simeone; **© 06/687-9694**). You can eat outdoors or in at this simple but elegant place that's also quite "in." Lunch for two costs about 64€ ($83). Don't let the address throw you; it's right on the Via dei Coronari. Or try **Le Streghe** (Vicolo del Curato 13; **© 06/687-8182**) if you want to spend less; I eat there—often outside—for about 20€ ($26).

Campo dei Fiori Campo dei Fiori is one of those neighborhoods that is beginning to attract tourists and will certainly be ruined in no time at all; right now it is a genuine daily fruit and flower market that packs up by about 1pm. Get here by midmorning, browse the stalls and photograph the fruits, and then plop down at any of the dozen or so cafes nearby. There are also pizza places, if you don't want to spend 48€ ($62) on lunch.

Aside from the market, you are in the midst of an old Roman neighborhood, where rents are lower and fun shops are opening up. A number of food and cookware stores surround the Campo dei Fiori; the Piazza Navona is just a few blocks away, which gets you to the **Rancé** soap shop and a stroll around the piazza, of course. Note that there is no market at Campo dei Fiori on Sundays.

Via del Governo Vecchio This is sort of a hidden street, between the Piazza Navona and the Campo dei Fiori. Before you attempt to find it on foot, first try to locate it on a map. The street is dark, narrow, medieval, and blessed with a few vintage-clothing shops. Some are the army-navy type; others sell serious vintage. Aside from the vintage stores, there are

Via dei Coronari

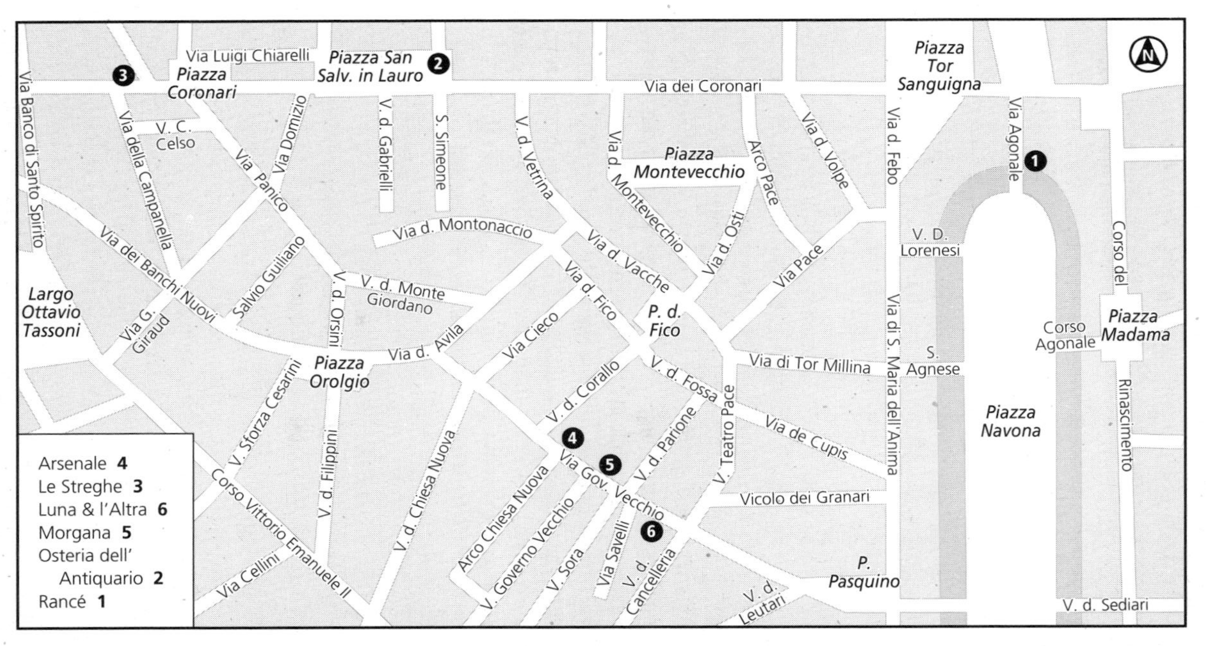

some cutting-edge fashion boutiques. I like **Morgana** (no. 27) and **Arsenale** (no. 64); both are hot and happening. This neighborhood is easy to reach, is fun to shop, and gives you a less touristy perspective on Rome.

The Ghetto This is a far cry from the Grand Hotel, but for those of you who want to stay in a fabulous hotel but then travel to the grittier parts of the city, you are off on a crazy adventure. Take a bus from the train station to the Vittorio Emanuele monument and walk, or just taxi, right to the oldest part of Rome, where the ghetto was.

Take the Via delle Botteghe Oscure for 2 short blocks, note all the fabric jobbers (wholesalers), and then turn left at the Piazza Paganica. You'll now enter a small neighborhood that seems very residential. Wander the streets and look for the shops that interest you. This is the kind of adventure that is welcomed by a true *garmento,* someone who likes to see bolts of fabric piled up in store windows and doesn't care about fancy architecture or salespeople in matching uniforms. The area is charming, crumbling, and undiscovered by tourists. All of these stores are jobbers; you'll find jeans and underwear and sweats and even a few jewelry shops. Don't miss the discounter **Leone Limentani** (Via Portico d'Ottavia 47), which has mounds of dishes and china—even Richard Ginori patterns.

ROME RESOURCES A TO Z

Antiques

While I can't go so far as to suggest you actually buy antiques here, Rome is the Italian center of fancy antiques shops. There are several streets where stores abound, including **Via del Babuino** and **Via dei Coronari** (see above). If you're shopping for serious antiques and looking for a dealer to trust, look for the gold seal representing the Associazione Romana Antiquari. Note that the shops on Via dei Coronari are usually open at night for short periods in May and in the fall; there's an antiques market at Pala Parioli.

Beauty

Also see "Pharmacies & Soaps," later in this chapter.

Aveda

Rampa Mignanelli 9 (Metro: Spagna).

Although this address sounds screwy, *rampa* very well describes the fact that the shop is on a ramp to the Spanish Steps. This is an American brand, and prices are slightly higher in Rome than in the U.S., but it's a high-quality line and good for travel sizes if you're in need of products. ✆ **06/6992-4257.** www.aveda.com.

Beauty Planet

Grand Hotel Palace, Via Veneto 66–70 (Metro: Veneto).

A full-service spa and beauty center, this is not one of the new, low-rent rip-offs of Sephora, but a very fancy, high-end shop with expensive brands and some expensive accessories, such as hair clips and bands. You need not be a guest at the hotel to shop here. Closed Sunday. ✆ **06/481-7149.**

Books

The large news kiosks on the Via Veneto sell paperback books in many languages, including English.

Feltrinelli

Via Vittorio Emanuele Orlando 79–87 (Metro: Repubblica).

This famous chain has stores here and there in busy shopping districts. This location is divided into a few stores in a row; the international shop, with books in English, is at no. 87. There's also a ton of guidebooks and a wide selection of videos and DVDs of famous Italian movies. Also open Sundays from 10am to 1:30pm and 4 to 7pm. ✆ **06/482-7878.**

RIZZOLI ROMA
Largo Chigi 15; Via Tomacelli 156 (Metro: Spagna).

This is Italy's best bookstore with books in all languages. Tomacelli is the larger of the two shops; both are open on Sundays from 10:30am to 1:30pm and 4 to 8pm. During the week, hours are nonstop. To reach the Largo Chigi location, call ✆ **06/679-6641.** For the Tomacelli location, call ✆ **06/6882-8513.**

Cashmere

AMINA RUBINACCI
Via Bocca di Leone 51 (Metro: Spagna).

Visitors to Capri will know the name of this famed Neapolitan source that has recently opened a small shop in Rome. It specializes in cashmeres but also sells cottons and cashmere blends. To die for. ✆ **06/679-5354.** www.aminarubinacci.it.

MALO
Via Borgognona 5 (Metro: Spagna).

The flagship of the famed brand has home style, gift items, accessories, and more cashmere than you can dream of. Malo even has an outlet store outside of Florence; see p. 166. ✆ **06/679-1331.** www.malo.it.

Department Stores

Italy doesn't have great department stores, and I don't suggest you go out of your way to shop in one. In Rome, two are somewhat convenient to mainstream tourist shopping: a branch of **La Rinascente,** at Via del Corso 189; and a branch of **Coin,** at Piazzale Appio, which is across the street from the Via Sannio market, and may be on your itinerary (if you can't stand to look at another fountain).

UPIM, the dime-store version of an Italian department store (which may be a contradiction in terms), has stores at

Via del Tritone 172 and Via Nazionale 211. The **Standa** on Viale Trastevere 60 has a supermarket downstairs.

Designer Boutiques

The best Metro stop for all these addresses is Spagna. For details on many of these well-known brand names, check out the "Dictionary of Taste & Design" (p. 55).

Continental & U.K. Big Names

BURBERRY
Via Condotti 59–61.

CARTIER
Via Condotti 83.

CELINE
Via Condotti 20a.

CHANEL
Via del Babuino 98–101.

DIOR
Via Condotti 1–4.

ESCADA
Piazza di Spagna 7.

HERMÈS
Via Condotti 67.

KENZO
Via del Babuino 124.

LOUIS VUITTON
Via Condotti 13.

YVES SAINT LAURENT RIVE GAUCHE
Via Bocca di Leone 35.

ITALIAN BIG NAMES

ALBERTA FERRETTI
Via Condotti 34.

BENETTON
Piazza di Spagna 67–69.

BOTTEGA VENETA
Piazza San Lorenzo in Lucina 9.

BRIONI
Via Barberini 79–81.

D&G
Piazza di Spagna 93.

DOLCE & GABBANA
Via Borgognona 7d; Via Condotti 51.

EMPORIO ARMANI
Via del Babuino 140.

ERMENEGILDO ZEGNA
Via Borgognona 7.

ETRO
Via del Babuino 102.

FENDI
Via Fontanella di Borghese 48; Via Borgognona 39.

GF FERRÉ
Piazza di Spagna 70.

GIANFRANCO FERRÉ
Via Borgognona 6.

GIORGIO ARMANI
Via Condotti 77.

GUCCI
Via Condotti 8.

HOGAN
Via Borgognona 45–46.

JUST CAVALLI
Piazza di Spagna 82–83.

LA PERLA
Via Condotti 79.

LAURA BIAGIOTTI
Via Borgognona 43–44.

LES COPAINS
Piazza di Spagna 32–35.

MAX & CO.
Via Condotti 46.

MAX MARA
Via Condotti 17–19; Via Frattina 28.

MISSONI
Piazza di Spagna 78.

PRADA
Via Condotti 92–95.

ROBERTO CAVALLI
Via Borgognona 7a.

SALVATORE FERRAGAMO
Via Condotti 66–73.

TRUSSARDI
Via Condotti 49.

VALENTINO
Via Condotti 13.

Discounters

Also see "Outlets" (p. 99) for more bargain-hunting destinations.

DISCOUNT SYSTEM
Via Viminale 35 (Metro: Repubblica).

This store is possibly owned by the same people who own Il Discount Dell Alta Moda (see below), or else it is just patterned after it. It has a very similar brochure and the same pricing system, which means that, to get the accurate price, you must deduct 50% from the marked price on the tag (so don't let the price tags throw you).

Discount System is a larger store and has a much, much, much greater selection. I spent an hour here touching everything and trying to buy something but left empty-handed. You'll see menswear, women's wear, shoes, handbags, luggage, belts, ties, dressy dresses, and every big-name Italian designer. The clothes are at least a year old.

The location is convenient—around the corner from the Grand Hotel and down the street from the main train station; you can take the Metro to Repubblica and walk. The same Metro will also take you to Piazza di Spagna and the Spanish Steps. ✆ **06/474-6545.**

IL DISCOUNT DELL ALTA MODA
Via di Gesù e Maria 16 and 14 (Metro: Spagna).

I'm leaving this store in the book for now, but my last visits have been very disappointing. The problem is lack of range, lack of sizes, and sometimes high prices (even at a discount, some of these prices will make you wince). ***Important note:*** The price is half of what's marked on the ticket. So if you're going to wince, at least do so accurately.

Now for the good news: There are plenty of big names. The handbags are probably the best deal. And the men's store, two doors down at no. 14, is huge and well stocked. The styles, colors, and sophistication of the men's suits were beyond compare. ✆ **06/361-3796.**

Gifts

FABRIANO
Via del Babuino 173 (Metro: Spagna).

Another find from Milan, this store sells pens, writing goods, bound notebooks, and papers. There are some great gifts with tons of style for not much money. ✆ **06/3260-0361.** www.fabrianoboutique.com.

Gloves

MEROLA
Largo Goldoni 47, off Via del Corso (Metro: Spagna).

This is the oldest glove shop in Rome and a far cry from much of the rest of the fare on Via del Corso, which nowadays seems to cater to teens. Yes, Audrey Hepburn's gloves in *Roman Holiday* came from here. ✆ **06/679-1961.** www.merolagloves.it.

Handbags

What's a trip to Italy without a touchy-feely session with 1,001 handbags? There may be better buys north of Rome, but Rome is a good place to start to look.

CARPISA
Via del Corso 164, Via Belsiana 59 (Metro: Spagna).

This is a chain that began in Naples and now has stores all over Rome and most of Italy—they are hugely popular due to low prices and lots of great colors, and appeal more to the younger set. Most of the summer bags are canvas; fabrics are also used in fall and winter—this, of course, helps keep prices down. Indeed, where else can you find a great bag for 20€ ($26)? ✆ **800/777-155** toll-free in Italy. www.carpisa.it.

FRANCESCO BIASIA

Via di Torre Argentina 7 (Bus: Largo Argentina); Via Due Macelli 62 (Metro: Spagna).

This brand is well known for its *ooh la la* interpretation of southern Italy. It's often sold in department stores throughout the country. The brand is also often sought at discount sources because it tends to be a little pricey. The Largo Argentina location, by the way, is within walking distance of the Trevi Fountain and the area around San Silvestro. ✆ **06/679-2727.** www.biasia.com.

FRANCESCO ROGANI

Via Condotti 47 (Metro: Spagna).

This is a very fancy tourist trap (TT) and may not be your cup of Hermès copy, with many versions of both Kelly and Birkin styles and even a Bugatti or two. Prices are fair.

The store locks the doors when it thinks there are too many shoppers, it does not have a very service-oriented attitude, and it offers sales that may or may not be real. I found great stuff and am thrilled with my buys, but I don't know if I believe that the marked-down price isn't the price the goods originally sold for. The bags I bought were great because of the ratio of quality to price; at twice the price (as marked on the tags), I would not have pounced.

Rogani uses a pebble-grain leather, which is good for travel because it doesn't mark up that easily and wears well. You can also buy the croc-stamped leather that comes in yummy colors—this is the latest trickle-down trend from the Lana Marks bags. You'll pay about 230€ ($300) for a medium-size Birkin-style bag. ✆ **06/678-4036.**

FURLA

Piazza di Spagna 22 (Metro: Spagna).

This Italian chain with stores all over the world—including a dozen in Rome—is known to offer high style and some glamour at realistic prices. Sort of the poor man's Prada, with bags that sell for under 160€ ($208). There are outlet stores in various malls covered in this book. © **06/6920-0363.** www.furla.com.

Home Style

For details on the fabulous **Lisa Corti** and **Tad,** see "The Five Best Stores in Rome" (p. 79).

C.U.C.I.N.A.

Via Mario de'Fiori 65 (Metro: Spagna).

This store is actually similar to Pottery Barn or Crate & Barrel in the U.S., or even Conran's in London, but this is the Italian version. It's a must for foodies and those seeking gifts for cooks and gourmands—lots of little doodads. © **06/679-1275.**

Frette

Piazza di Spagna 11 (Metro: Spagna).

This is a branch of the famous Italian linen house that sells both luxury bedding and a hotel line. The latter is high quality but less expensive. © **06/679-0673.** www.frette.com.

Malls

Especially if you arrive by rail, your first mall stop may just be the very fine **Forum Termini,** in the central train station (see "The Five Best Stores in Rome" on p. 79).

Piazza Colonna

Galleria Alberto Sordi (Metro: Spagna).

This mall is V-shaped, stays open on Sundays (and until 10pm most nights), and has cafes and some fun stores. What's not to like? The anchor is a large **Zara.** The location near the Spanish Steps and the San Silvestro bus stop make it ideal. The bookstore, **Feltrinelli,** has books in English.

Markets

Although Rome's main flea market at Porta Portese is famous, I've never found it that good—except when I needed to buy extra luggage because I'd gone wild at Fendi. The biggie is held on Sundays from 6am to 2pm. You can get here at 8am and do fine; this is not like the Bermondsey Market in London, where you must arrive, in the dark, with a flashlight in your hand. In fact, in Rome, go to flea markets only in daylight.

The big flea market is officially called the **Mercato di Porta Portese;** it stretches for about a mile along the Tiber River, where about 1,000 vendors are selling everything imaginable—a lot of which is fake or hot (or both). Enter the market about halfway down Viale Trastevere, where the old clothes are. This way you avoid miles of auto accessories, which, as far as I am concerned, you can give a miss.

The big news in Rome, though, is that "private" flea markets are popping up—real people just rent a table and sell off last year's fashions or whatever turns up in Grandma's palazzo. Often the sellers are aristos or celebs. Check the Friday edition of the local newspaper, *La Repubblica,* for the weekend market schedule, listed under a heading called *Mercatini* (Markets) on the weekend events page.

Typically, these events are held on Sunday, may cost 3€ to 10€ ($3.90–$13) to attend, and have a few hundred vendors. They do not start super early, but rather struggle to open around 10am, and are hottest from noon to 1pm; most are in areas off the beaten track and may require a bit of a taxi ride.

The newest flea market, which most people call the **Ponte Milvio Market,** is held monthly. It begins on Saturday afternoons (3–7pm) and runs all day on Sundays, starting at 9am on the banks of the Tiber between Ponte Milvio and Ponte Duca d'Aosta.

Via Sannio is a busy real-people market area with all kinds of fabulous junk. Everything is cheap in price and quality. The goods are all new, no antiques. Many of the vendors who sell on Sunday at Porta Portese end up here during the week, so if you miss Sunday in Rome, don't fret. Just c'mon over here.

Pickpockets seem fewer during the week, also. There's a **Coin** department store on the corner. You can get here by bus or Metro (the stop is Sannio); because it's in a corner of central Rome, the taxi fare can be steep.

Piazza Fontanella Borghese, not far from the Spanish Steps, has 24 stalls selling prints, maps, books, coins, and some antiques. Good fun; a class act. Open Monday through Saturday from 9am to 6pm, possibly later on summer evenings.

Outlets

CASTEL ROMANO DESIGNER OUTLET
Via del Ponte di Piscina Cupa 51, Castel Romano.

Also called Pontina (a nearby location), this is the Rome area's grandmother of outlet malls. More and more outlets are coming on board, although outlet malls to the north are still larger. This mall is owned by McArthur Glen, which also built Serravalle Designer Outlet (between Milan and Genoa), though it's not nearly as large, with fewer than 100 stores. It's located some 12 miles south of Rome, accessible via various tours. Of the two malls south of Rome (see below for the second), McArthur Glen has the more upscale names. © **06/505-0050.** www.mcarthurglen.it.

FASHION DISTRICT
Via della Pace, Pascolaro, Valmontone.

The good news about this mall is that you pass right by it while on the highway that connects Rome and Naples. There really isn't any bad news, though the mall is not a great one. It's worth a stop and should improve in years to come, as it was built to handle more than 200 stores. © **06/959-9491.** www.fashion district.it.

Papal Shopping

Papal merchandise ranges from the serious to the kitsch. The shopping falls into three categories: There are a number of gift stands and shops scattered throughout the Vatican; there is a string of stores in Vatican City; and there are vendors who sell from card tables on the sidewalks as you walk from the entrance/exit of the Vatican Museum (this way to the Sistine Chapel) to the front of St. Peter's.

If you are on a quest for religious items (of the non-antique variety), a dozen shops surrounding St. Peter's Square offer everything you've been looking for. Bottle openers with a bas-relief portrait of the pope, anyone?

Most of the shops will send out your purchase to be blessed by the pope. Allow 24 hours for this service. Some of the stores will then deliver the items to your hotel; others ask you to return for them. If you are having items blessed, be sure to find out how you will be getting your merchandise back.

Pharmacies & Soaps

Also see "Beauty," earlier in this chapter.

FARMACEUTICA DI SANTA MARIA NOVELLA
Corso Rinascimento 47 (no nearby Metro).

Yes, this is a branch of the famous Florentine address (p. 171). It has expanded enormously in recent years, with stores in many European capital cities. This one, small and new, is a block from Piazza Navona. The salespeople do not speak English, but if you give it some time and some mime, you'll sample everything and figure it all out. Weekend Soap, for 9€ ($12), is one of my favorite gifts. © **06/687-2446.** www.smnovella.it.

RANCÉ
Piazza Navona 53 (no nearby Metro).

This firm was from the south of France, where its ingredients originate, but is now Italian. It is most famous for its soap, although now there is a full line of bath and beauty products as well as scents. The brand is sold mostly through catalogs in the U.S., but you can save 50% if you shop the boutiques in Rome and Milan. ✆ **06/6880-9705**. www.ranceusa.com.

Plus Sizes

ELENA MIRÒ
Via Frattina 11–12 (Metro: Spagna).

This Italian line begins at size 46 (about a size 14). The chain has stores popping up all over Europe, selling chic and stylish work and play fashions for less money than Marina Rinaldi. It also has a presence in many of the new outlet malls around Italy. ✆ **06/678-4367**. www.elenamiro.com.

MARINA RINALDI
Largo Goldoni 43 (Metro: Spagna).

A division of Max Mara, Marina Rinaldi is now a global brand with chic fashions for the large-size woman. Its sizing system is strange, so please try on before you buy. Even if you use the chart that compares its sizes to American sizes, you may be in for a surprise. ✆ **06/6920-0487**.

Shoes

There are scads of little shops selling leather goods all over Rome, and all over every other major Italian city, for that matter. Note that there is also a section of this chapter called "Handbags," although most shoe stores sell handbags, too.

BOTTEGA VENETA

Piazza San Lorenzo 9 (Metro: Spagna).

This gorgeous Bottega shop is across the way from the newer Louis Vuitton that has since become luxe headquarters of the Spanish Steps shopping district; it is hard to find unless you know where to look. Is the store worth finding? Well, yes. Prices are lower than in the U.S., but there are no bargains here. That won't shock anyone, as Bottega has never had inexpensive merchandise. The store has two levels, many collections, and is to drool for. The prices are so high you could drool, and then faint. ✆ **06/6821-0024.** www.bottegaveneta.com.

FRATELLI ROSSETTI

Via Borgognona 5a (Metro: Spagna).

The Rossetti brothers are at it again—shoes, shoes, shoes, and now at somewhat affordable prices. There are men's and women's shoes, as well as belts and even some clothes. ✆ **06/678-2676.** www.rossetti.it.

HOGAN

Via Borgognona 45–46 (Metro: Spagna).

Here we have the Hogan line of sports shoes, high heels from the Tod's line, and very fancy (and expensive) leather handbags. Shoes begin at around 160€ ($208). ✆ **06/678-68-28.** www.todsgroup.com.

TOD'S

Via Condotti 14 (Metro: Spagna).

The original driving shoe, Tod's has become part of an international uniform of casual chic, and is even knocked off by the makers of fake brands. It carries men's and women's casual shoes, as well as some heels and handbags for women. ✆ **06/678-68-28.** www.todsgroup.com.

Chapter Five

BEYOND ROME: NAPLES & THE AMALFI COAST

NAPLES

Welcome to Naples, where some shopkeepers told me to take off my watches (yes, I do wear two), lest I attract a thief . . . or two. Welcome to Naples, where the clerks at Ferragamo were not only rude but also refused to redo my tax-refund papers when I decided to buy *more.* Welcome to Naples, where I had the best pizza of my life, where I fell madly in love with the scarves at Rubinacci, and where you are less than an hour away from Capri—or Amalfi. If you come by cruise ship, welcome all and mind the valuables.

Getting There

From Rome, you can rent a car for the 2-hour trip to Naples; this gives you a car for driving along the Amalfi Coast as well. If you drive from Rome, note that you will pass some outlet malls along the way, such as the **Castel Romano Designer Outlet** (p. 99).

You can also take the train from Rome. The Naples train station is clean, modern, and not frightening. But just for the hell of it, watch your valuables.

If you arrive by cruise ship, the port of Naples (Maritime Station) is next to the heart of town. Note that the ferries and hydrofoils to the islands (Capri, Ischia, and so on) use different piers in other parts of town.

If you fly in, you'll love the small, neat Naples airport. It probably doesn't pay to connect directly to Naples from a long-haul flight, but you can easily get here from any European hub in just an hour or two. Several low-cost carriers serve Naples, such as Volare, BMI, easyJet, and Vueling, covered on p. 16.

Getting Around

For cruisers, you can find taxis at the gates of the Maritime Station; do be clear with the driver about where you are going and be vigilant about the meter lest you get cheated.

All hotels can get you a taxi, and there are also taxi stands, usually at big squares. If the driver is honest and goes by the meter, round up the tab as a tip. To call a radio taxi, dial ✆ **3296.** Remember that traffic is fierce during rush hour and can run up the tab on the meter.

There is a Metro, but it's of better use to residents or sightseers, not shoppers, so I don't refer you to Metro stops in this chapter. Also, when it's hot, you do not want to go into a hole in the ground.

For out-of-town trips, there are several train stations. The main one, Centrale, has trains that will take you to Pompeii and as far as Sorrento.

You may also want to book a car and driver for the day; your hotel can do this for you. If you rent a car, don't try to drive in town. And remember, when driving the Amalfi Drive: No limoncello for you, *cara.*

The Lay of the Land

Naples is an enormous city. On a day trip, you will probably only want to visit the nice shopping areas and then have a look at the museums, the palm trees, the castle fortress jutting out into the sea, and the sea itself. Watch your handbag.

Naples

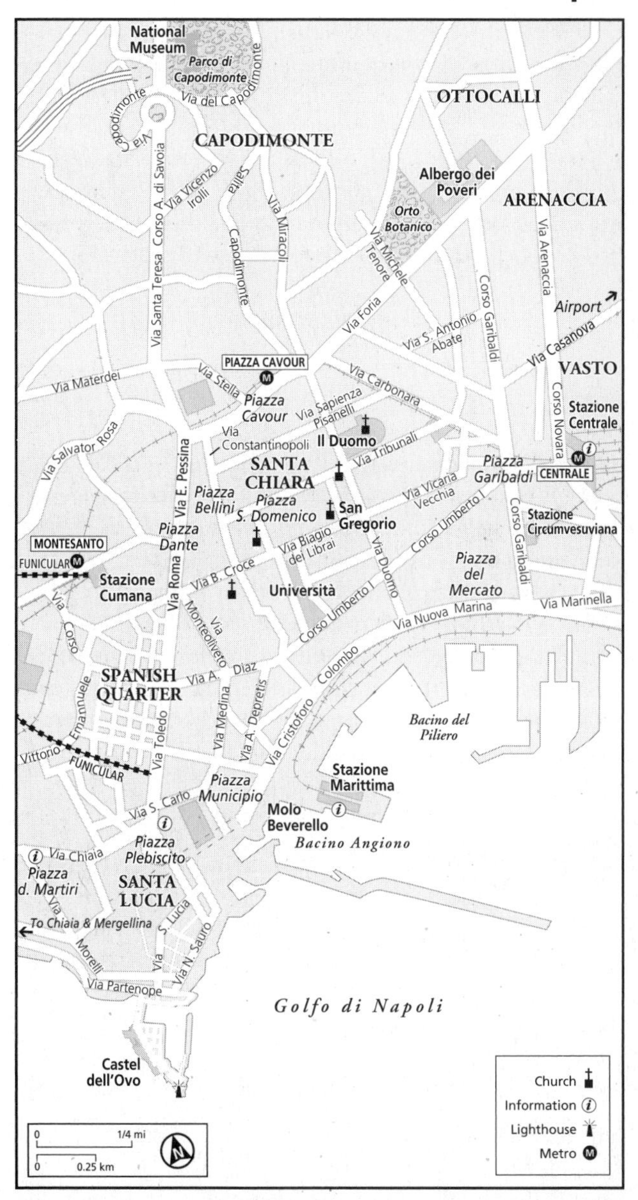
National Museum
Parco di Capodimonte
Via del Capodimonte
Via Capodimonte
CAPODIMONTE
OTTOCALLI
Corso A. di Savoia
Via Vicenzo Irolli
Salita Capodimonte
Via Miracoli
Albergo dei Poveri
Orto Botanico
ARENACCIA
Via Michele Tenore
Via Arenaccia
Via Santa Teresa
Corso Garibaldi
Airport
Via Foria
Via S. Antonio Abate
Via Casanova
VASTO
PIAZZA CAVOUR
Via Materdei
Via Stella
Via Carbonara
Piazza Cavour
Via Sapienza Pisanelli
Corso Novara
Stazione Centrale
Via Salvator Rosa
Via Constantinopoli
Il Duomo
Via Tribunali
Via E. Pessina
SANTA CHIARA
Piazza Garibaldi
CENTRALE
Piazza Bellini
Piazza S. Domenico
San Gregorio
Via Vicaria Vecchia
Stazione Circumvesuviana
Piazza Dante
Via Biagio dei Librai
Corso Umberto I
MONTESANTO
FUNICULAR
Via Duomo
Piazza del Mercato
Stazione Cumana
Via B. Croce
Via Roma
Università
Via Monteoliveto
Via Nuova Marina
Via Marinella
Via Corso
Corso Umberto I
Colombo
SPANISH QUARTER
Via A. Diaz
Via Medina
Via A. Depretis
Via Cristoforo
Bacino del Piliero
Vittorio Emanuele
Via Toledo
FUNICULAR
Stazione Marittima
Piazza Municipio
Via S. Carlo
Molo Beverello
Bacino Angiono
Via Chiaia
Piazza Plebiscito
Piazza d. Martiri
SANTA LUCIA
Via S. Lucia
To Chiaia & Mergellina
Via Morelli
Via N. Sauro
Via Partenope
Golfo di Napoli
Castel dell'Ovo
Church
Information
Lighthouse
Metro
0
1/4 mi
0
0.25 km

Warning: Please study a map of Naples before you go off on your own; learn where everything is in relationship to the main icons. If you think of the Castel dell'Ovo as the heart of the world, then the various areas to visit can be read as you tell time: The castle is at 6 o'clock, the Maritime Station is at 5 o'clock, the Via Constantinopoli and the National Museum are at 1 o'clock, the historic old town and street of angels are at 2 o'clock, and the fancy shopping is at 10 o'clock.

Sleeping in Naples

If you're visiting for longer than a day trip, here are a couple of hotels to consider:

- **Grande Hotel Vesuvio** (Via Partenope 45; © **081/764-0044;** www.vesuvio.it): This is the leading hotel of the city, located right on the Bay of Naples with a view directly to heaven. There's a spa, you can eat on the rooftop, and you're within walking distance of much of the fancy shopping.
- **Hotel Excelsior** (Via Partenope 48; © **081/764-0111;** www.starwoodhotels.com): The ornate Excelsior has an oceanside location with great views; each room is furnished with antiques. Cruise passengers enjoy lunch at La Terrazza—you can even see your ship.

The Shopping Scene

Walking up and down and around the fancy shopping district in Naples is a treat. There are gorgeous antiques stores and great places for a gelato. It makes a nice half-day shopping excursion, after which you can eat, quit, or move to secret sources or even museums (all with good gift shops). Note that it takes more than a weekend to have a custom-made suit made.

Shopping Hours

Stores are normally open from around 9am to 1:30pm and 4:30 to 8pm. Nothing is open on Sunday. On Monday, nothing is open in the morning, and some things will open around 4 or

4:30pm. Even street markets get going late here: Don't go to a flea market before 9:30am.

On Saturday in summer, stores will close for the day at 1:30pm, but in winter they reopen in the afternoon. If you need a pharmacy during off hours, ask your concierge or check the listing in the newspaper for the open stores.

Most stores are closed for the first 3 weeks of August, or longer. Only mad dogs and tourists go out in the midday sun.

Shopping Neighborhoods

Maritime Station & Hotel Heaven Cruise passengers disembark at the clean, modern Maritime Station, right in town near the Castel dell'Ovo, a 2,000-year-old fortress—a nice touch, adding a little romance to a commercial seaport. There are several shops in the terminal, along with a bank and a currency exchange office. When a large ship comes to port, street vendors set up outside.

Castel dell'Ovo Located directly across from the Hotel Vesuvio, right near the Maritime Station, the Castel is on a small island, which also houses several adorable alleys for exploring (no shops, sorry) and many bars, seafood restaurants, and pizza places. It's great fun. There's a tourist info stand here, too.

Luxury Shopping The main upscale shopping district is a few blocks from the strip of luxury hotels on the waterfront. Just walk along the water (with the castle to your rear) until you come to a clump of palm trees that represents the Piazza Vittorio, turn right, and head "up."

Now it gets slightly tricky as this is a district, and you don't want to miss all the parts—you can, and will, miss part of it if you don't look at a map. The Via Calabritto is one of the main tony shopping streets, with many of the big-name designers (**Prada** is at no. 9), but not all. It stretches from the Piazza Vittorio to the Piazza dei Martiri and the large **Ferragamo** shop.

There are a few side streets off the Piazza dei Martiri that will remind you that you really *are* in Italy; some antiques shops are located down the Via Domenico Morelli. The area is not without charm, and you can easily segue to the Via dei Mille and Via Gaetano Filangieri, which have the rest of the luxury shops—**Bulgari, Zegna, Hermès, Frette,** and more.

Via Chiaia This is a real-people shopping street that's between the luxury district and Via Roma. Use it to cross over from one neighborhood to the other or to get to Via dei Mille—it's all an easy walk. Shopping-wise, there's very little to distract you. Italy-wise, it's great fun.

Via Roma Via Roma is the commercial heart of town; it is called Via Toledo lower down and becomes Via Roma near Piazza Dante. This street stretches for 3km (2 miles) from the Piazza del Plebiscito, right near the Maritime Station, through the center of town, passing the Piazza Carita on its way to the Piazza Dante and then ending near the National Museum.

La Pignasecca This is foodie land: Just follow Via Pignasecca and Via Portamedina up and down, checking out all the tiny specialty shops. This is a central area in the real-people part of town.

Centro Antico The core of the old town *(centro antico)* includes the famous Via San Gregorio Armend, the street of angels, where all the miniatures and *presepios* (crèches) are made. But don't look for Via San Gregorio Armend on your map, as it's a small area around the church of the same name. Instead, you want to find the rectangular area between the Piazza Gesù and Piazza Dante, reaching over to the Duomo as its other border. The main streets for shopping, gawking, sightseeing, and absorbing the soul of Naples are Via Croce and Via Tribunali. Via Croce will change its name a few times, so fret not. The area is part of a living-history, outdoor-museum program that labels the buildings and tells you the path to walk (and shop).

Port Alba Adjacent to the old town is Port Alba, a medieval doorway that leads to a million bookstores. Just beyond this is Via Constantinopoli, filled with antiques shops. Once a month, there's an outdoor flea market on the weekend (except in Aug).

Antiques & Flea Markets

FIERA ANTIQUARIA NAPOLETANA
Via Caracciolo.

Getting to this antiques fair is a little tricky, as there is often confusion about the dates; the listing in *Dove* magazine is also unclear. Luckily, you can call the market offices directly at © **081/621-951** and get the dates for the year. A weekend event, the fair is considered the best in southern Italy; it runs from 8am to 2pm.

MOSTRA MERCATO CONSTANTINOPOLI
Via Constantinopoli.

A weekend fair never held on the same weekend as the other fair (Via Caracciolo, above), this is a more casual event in the street of antiques shops, with dealers set up on sidewalks and under tents. Don't bother going if the weather is bad. © **0347/486-37-15.** antiquario@tightrope.it.

Local Heroes

MARIANO RUBINACCI
Via Filangieri 26.

This shop offers a sort of Ralph Lauren/local-preppy look, complete with silk scarves that would make Mr. Dumas-Hermès weep with envy. The scarves depict various scenes in Neapolitan history, geography, or iconography; they're sold in some hotel and museum gift shops as well. Prices range from 120€ to 200€ ($156–$260). The best luxury souvenir in town. © **081/415-793.** www.marianorubinacci.it.

MARINELLA
Riviera di Chiaia 287.

This itty-bitty tie shop is one of the most famous addresses in Naples. Come holiday season, lines stretch down the street, there are no ties in stock, and shoppers are issued chits, which

Shoppers Beware

Whether you are on your own or on a ship tour, you may be taken to "factories" to go shopping. Be careful—they may or may not offer the real thing, or real deals. They certainly offer kickbacks to your guide.

they gift-wrap to present. The store creates custom ties, as long, short, wide, or thin as you want or need. © **081/764-4214.**

MAXI HO
Via Nisco 20; Riviera di Chiaia 95; multiple other locations.

Despite its silly-sounding name, this is one of the best stores in Naples. The various addresses are mostly in the luxury district and are not branches of the same store but extensions of the store that feature different looks. Each sells a different group of designer brands geared for a certain look or age group. © **081/414-721** or 081/247-0072.

UPIM
Via Nisco 11.

This branch of the dime-store chain is right in the heart of the shopping area, with tons of clothes, home fashions, and even underwear. I buy a lot of La Perla copies at UPIM and love them. © **081/417-520.** www.upim.it.

CAPRI

In Capri, I'm always too busy with the jewelry stores, the sandals, the latest incarnations of Tod's shoes and handbags, the cottons and the cashmeres, and even the lemons to get to the beach or to notice who's not wearing what. Capri is a shopping port. Capri is a shopping day trip. Capri is a spree. This is a town that has streets that are more like alleys, where you stroll in total contentment, remembering Jackie O, and you happily get lost and found in this maze.

You can research and buy lemon booze from a so-called lemon factory or two, ride in a '57 Chevy stretch convertible (with fins), buy plastic pens with your name on them in Italian, or sink deeply into **Gucci, Prada, Fendi, Hermès,** and all the better names of international and Italian fashion. In between, of course, you eat, sip, stare, and take a nap. The place to hang out? La Piazzetta in the center of Capri.

Getting There

You may arrive by cruise ship (and tender ashore) or by hydrofoil from Naples, Amalfi, Sorrento, or another port or resort town. Regardless of how you actually arrive, you'll land near the funicular that takes you up to Capri proper. Sunglasses, please.

If you have luggage, there are porters at the pier. They happen to be very honest, so don't fret.

Although I usually get to Capri via cruise ship, on my last visit I took the hydrofoil from Naples. The trip lasts about 45 minutes, costs about 12€ ($16), and is most pleasant if you are on a larger vessel with space around you. There's a ferry or hydrofoil almost every hour; they all arrive at the same place in Capri, but they depart from different stations in Naples, depending on which line you book.

If you want to go by private boat, contact **Gianni Chervatin** (✆ **081/837-6895**), former general manager of the Grand Hotel Quisisana in Capri, who arranges jet-set details for the rich and famous. Or seek out **Capritime** (✆ **32/9214-9811**; www.capritime.com), a firm run by American Rebecca Brooks, who offers private boat tours.

You can also copter in from Rome or Naples by booking with **SAM** (✆ **082/835-4155**; www.capri-helicopters.com).

The Lay of the Land

The island of Capri is rather big and has much more to it than just the resort town of Capri. From a serious shopping perspective, you can skip Anacapri, although it's fun visually.

In fact, I think you'll be surprised by the sprawl of downtown Capri. Best yet, a lot of it is hidden in back alleys, so take some time to look at a map. If you follow the main tourist trail, you'll miss the best stuff.

Sleeping in Capri

The most famous hotel in town is the **Grand Hotel Quisisana** (Via Camerelle 2; © **081/837-0788;** www.quisi.it), right in the heart of the shopping district. Another option is the **Hotel Punta Tragara** (Via Tragara 57; © **081/837-0844;** www.hoteltragara.com), which overlooks the sea. And **J. K. Place** (Via Prov. Marina Grande 225; © **081/838-4001;** www.jkcapri.com), with a twin in Florence, is divinely stunning and very much the hip place to be—plus it's the only hotel with a seaside location.

The Shopping Scene

As cruise ports go, Capri ain't bad. It has a lot of stores and a sprinkling of designer shops—small branches of **Prada, Gucci, Fendi, Ferragamo, Malo, Alberta Ferretti, D&G, Tod's, Hermès,** and so on.

The emphasis in Capri is on high-quality goods and cheap sandals (as a beach town, Capri has become famous for its sandals, and there are scads of no-name shops selling the latest looks, as well as copies of the latest looks). The resort fashions are very body-revealing, in the southern Italian style.

Capri is also home to several perfume shops. Each one carries several brands on an exclusive basis, but no single shop carries every brand. If you inquire about a brand that a store doesn't carry, the clerk is likely to try to trade you over to the brand it sells, rather than tell you to walk down the street or around the corner. There is also lemon perfume.

Note that the style of goods and the shopping experience is so totally different from Positano (covered later in this chapter) that there is virtually no overlap.

The Best Buys in Capri

Cottons & Cashmeres Despite the heat, cashmere is one of the leading lights of Capri. There are several specialty shops that sell premium cashmeres; some also sell cottons.

Jewelry Until I visited Capri and saw its magnificent jewelry, I'd never been one for important (or even real) jewelry. Now I've been converted. There's a good bit of latitude on price. If you have a few thousand dollars, you may be very happy.

Lemons We're still in southern Italy, so there's limoncello galore. I also buy fresh lemons in the market down near the port.

Shoes Capri has all sorts of shoe stores, from the fancy **Ferragamo** shop and places that sell **Tod's** to little hole in the walls with 24€ ($31) sandals. For locally made sandals, there are stores in Capri as well as Anacapri. **Sandalo Caprese** is the most famous—this is the cobbler who fit Jackie O and Sophia L.

Shopping Hours

Stores open around 9am and close at 1pm, though more and more stay open during lunch. Those that close will reopen from 3:30 to 7pm. Big names tend to be open nonstop. Stores in Capri are open on Sundays, too.

The tourist traps (TTs) down by the port usually stay open during lunch and are often open until 8pm in the summer.

Note that the season begins March 15 and ends October 15; most stores are closed out of season.

Shopping Neighborhoods

Marina Grande This is where your ship's tender or your ferry or hydrofoil comes to port; on the pier, there's a Customs office and a pushcart vendor selling ices and fresh fruit in newspaper cones. You'll also find several TTs (teeming with Blue Grotto souvenirs), a liquor store, a minimart, and the funicular, which takes you up to Capri proper.

Main Street Capri Capri has two main streets, Via Vittorio Emanuele and Via Camarelle. The former dead-ends to the latter when you hit the **Grand Hotel Quisisana.** If you are facing the hotel from Via Vittorio Emanuele, bear left to explore Via Camarelle, where most of the designer stores are located. The island's toniest shops can be found in this district, with everything from antiques and jewelry to expensive resort wear and affordable sandals.

Back Street Downtown Hidden from view, but running parallel to Vittorio Emanuele, is a pedestrian alley—Via Fuorlovado—that is crammed with real-people shops. Don't miss the chance to prowl this street; it's far more charming than the main tourist thoroughfare.

Via Roma The Via Roma in Capri is what the British call a high street; it's where you'll find the bus station and the main thrust of the town's real-people shopping. As well as some of the limoncello shops.

Anacapri This is a different city from Capri, easily accessible by bus. The sandal maker **Sandalo Caprese** is here. The largest and fanciest boutique in town is **Mariorita,** where you go for clothes, home style, local coral, and ceramics.

Finds

ALBERTO & LINA
Via Vittorio Emanuele 18.

This is one of the leading jewelers in town. In case you haven't already guessed, Italian women define themselves and their success in life vis-à-vis their jewelry, which they buy in places like this and wear all of the time. Yes, even to the beach and right into the sea. That's how we all know it's real gold. © **081/837-0643.** albertoelina@libero.it.

Amina Rubinacci
Via Camarelle 13.

This is my favorite shop in Capri—I come here first to stare at the colors, touch the cashmeres, sigh about the quality, and then buy a few T-shirts. Because the T-shirts are about 40€ ($52) each, this is my idea of extravagance. Hand-wash your cottons from this store; I had big-time shrinkage when I used the washer/dryer. This brand has expanded and now has stores in Naples, Rome, and elsewhere around Italy. ✆ **081/837-7295.** www.aminarubinacci.it.

Carthusia Profumi
Via Camerelle 10.

I am more amused by this store than serious about it, but I have met people who make this a ritual stop when they are in town. Before she had her own perfume line, Liz Taylor was supposedly a regular. This perfumer makes a local scent that you can only get here; it's very lemony. Cute gifts, too. ✆ **081/837-0368.** www.carthusia.it.

La Capannina Più
Via Le Botteghe 12–14.

This very fancy gourmet-food store sells all sorts of imported goods (skip the English brands)—much to see, touch, and taste. ✆ **081/837-0732.** www.capannina-capri.com.

SORRENTO

Most of you will probably arrive by car, train, or tour bus from Naples or Pompeii. A few lucky ones will arrive by cruise ship. However you come, you should stay long enough to see my favorite limoncello.

Of course, Sorrento is more than a chance for a dime store. The little square and the carriages that are pulled by donkeys in fancy dress hats, the narrow alleys crammed with crates heaped with fruits and vegetables, the faience spilling from the stores, the overlook with the view down into the Bay of Naples . . . hmmmm, this is what we saved all that money for. This is what southern Italy is all about.

Sorrento is also the gateway to Positano and the rest of the Amalfi Coast. You can rent a car in Sorrento and drive yourself there. If you're feeling more adventurous, take a bus from the station in Sorrento. Even if Gore Vidal hasn't invited you to the villa for lunch, you're going to want to spend as much time as possible in these gorgeous, adorable, and ever-so-chic hill towns.

Getting There

From Naples, you can take the train or bus, rent a car, hire a car and driver, or take the hydrofoil. Or hop on the ferry from Capri, a mere 8km (5 miles) away.

If you are driving, forget all this hillside nonsense; you'll arrive right at town level and can ignore the port itself. If you're staying only a matter of hours, head right to the **Grand Hotel Ambasciatori** (Via Califano 18; ✆ **081/878-2025**), which has parking. Or leave the car near the Via Fuorimura, in the heart of town, and then walk. Parking in town is difficult.

The Lay of the Land

Like many Italian resort cities, Sorrento is built on a hill above the harbor. You will come to port at Porto Marina Piccola, and then catch a shuttle bus up to the heart of town, Piazza Tasso. You can walk, but it's pretty far, very steep, and the road is curvy and dangerous.

Cruise passengers can take the ship's shuttle bus. If you miss it, or need instant gratification, a taxi to and from town and the marina costs about 8€ ($10). Like the taxi drivers in Naples, they'll try to run up the meter. (For less than a couple of euros each way, you can take a public bus.) Taxis in town congregate at the Piazza Tasso, lining up on Via Fuorimura.

The Shopping Scene

Sorrento has a lot of charm to it. There's no serious shopping, but there are several opportunities here that you won't find elsewhere.

While Sorrento has only one or two designer shops (there's an **Emporio Armani**), it does have a branch of **Standa,** one of the best dime stores in Italy, so you can have some serious fun here. Along with a main shopping street, there's a pedestrian back street that's shady and picturesque.

And there are lemons to buy. And where there are lemons, there's limoncello. Don't drink limoncello and drive, of course—especially when we're talking about the Amalfi Drive!

Shopping Hours

Stores open at 8:30 or 9am and close from around 2 to 4pm for lunch. When there are ships in port, hours can be a little more flexible. The major department store in town, **A. Gargiulo & Jannuzzi** is open (nonstop, mind you) from 8am to 10pm in season. This town is closed on Sunday.

Shopping Neighborhoods

Piazza Tasso This is the proverbial town square: It's in the middle of everything, and many streets branch off in various directions, with each offering different shopping opportunities. You'll also see the donkey carts that you can rent for a trot about town.

Corso Italia This is the main real-people shopping street. It goes across the city and has two different personalities.

The portion that stretches to your right, if your back is to the sea and the donkeys are in front of you, is the main shopping street, with branches of **Lacoste** (very expensive!), the leather-goods and shoe store **Pollini,** and a few cafes.

Via Fuoro This is everyone's favorite street because it's a pedestrian alley: no cars, just tourists. There are drugstores, grocery stores, ceramics shops—in sum, everything that's authentically Italian.

Via de Maio This is the road that leads to the main square from the marina; the 2 blocks before you get to the square are filled with stores—some of them quite nice. There are also two excellent pharmacies here.

Via Fuorimura Leading away from town, this street is home to just a few stores and a hotel or two, but it's where you'll find **A. Gargiulo & Jannuzzi.**

Finds

A. GARGIULO & JANNUZZI
Viale E. Caruso 1.

This is the largest department store in Sorrento, and it was designed for tourists. In business since 1853, it's open from 8am to 10pm nonstop, it's air-conditioned, and it's accustomed to foreign visitors (the folks here speak English perfectly). This is not a TT, but rather a sprawling space with entire departments devoted to different crafts of the area: ceramics, exquisite linens (some of it deservedly very, very expensive), the local inlaid-wood marquetry, and more. ✆ **081/878-1041.** www.gargiulo-jannuzzi.it.

LIMONORO
Via San Cesareo 49–53.

This is my favorite limoncello factory; it's pretty—lots of white tile—and has a great selection. There are many different products, gift packages, and beautiful lemon-laden wrapping paper. ✆ 081/878-5348. www.limonoro.it.

POSITANO

The famed Amalfi Drive begins shortly after you bypass Sorrento and enter the kingdom of the curves, a twisty road that skirts the coast from above and often makes me queasy . . . and very grateful for my regular driver, Franco, who is always booked for me by the Hotel Le Sirenuse.

I never need go farther than Positano, but you can go all the way to Salerno, shopping as you go. Me? Bury my heart in Positano, where it simply can't get much better. And everyone speaks English.

Visitors say Positano; locals say Posi. So, while a day in Sorrento is a pleasant enough way to spend some time, if you're a do-everything kind of person on a cruise or a limited schedule, you can get through the pleasures of Sorrento (pleasurably) in 2 hours, and then be on your way to Posi, via the Amalfi Drive.

Cruise passengers can rent a car for the day, take a taxi, or, for the truly determined, hop on the public bus from Sorrento.

Some of the stores in Posi close for lunch from 1 to 3pm, so make sure to allow time for shopping beforehand. Then again, you can avoid the pressure by simply booking yourself into town and staying for a few days. There is water transportation directly from Naples, weather permitting.

The Lay of the Land

Positano is one of the famed hill-clinging towns; it is literally dug into the side of a cliff and is terraced from the beach to the top of a small mountain. There are some main streets, but most of the shopping is along pedestrian alleys and walkways. What I call "uptown" is the Via Colombo; what I call "downtown" is the Via dei Mulini. In this city, you are either up or down (or prone). Visitors with limited mobility and those who are infirm, short of step or breath, or simply lazy might want to reconsider. The lay of the land is vertical, not horizontal.

The Shopping Scene

If you haven't already learned the International Rule of Inaccessibility, this is a good time to get acquainted. What makes

The Lay of the Clay

Maybe it has something to do with thousands of years of lava and ocean spray and shifting earth and great good luck, but the Amalfi area is home to fabulous clay and is therefore the place to buy dishes. Every other store in Positano sells dishes, but every town in the area has its share. Remember when buying dishes that prices may be low, but shipping ain't.

A few years ago, a hand-painted look caught on and was sold at every store. That theme is passé now and solid rustic colors are in style, with a contrast raw border through which you can see some of the baked terra cotta.

For the most fun, head to **Vietri** (© 800/277-5933; www.vietri.com) in the town of Vietri sul Mare, near Salerno. The entire town is filled with factories and stores, but Vietri itself (a popular brand with strong U.S. distribution) allows you into the factory to buy or to design your own wares.

Solimene (© 089/210-243; www.solimene.com) is another firm that does much of the same.

a city into the kind of haven that the rich and famous like to visit is its inaccessibility to the masses. All the great resort cities of the world, especially in the Mediterranean, are hard to get to.

This being understood, Positano is the center for the rich and famous along the Amalfi Coast. It is adorable, and its stores sell fun things. There are very few TTs and no branches of Gap. On the other hand, the selection gets to look uniform in short order; there are only a handful of stores that sell designer clothes or nonresort items that you might wear in the real world if you don't live in the U.S. Sunbelt.

The scene is antithetical to what's happening on Capri. Here it's more laid-back, and the look is sort of rich-hippie casual. It's a movie set, and stores display their wares to enchant . . . and sell. Flowers pour out of flowerpots, cottons fly in the slight breeze, and lemons are dancing everywhere.

Dishes and pottery are big things; many stores sell them, and all stores seem to sell so much of the same thing that you soon get dizzy. There aren't as many jewelry shops as in Capri—the emphasis here is less on the body and more on comfort or home style. There are bathing-suit and clothing boutiques, but they sell funky fashions and comfortable things, even comfortably tiny bikinis. Many of the stores specialize in what I call Mamma Mia fashions: clothes made for short, wide women with a large bosom. I buy these clothes because they hide the waist and hips and allow for great comfort and eating space. Pass the pasta, please.

Shopping Hours

Stores open at 9am, close for lunch from 1 to 3 or 4pm, and stay open until 7 or 8pm. Many stores are closed from mid-October to mid-March. Stores do open on Sunday and on Monday morning.

Finds

Ceramica Assunta
Via Colombo 97.

Just a few doors downhill from Le Sirenuse, this shop has a wide selection of local ceramics in assorted styles. Most of the ceramics shops sell more or less the same wares, but this place is large enough for you to see everything. They pack and ship and will deliver to your hotel. ✆ **089/875-008.** www.ceramicassunta.it.

Emporio Le Sirenuse
Via Colombo 30 (across from Hotel Le Sirenuse).

This is where I first discovered my idol, Lisa Corti, and where I first fell in love with my dear friend Carla, who buys for the shop and has the eye of a maven, and whom I trust with all things Italian.

The tiny shop is a mélange of gorgeous tiles, hand-painted armoires, and merchandise in colors chosen to reflect the energy of the resort and the passion of the sea. While perhaps 30% of the merchandise is from Lisa Corti (thank God), the clothes come from Missoni, Etro, and many smaller designers that Americans may not know. Prices are fair—certainly no higher than elsewhere, despite this being a fancy resort.

This is one of the best stores in Italy and is worth the trip to Posi if you love color and flair and the art of the unique. There is also a catalog and online business. ✆ **089/812-2026.** www.emporiosirenuse.com.

Chapter Six

FLORENCE

WELCOME TO FLORENCE

I love Florence and its art treasures (including stores, of course), but I hate the tourist crowds, the prices, and the atmosphere in which local shopkeepers know that you will buy or eat or favor their firms, and so provide little as they laugh all the way to the *bancomat.*

If you haven't been to this part of Italy recently, note that Florence has changed enormously—even Siena has changed. In the old days, we used to go to Siena to find what we all used to go to Florence to find (charm). Now Siena is so popular that smart visitors are headed for Lucca. More on Lucca in "Beyond Florence," later in this chapter.

I'm not bad-mouthing Florence—or Siena—I'm just warning you. And asking you to note that I am reporting in these pages on several different faces of Florence, as I search for hidden values and hidden finds. There is much in Florence to enjoy, so step this way.

ARRIVING IN FLORENCE

By Plane

Before small intra-European airlines were fashionable, you had to fly into Pisa to fly to Florence. While you still have that option, and the Pisa airport is larger, you can now fly directly into Florence. Pisa is now served by some low-cost carriers as well as by the major E.U. airlines.

The Florence airport is lovely (good shopping for such a small airport) and only about 15 minutes by taxi from the heart of town, but there are often weather problems. You can't count on a timely arrival or departure.

Many travelers still use the Rome airport because you get your long-haul flights there and can easily connect to Florence by train, although there is no longer a train from the Rome airport straight to Florence. Still, you can connect through Rome's central station quite easily.

The real trick is to take one of the many low-cost carriers into Bologna and then catch one of the hour-long trains to Florence.

By Train

If you are coming to town by train, do pay attention: You want the **Santa Maria Novella** (often written as S.M.N.) rail station. The train may stop at another local station; do not panic. Wait until you get to S.M.N.

The Florence train station is smaller than the one in Milan and less intimidating. To get a taxi, follow signs to the left side of the station (left, that is, if you are arriving and walking toward the front of the station). There are a few stores (and a McDonald's) in the arrivals area; there's a small mall beneath the station. Yes, you can check your e-mail while at the station at an Internet cafe downstairs.

The train ride from Rome takes about 2 hours; from Milan, about 4 hours. Bologna is slightly more than an hour away.

Note that there are both Eurostar trains and IC (InterCity) trains to Florence; the IC from Rome is a half-hour longer but may be less expensive or included without a supplement in your travel pass.

By Car

Driving into Florence is relatively easy but made better if you have a computer printout with exact directions—and if you have a passenger along who is a quick navigator with good eyesight who can find the street names. This actually takes a wizard sometimes.

If your hotel is in the heart of the historic center, call before you arrive to provide your license plate and car information so the staff can inform the police. Cars without special permits are not allowed in the city center.

Once you are at your hotel, you will park the car and leave it—you are not allowed to drive around downtown. You can, of course, use your car to get out of town and travel to the outlets.

GETTING AROUND

It's a good thing you can walk just about everywhere in central Florence, because more and more bans are being put on vehicular traffic. This is true not only in Florence but also in Siena and other nearby towns. To enter the historic parts of town, a car must have a specific sticker on the windshield. Rental cars do not come with these stickers.

By Taxi

You can get a taxi at the train station; taxis have stickers that allow them to drive anywhere in town. There are no free-roaming taxis driving around town—you don't just hail a cab. You must call ahead.

If you need a taxi to pick you up somewhere, call © **055/43-90** or 055/42-42. Your hotel probably has a direct hot line that will summon a taxi in a matter of minutes. Note that with a radio taxi, the meter starts running when the driver gets the call to fetch you, so he may arrive with 6€ to 8€ ($7.80–$10) already on the meter.

By Bus

For your day trip to Siena or Lucca (see "Beyond Florence," later in this chapter), you may want to take the **SITA bus.** The SITA station (© **055/214-721**) is across from the Santa Maria Novella train station, an easy walk from most hotels.

For your day trip to Forte dei Marmi (again, see "Beyond Florence"), you'll need the **LAZZI bus** (© **055/215-154**), also located near the Santa Maria Novella station.

By Car Service

Most hotels will offer car service, but it can be rather pricey. I prefer to book through Maria Teresa Berdondini of **Tuscany by Tuscans** (©/fax **0572/70467**; www.tuscanybytuscans.it) because she has better rates and because most of her drivers speak English. Any legit car service will have the proper license to enter city streets that are forbidden to regular traffic.

About Phones & Addresses

Florence is more strict than many other Italian cities about its numbering system; stores (to differentiate them from residences) are zoned red, or *rosa,* and therefore usually have an "r" after their street number. The same number in black (to depict a residence) is somewhere else entirely on the street. Go figure.

Some local phone numbers have six digits, while some have seven. Don't freak.

Florence

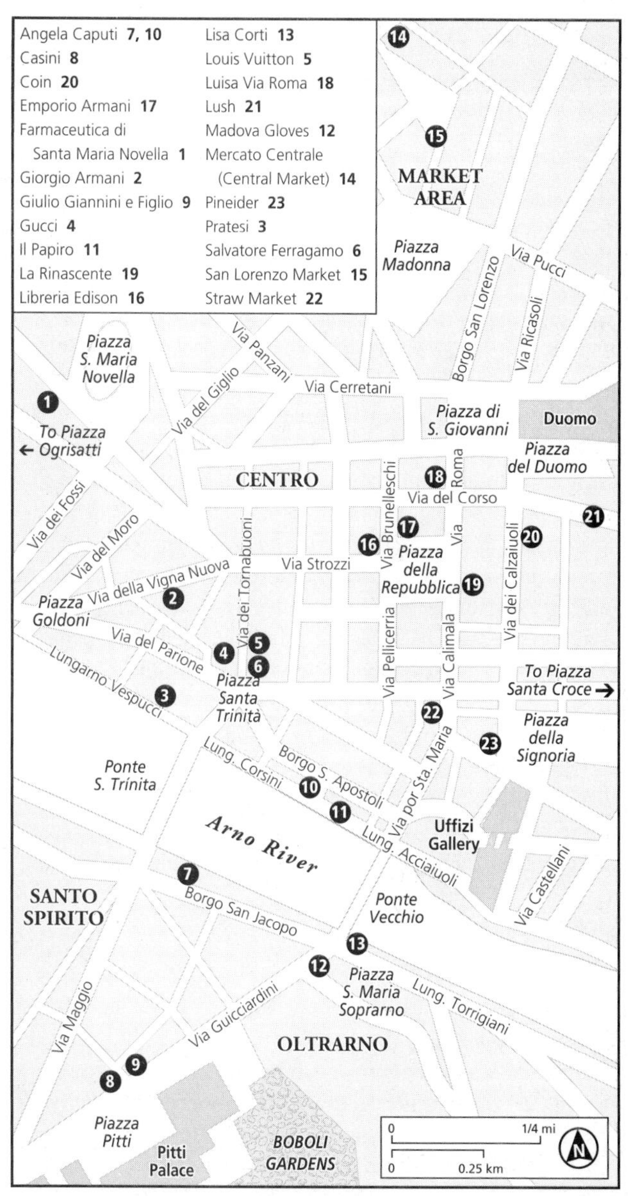

Angela Caputi 7, 10
Casini 8
Coin 20
Emporio Armani 17
Farmaceutica di Santa Maria Novella 1
Giorgio Armani 2
Giulio Giannini e Figlio 9
Gucci 4
Il Papiro 11
La Rinascente 19
Libreria Edison 16
Lisa Corti 13
Louis Vuitton 5
Luisa Via Roma 18
Lush 21
Madova Gloves 12
Mercato Centrale (Central Market) 14
Pineider 23
Pratesi 3
Salvatore Ferragamo 6
San Lorenzo Market 15
Straw Market 22
MARKET AREA
Piazza Madonna
Via Pucci
Borgo San Lorenzo
Via Ricasoli
Piazza S. Maria Novella
Via Panzani
Via Cerretani
Via del Giglio
Piazza di S. Giovanni
Duomo
Piazza del Duomo
To Piazza Ogrisatti
CENTRO
Via Brunelleschi
Via Roma
Via del Corso
Via dei Fossi
Via del Moro
Via dei Tornabuoni
Via Strozzi
Piazza della Repubblica
Via dei Calzaiuoli
Piazza Goldoni
Via della Vigna Nuova
Via del Parione
Lungarno Vespucci
Piazza Santa Trinità
Via Pellicerria
Via Calimala
To Piazza Santa Croce
Piazza della Signoria
Ponte S. Trinita
Lung. Corsini
Borgo S. Apostoli
Via por Sta. Maria
Uffizi Gallery
Arno River
Lung. Acciaiuoli
Via Castellani
SANTO SPIRITO
Borgo San Jacopo
Ponte Vecchio
Piazza S. Maria Soprarno
Lung. Torrigiani
Via Maggio
Via Guicciardini
OLTRARNO
Piazza Pitti
Pitti Palace
BOBOLI GARDENS
0
1/4 mi
0
0.25 km
N

SLEEPING IN FLORENCE

Grand Hotel Villa Medici
Via Il Prato 42.

I have been hanging out at this hotel for years, and while the location at first seems slightly off, it's actually great—within walking distance of the train station, bus station, and city center, and, importantly, not far from the autostrada. ***Note:*** Do not confuse this hotel with the Grand Hotel.

This is the place to pick if you want to travel outside of Florence, if you are headed to the outlets or to the countryside. It's also near the Tuesday Cascine open-air market and a 10-minute taxi ride from the airport. Traffic problems in Florence cannot be underestimated, thus location becomes one of this hotel's major selling points.

The Grand Hotel Villa Medici has just been renovated, so it features old-fashioned villa architecture with new modern interiors and lots of electronic amenities, including flatscreen TVs. On a recent visit, I stayed in what's called an apartment, which is sort of a suite, with two bathrooms and a sofa bed in the living room—great for those traveling with kids.

The property has numerous rates and promotions based on the season; doubles are about $400 regularly. You can book through the Leading Hotels of the World (© **800/233-6800** in the U.S.; www.lhw.com/ghvmedici), call the hotel directly (© **055/277-171**), or log on to www.villamedicihotel.com.

Hotel Bernini Palace Baglioni
Piazza San Firenze 29.

Totally redecorated in Orientale modern chic, the Bernini Palace is the poshest thing in town: not too big, not too small, and very dark and Venetian and dramatic and bold. If you want digs in the historic center of town, you cannot find a place with a better location or a more you-ain't-seen-nuthin'-yet style.

Rates vary between $300 and $400 depending on the season; look for various promotional offers and online deals. ✆ **055/288-621.** www.baglionihotels.com.

JOLLY HOTEL FIRENZE
Piazza Vittorio Veneto 4a.

I frequent the Jolly chain because it covers Italy and has good, dependable four-star hotels. This one, on the edge of Florence, is modern and ugly from the outside, but great on the inside and well priced.

Being on the edge of town is a blessing due to the traffic problems—you can still walk or bus into the historic center, but you can also get out of town quickly. The hotel has a shuttle that will take you into town, and you can buy bus tickets for public transportation at the front desk. The Jolly is also directly across from the Tuesday Cascine open-air market I love so much. If you're into supermarkets, you can take a 20-minute walk across the Arno and into real-people Florence and shop at a big grocery store.

Prices vary by season. For my last visit, I used Expedia.com and sprang for the highest-quality room available, which was 199€ ($259) for two including full buffet breakfast. ✆ **800/247-1277** in the U.S. Local phone ✆ 055/2770. www.jollyhotels.it.

J. K. PLACE
Piazza Santa Maria Novella 7.

New hotels continue to pop up in Florence—or rather, new old hotels—they are new, but put into old buildings! This one is ready for its close-up in any international design magazine—a slew of small salons on the ground floor welcome you, there's a restaurant that's already the talk of the town, and bedrooms (some are apartments) are modern and luxe and cozy. This is truly a boutique hotel in all ways.

The location is a block from the train station, so you are near everything, but isolated by the famed medieval church of the same name as the piazza. The clientele is so glam that you will want to stop by for a meal even if you aren't staying here.

Low-season rates are $400 for a double superior; that same room costs $500 in high season. Rates include breakfast, online services, coffee, tea, soft drinks, and other extras. ✆ **055/ 264-5181.** www.jkplace.com.

SNACK & SHOP

Busy shoppers might want to grab a bite at any of the stalls—some have counters—in the food market at San Lorenzo or any of the tiny cafes behind the stalls in the open-air portion of this market. I often stop for pizza at one of the pizza places on the main streets, and then follow up with a gelato. In the area around the Straw Market, you'll see several pizza places (you buy it by the slice) and gelato dealerships.

THE SHOPPING SCENE

If you're in Florence for the first time, you may be overwhelmed—or just plain faint. It's the heat! It's the crowds! It's the handbags! If you are combining art, culture, and shopping on a short time schedule, you will most certainly be dizzy.

If this is a repeat trip and you have a discerning eye, you may want to take shortcuts. Certainly the shopping scene is changing quickly, and sophisticated travelers may not be pleased. Fret not; just follow me. And remember, we don't buy junk anymore—those days are gone. We're counting our dollars, our euros, and the number of shoes in the closet.

This city does not offer as many of the classic, big-name, big-ticket Italian designer stores as Rome or Milan, although Florence does have a street of dream shops and a side street of fashionable big names. You won't go naked if you hit Florence without a garment to your name, but you won't find Chanel, either. Not to worry, though—Zara has arrived.

In many ways, you must expect your shopping finds to reflect the geopolitical situation. Florence is the unofficial beginning of the south of Italy. Few people here wear black; there is no hard-edged fashion. In fact, you are more likely to find that the locals with money and pedigree wear English-influenced country styles.

This is not a case of keeping Italy for Italians or keeping out northern, big-city style. It's cultural. Strangely enough, you will find that many French chains have invaded not only the tourist shopping areas but also the real-world parts of town, and you'll also see Blockbuster stores—an American contribution—in residential areas. Even French super-chef Alain Ducasse has opened a restaurant in Tuscany as the area becomes more international and less related to Milan.

Best of all, Florence serves as the gateway to some superlative factory outlets and the wonders of everything else under the Tuscan sun. The bargains and buys are just outside Florence; the city is a good jumping-off point for many adventures. Rent a car; get outta town. Get lost; get found.

The Best Buys in Florence

Junk I love junk; I love $5-to-$25 gift items. But we don't want it to look cheap or tacky or end up at someone's yard sale next summer.

Junk that doesn't look like junk? How about those silk ties I found in San Lorenzo for 5€ ($6.50) each? Not only are the same ties sold elsewhere in Italy for $25 to $35, but these ties also compete with $50 ties. And yes, I do tie my hair back with a men's tie—so don't think these are just for those who wear suits or haven't discovered dress-down days. The fashionable ties are textured solids in gelati colors.

Smalls This is what I call small stylish items with low prices that are easy to pack. The markets are a good source if you have a discerning eye. Grocery stores are filled with choices. Even Lush, the British bath-and-beauty chain, has Italian-influenced products. Florence provides better high-quality, easier-to-get-to smalls than any other major Italian city.

Ceramics & Faience If you get into the hill towns and pottery towns, you will save off Florence prices. If you don't have the opportunity to get out of town, you'll find plenty to choose from in Florence—from huge jardinières to little rooster jugs. I am horrified by how expensive these items have become (40€/$52 for a plate to hang on the wall), but you can still get a salad serving set for 4€ to 6€ ($5.20–$7.80). Some items are sold in the two town markets; better-quality items are sold in specialty shops around town. But prices for ceramics are lower in Siena, just an hour away. And they are even better in Deruta (p. 178), 2 hours away.

Olive Oil Olive oil is much like wine, with olives very much like grapes. Often, vineyards that make wine also make olive oil, and have wine shops *(enoteca)* that sell it. The airport in Florence has an excellent selection; otherwise, you can try a wine shop, a grocery store, or even some of the specialty sources directly. The selection at **Baroni** at the Mercato Centrale (Central Market) is excellent. There are many tours and tastings that help educate your palate (see "Out-of-Town Touring," later in this chapter).

Remember, the good stuff isn't cheap; it usually comes in a glass bottle and is heavy and fragile. Expect to pay 15€ to 40€ ($20–$52) per bottle. ***Note:*** You can no longer carry olive oil on the plane with you. When you pack it in your suitcase, tape the bottle at the neck, wrap it in bubble wrap, and then roll it in plastic bags and washable clothes.

Paper Goods If you didn't get your fill of Italian-style papers in Venice, you can buy more in Florence. The assorted merchandise is so classy-looking that it makes a marvelous gift; pencils cost less than $1 each. There are about half a dozen stores in central Florence that specialize in Florentine paper works; items of lower quality are sold at souvenir stands and in the markets.

Cheap Handbags I am only slightly ashamed to tell you this: The triumph of one trip to Florence was a faux reptile-printed plastic Birkin-style handbag for $30 that is so stunning you could faint. Because it is textured, it's harder to detect that it's plastic, and it's absolutely fabulous with gray flannel. It's also great for travel because it's not too fragile. In subsequent visits I have never found anything to rival this buy, but I keep looking. You just never know.

Designer Brands at the Outlets It takes some time and trouble, but it's worth it. Buy clothes, shoes, cashmeres, handbags, and bed linen from a variety of nearby sources. See p. 165.

Shoppers Beware

Be careful when buying the following items:

Gold There are plenty of jewelers on the Ponte Vecchio, but prices are competitive to those in jewelry marts in the U.S. I can't tell you why you should buy from them unless you have romance in mind and are willing to pay for it. But wait; if you're looking for 18k gold as opposed to 14k, this is the place to find it. Yes, the prices are high, but most merchants will deduct the VAT and give you an additional discount for a cash sale.

If you are looking for a Nomination bracelet—gold or silver—try jewelers on the side streets. I was shocked to discover that you can now buy fake Nomination bracelets from those guys with blankets on the streets. Oh my!

Leather Goods I know, I know, Italy, especially Florence, is famous for its leather goods. I'm not telling you to refrain from a leather purchase. I merely ask that you purchase slowly and carefully. There are so many fake-leather factories in Florence and so many handbags for sale in markets and on the street that you will lose your mind in short order. More important, leather goods in Italy are well made but expensive. If it's not expensive, it might not have been made in Italy.

For real value in leather goods, you'll do far better spending a little more money and buying from a big-name leather-goods house with a reputation to back up the goods. And forget about those so-called outlets that stretch from downtown to the Leather School. I'm not even that impressed with the Leather School.

Do note that there is a huge territory of no man's land: no-name, no-brand handbags and leather goods that are not inexpensive ($250 and up) but offer great value if bought properly. Buying and bargaining for them is tricky.

Silk For affordable silks that won't embarrass you, avoid fake designer scarves; instead, check out the ties. ***Warning:*** While you may associate silk with this part of Italy (as well as to the north), most of the market stock comes from Asia. Check edges to see if they are hand-stitched, and make sure it's silk and not polyester—unless you want polyester, which is less expensive.

Secret Dealings

To compensate for lack of sales in off periods, many store owners, especially those outside the deluxe brands, will make deals. I saved about $100 on a handbag once because I was able to go down the street to the ATM and pay in cash and was equally willing to waive the tax-refund paperwork.

Hidden Finds in Florence

If you are offended by all the tourist junk in Florence, fear not. There are a handful of hidden places that are yummy and worth the slight trouble it takes to find them.

ALESSANDRO DARI
Via San Niccolo 115r.

I found my visit to this shop to be a religious experience—or at least a very spiritual one. I don't mean because it carries religious merchandise, but I felt myself surrounded by the work of a master, perhaps the Michelangelo of our time; I felt as if Dari's work came straight from the angels or even God.

This is basically a jewelry shop with a workshop, so you can commission a piece or buy from the display cases. Prices start at 400€ ($520) and go up, but for less than 1,000€ ($1,300) you can have some serious work. There are rings that are buildings, rings that do tricks, and pieces with hidden mechanisms and secrets.

The shop is away from central Florence but within easy walking distance of the Ponte Vecchio. ✆ **055/244-747.** www.alessandrodari.com.

Antico Setificio Fiorentino
Via Bartolini 4.

Within easy walking distance of the center of downtown, this factory is truly hidden in an industrial neighborhood, behind a high fence. Once through the gate, you will step back in time to the 18th century. The compound includes a private house, a factory (hear the hum of the shuttles?), and a showroom laden with fabric and ribbons. The showroom is organized by price and by type of silk and cotton: Prices are not low. To visit this factory is an experience all its own. If you don't intend to buy $100-a-yard (or more) goods, don't worry—you can still afford a small bag of potpourri.

You may want your concierge to phone ahead, as you need an appointment; you may be asked to pay for the right to visit. ✆ **055/213-861.** www.setificiofiorentino.it.

Chianti Cashmere Company
Siena.

American Nora Kravis breeds cashmere goats in the hills outside Florence; she uses the milk from these goats to make soap and skincare products. Check it out on her website and arrange ahead of time to visit. ✆ **0577/738-080.** www.chianticashmere.com.

Farmaceutica di Santa Maria Novella
Via della Scala 16r.

This is by no means a new source or much of a secret, but it is a little hard to find and fits with the mood of most of the other shops in this list—entering the former convent that looks like a museum feels like a step back in time. The usual soaps and skin creams are sold in the front rooms; in the rear, a newly opened room features herbal cures. ✆ **055/216-276.** www.smnovella.it.

GREVI
Via della Spada 11–13r.

This centuries-old family business makes hats outside of Florence and sells from a small shop in the heart of town. There are a wide variety of styles, with some exotics and many plain old useful items. The packable hat is good for travel. Expect to pay about $100. ✆ **055/264-139.** www.grevi.com.

LORENZO VILLORESI
Via dei Bardi 14.

This place is as hidden and private as they get, and you must telephone for an appointment at least a day in advance. Mr. Villoresi has a nose for some big-time scents, and he's created them for some big-time firms, but he will allow you a private workshop with him. It costs 250€ ($325) and takes as long as it takes because the two of you are creating your own fragrance from scratch. Heaven scent. ✆ **055/234-1187.**

Florentine Choices

Because Florence has so many faces and opportunities, you will have to make choices in terms of what kinds of sights you want to see and stores you want to shop. And because prices are so high, you may want to change your orientation a bit to get the best experience for your euro.

- Choose a hotel on the edge of town if you want to get onto the road or into real-people parts. If you want to be in the thick of it all, choose a hotel well located in the city center.
- Choose the one great handbag you promised yourself based on its quality, not its label.
- Spend some money gaining experience as a souvenir instead of handbags. Book a day with Faith Heller Willinger, the

famous American food maven living in Florence, who now takes on visitors (p. 150), or Maria Teresa Berdondini (www.tuscanybytuscans.it), who can arrange other cooking classes.

- Think foodstuffs in terms of shopping and gifts to bring home; think tastings in terms of sightseeing. Get back to the land.
- Shop at outlets. Window-shop in Florence if you want, but get a car—or a car and driver—and take a day trip to the nearby outlets for serious savings. You can even take a bus, a free shuttle, or an official tour to outlets; outlets are the number-two most-visited Italian cultural sight these days.
- Look beneath the surface. Head to the fringes of the tourist districts. Find the hidden gems. You may want to book a day with Maria Teresa Berdondini (www.tuscanybytuscans.it), who does a Hidden Florence tour that will touch your soul and show you artisans and craftspeople behind closed doors—it makes shopping into a religious experience.

Comparison Shopping

Many designer big names keep coming to town to stake a share of the crowds; existing stores are constantly renovating. Best plan: Do your serious fashion shopping in other cities and save Florence for specialty goods, unique items, and shopping experiences you simply can't get elsewhere. And keep in mind the following:

- Rome and Milan have more designer stores.
- Florence and the surrounding area are good destinations for buying under-$10 gifts that don't look junky (see "The Best Buys in Florence," earlier in this chapter).
- Museums all have gift shops, most of which offer unique items at reasonable prices. Crowds may be thinner here, too.
- The Straw Market and the San Lorenzo market are both wonderful fun, but they have very, very similar merchandise—and, let's face it, it's mostly junky and touristy. If your time is truly limited, choose one. It won't hurt you to miss

them both. Foodies should pick San Lorenzo; in fact, I'd pick San Lorenzo no matter what.

Shopping Hours

Like all Italy, Florence is celebrating a new world in shopping hours. The two big department stores stay open on Sunday, and there's a lot going on that didn't used to happen. Many stores still close at lunchtime during the week, but Florence doesn't close tight for lunch. You can find some life if you look for it.

Shops are basically closed Sunday and Monday, or at least on Monday until 3:30pm. In summer, they also close on Saturday afternoon at 1pm. Sunday is now livelier than Monday morning (even Sun morning), so don't stay home making false assumptions—get out there and shop.

Sunday hours for those stores that stay open are 10am to 4pm or 11am to 5pm. Outlets are open on Sunday, but get the exact hours, as they vary and you can plan your schedule with finesse.

Nearby outlets may be closed Mondays until late afternoon. Don't venture out of town on a Monday without checking it out first.

Also note that the last Sunday of the month is a special day in retail, so more stores are open than on the first Sunday of the month (there's also a cute flea market that day); the suburban American-style shopping mall is open as well.

Markets always close for holidays but do not necessarily close for lunch. The San Lorenzo market is closed on Sunday and Monday but is open during lunch on other days. The Straw Market is open but not in full bloom on Monday; it is open during lunch every day—except Sunday.

Food stores are open Monday morning. In winter, food stores are also open on Saturday afternoon but are closed on Wednesday afternoon. In June, the pattern switches, and the food stores close on Saturday afternoon and stay open on Wednesday afternoon.

Speaking of summer hours, everything except major tourist traps (TTs) is closed from mid-August through the rest of the month.

Sunday Shopping

While Sunday isn't a big shopping day in most of Italy, if the weather is nice, or if the tourists are in season, you'd be surprised at just how much business goes on. Here's how you can spend your day:

The **Straw Market** (p. 163) has sellers who open up their carts. A big bookstore, **Libreria Edison** (p. 149), stays open every Sunday. And many stores do open on the last Sunday of each month.

In town, there is action on the **Ponte Vecchio.** The usual shops are indeed shuttered, but on the walkway over the bridge, standing shoulder to shoulder on both sides of the walk, is an incredible array of vendors—from boys with imitation Louis Vuitton totes to hippies with poorly made jewelry to real artisans with crafts pieces. Much of what you will see here is delightful junk—the exact kind of thing you want to see on a Sunday. But there are a few buys as well.

There's also a vast amount of Sunday shopping available in the so-called in-town factory outlets and TTs that stretch from the Duomo to Santa Croce. I think the single-best store for Sunday shopping (if you have to pick one) is **Ducci** (Lungarno Corsini 24r), a dressed-up version of a TT that's more like an art gallery.

But the real factory outlets—outside of town—are also open, usually Sunday afternoons only. Some open at 2pm, others at 3pm, so check before you drive or hire a car service. Don't be surprised if there are lines out front before the outlets open. At Prada, you take a number, but the cafe is open before the shop, so you can queue or sip a coffee.

If you like upscale, tony shopping rather than touristy stuff, there's magnificent shopping in **Forte dei Marmi** on Sunday. It's just an hour from Florence. For the uninitiated, Forte dei

Out-of-Town Touring

If head-for-the-hills is your choice of neighborhood, you've picked a great part of Italy to explore. If you want someone else to do the driving, you need only call my friend Maria Teresa Berdondini and her husband, Giuseppe Mazza (©/fax **0572/704-67**; www.tuscanybytuscans.it), who have a tour company that accomplishes all miracles, from olive-oil tastings to trips to the outlets.

Prices include departure and return to any hotel in Florence. For example, a half-day (4-hr.) shopping tour to Gucci and Prada outlets with car and English-speaking driver costs 300€ ($390), while a half-day walking tour visiting Florentine artists in their showrooms with a personal shopper runs 260€ ($338).

Marmi is sort of the Palm Beach of Italy. It's a 1-hour drive from Florence; you can also take the bus.

Alternatively, you can go to **Montecatini,** where stores are also open; this is a town famous for its spa, but it is also adorable and real and very lush Italian. It's about an hour away and easily reached by train.

Sending It Home

If you don't feel like schlepping your purchases with you, a giant post office in the heart of town—right near the Straw Market—offers what's called Express Mail. Italian mail makes me nervous, though; you can use FedEx if you prefer or if cost is no object.

An in-town branch of **Mail Boxes Etc.** (Via della Scala 13r; © **055/268-173**; www.mbe.com) does shipping, packing, money grams, and more. Store hours are Monday through Friday from 9am to 1pm and 3:30 to 6:30pm.

On the Pitti side of the Ponte Vecchio, Via Barbadori is home to both a post office and the **Shipping Company** (at the corner of Via de Ramaglianti). Just out of curiosity, I priced the cost of sending six bottles of olive oil from Florence to San Antonio, Texas—the answer was 115€ ($150). The Shipping Company is open Monday through Saturday from 10am to 1pm and 3:30 to 7pm.

SHOPPING NEIGHBORHOODS

Tornabuoni The Via dei Tornabuoni is the whoop-dee-doo, big-time street for the mainline tourist shopping of the gold-coast kind. This is where most of the big-name designers have their shops, and where the cute little specialty stores and leather-goods makers cluster. This is where you'll find everyone from **Gucci** (Via dei Tornabuoni 73r) to **Ferragamo** (Via dei Tornabuoni 16r), but, alas, no Chanel. Who needs Chanel with the Ferragamo museum to keep you busy? If you have only an hour for seeing the best shopping in Florence, perhaps you'll just want to stroll this street.

The Tornabuoni area begins (or ends) at the Piazza di San Trinità, which is a small plaza with a very tall, skinny obelisk. Although most of the hotsy-totsy names are right on Tornabuoni, some are on nearby side streets, especially on **Via della Vigna Nuova.** The Via dei Tornabuoni itself leads easily into Via della Vigna Nuova, but don't think it ends there. Stay with the street as the numbers climb because **Profumeria Inglese** (no. 97r) is well past the thick of things, but it's a great place for perfumes and beauty supplies (assuming you are not going to France). Also check out **Via degli Strozzi,** the connector between Tornabuoni and the Piazza della Repubblica. **Emporio Armani** (Piazza Strozzi) is here.

Excelsior/Grand This neighborhood, home to the Westin Excelsior and Grand hotels, backs up to Tornabuoni, where the famed hotels are located. Many good stores are actually on **Piazza Ognissanti;** the rest line **Borgo Ognissanti** until it hits Piazza Goldoni and becomes Via della Vigna Nuova. If all this sounds confusing, don't panic.

The neighborhoods are close to each other and could even be considered one neighborhood, which is why staying at either of these hotels makes good sense if you love shopping, want to walk, and need a luxury property.

The shops in the Excelsior/Grand area are less touristy and more mom-and-pop than the big names on Tornabuoni, but the area does include a designer name or two, such as **Bottega Veneta** (Piazza Ognissanti 3).

Grand/Medici You can walk from the luxury hotels at Borgo Ognissanti all the way to the Grand Hotel Villa Medici, another luxury hotel only 2 blocks away. In doing so you will pass several local resources and a discount shop as well as two major American car-rental agencies, Avis and Europcar (National).

If you want discount shopping, check out **One Price** (Borgo Ognissanti 74r), where the lamb's-wool sweaters come in dreamy colors and sell for about $25—if you get lucky, of course (this is how you hit it shopping). I scored on my last trip at **Il Giglio** (Borgo Ognissanti 86r) with a pair of Tod's wannabes (mustardy suede!) for $45.

Excelsior/Grand Antiques There are two main antiques areas in Florence, one near the Pitti Palace and the other right beside the Excelsior/Grand area at **Piazza Ognissanti.** If you're facing the Excelsior Hotel (with the Grand Hotel to your rear, the Arno River to your right, and a church to your left) and start walking, you'll pass a small street called Via del Porcellana. From there, look across Borgo Ognissanti to **Fioretto Giampaolo** (no. 43r). Stop in, and then walk a block toward Tornabuoni until you get to the Piazza Goldoni.

At the **Piazza Goldoni,** you'll discover **Via dei Fossi,** which is crammed with antiques dealers. In fact, the area between the two streets and including the **Via del Moro,** which runs next to Via dei Fossi, is host to almost two dozen dealers. Most of these stores sell larger pieces of furniture and medium-to-important antiques; there's not too much junk.

There are some businesses that are geared to the design trade without being in the antiques business—such as **Riccardo Barthel** (Via dei Forri 11r), which does tiles. One Sunday each fall (ask your concierge for the exact day, as it varies from year to year), all the dealers in the area have open houses.

Arno Alley The Arno is a river, not a neighborhood; the main street along each bank of the river changes its name every few blocks. On the Duomo side of the river, the portion of the street named **Lungarno Amerigo Vespucci,** which becomes **Lungarno Corsini,** is crammed with shops, hotels, and even the famous Harry's Bar.

Some of these shops sell antiques; several of them sell statues and reproductions of major works; some sell shoes, clothes, and/or handbags; and one or two are just fancy TTs. *Note:* Several of these shops are open on Sunday.

Duomo Center As in Milan, there is excellent shopping around the Duomo. Naturally, this is an older, more traditional area. Locals as well as tourists shop here. Because this area has gotten so built up and is filled with an overwhelming number of stores, I now divide it into directions.

There are stores around all four sides of the church (there's even shopping in the church, in a little museum store downstairs) and in the little side streets stretching from the church as well. This is where **Pegna** is located.

Crosstown To me, Crosstown heads from the Duomo to the Arno and over the river (or vice versa). The main shopping street of this part of town is called **Via dei Calzaiuoli,** and it's directly behind the Duomo and runs right smack into the Uffizi. It is closed to street traffic, so pedestrians can wander freely from the Duomo to **Piazza della Signoria,** another large piazza filled with pigeons, postcards, incredible fountains and statues, visitors and locals, charm and glamour, and everything you think Florence should have. You can't rave about an area too much more than that, can you?

A second main shopping street, **Via Roma,** connects the Duomo and the Ponte Vecchio and runs past **Piazza della Repubblica,** where many traditional stores are located. This street runs parallel to Via dei Calzaiuoli, and you could mistake it for the main shopping street of town unless you knew better. The Savoy Hotel is on Via Roma.

Just before it reaches the Ponte Vecchio, Via Roma becomes **Via por Santa Maria.** Don't miss **Luisa Via Roma** (Via Roma 21r), which is sort of the local version of Barneys.

Deep Town Streets that run from the Duomo in the direction of Santa Croce in the city center are chockablock with cute stores. The best ones are **Via del Corso** (which becomes Borgo Albizi) and **Via Tavolini,** which will change its name each block and runs exactly parallel to Via del Corso. Be sure to take some time to look at the old houses here and to smell the coffee. You'll find the local branch of **Lush** in this part of town; many of the branches of French stores are here, as are a few discounters.

Ponte Vecchio If you keep walking a few hundred meters from the Piazza della Signoria right to the banks of the Arno River, you'll see the Ponte Vecchio. You'll zig to the right a few yards, and then walk left to get across the bridge. Or you can connect by continuing straight along Via Roma, which will change its name each block and become the Ponte Veccio 3 blocks after you pass the Duomo. By my definition, the Ponte Vecchio neighborhood includes the bridge and the retailers on the Duomo side of the bridge. Once you cross the bridge, you're in another neighborhood: Pitti.

The Ponte Vecchio is a distinct area, however, because the entire bridge is populated by jewelry shops. Prices range from high to very high, but there are deals to be found on big-name Italian designer jewelry. Sarah bought a classic 18k gold Fope necklace from **Carlo Piccini** (Ponte Vecchio 31r) for about two-thirds of what she'd pay in San Francisco. **Gioielleria Callai** (Ponte Vecchio 17) has a good selection of earrings, bracelets, and gold chains. Both of these shops offer a hefty discount if you pay in cash.

Over the Bridge (Pitti & Santo Spirito) Once you cross over the Ponte Vecchio, you reach a different retailing climate. You are now on the Pitti side of the bridge. The stores are smaller but no less touristy; you get the feeling that real people also shop here. You can wander, discovering your own personal finds; you can stop and get the makings of a picnic or grab a piece of pizza. The shopping goes in two directions: toward the Pitti Palace or uptown along the Arno. (If your back is to the Duomo, turn left along the Arno to head uptown.) See both areas, looking at shops on **Borgo San Jacopo** and on **Via Guicciardini.** Take time to explore the small streets in between, including **Via Barbadori,** where you'll find a post office with ATM, a photo lab (**Studio Luce,** no. 18r), a small grocery store (**Primirie Market,** no. 34), and the **Shipping Company** (at the corner of Via de Ramaglianti).

If you are headed to the once-a-month flea market or looking for antiques shops and crafts vendors, the Santo Spirito neighborhood—actually part of Pitti—is where you want to be. Santo Spirito may not be on the tiny freebie maps handed out all over town, but it is truly convenient and easy to find: If you are standing in front of the Pitti with the Pitti behind you, walk straight for 1 block.

If you are looking for **Lisa Corti,** it's on Via Bardi, which is the street to your left, if your back is to the bridge. The store is hidden, so immediately after crossing the Ponte Vecchio, dart into the bridge area from the side to find it.

Santa Croce & Bernini Back Alley A sneeze behind the Piazza Signoria is the Hotel Bernini Palace and the Borgo dei Greci, which leads to Santa Croce. Shoppers know this area mostly because of the famous Leather School located inside the Santa Croce church (see "Leather Goods," later in this chapter). It's nice to wander around this area because it feels like it's a little off the beaten track and seems more natural than the parts of town where tourists swarm (yet this is a major tourist area with many, many TTs). Face it—it's all tourist shops. There are also some cafes and pizza eats, more so-called leather factory outlets than you ever care to see in your lifetime, one or two fun antiques-cum-junk stores (the best kind), and a good bit of Sunday retail. If you are lucky enough to catch the Sunday flea market, it's even deeper into this area.

FLORENCE RESOURCES A TO Z

Antiques

As an antiques center, Florence gets pieces from the entire Tuscan area. The problem of fakes, which is so severe in Rome, is not as great here. Anyone can get taken—that's well known—but the chances are lower in Florence than in Rome.

Please note that the laws defining what is and is not an antique are different in Italy than in many other countries, so items made from old wood or from older items may be classified as antiques even if they were made yesterday! The craftspeople in the area are gifted at making repros that are so good you can't tell how old they are.

- Antiques are available at a flea market at the **Piazza dei Ciompi,** but this is really grandmother's attic, fun stuff. We're talking car-boot or tag-sale quality here, but you may uncover a find every now and then (or absolutely nothing). Note that there are two parts to this market: the regulars, who are open every day in the center aisles in little huts, and the people who set up on tables in the open air on the last Sunday of each month.
- For more serious stuff, check out any of the following streets: Via Guicciardini, Via Maggio, Via dei Tornabuoni, Via della Vigna Nuova, Via del Porcellana, Borgo Santi Apostoli, Via dei Fossi, Via del Moro, Via di Santo Spirito, or Via della Spada. There's a string of fun shops for everything from old postcards to 1950s jewelry on the Borgo San Jacopo right over the bridge. I happen to like Via dei Fossi for medium-range antiques—possibly affordable.
- Affordable antiques are best bought at flea markets that are regular events, most often held once a month. Better yet, they are best bought at markets that are out of town. Many locals like to go to **Viterbo,** a city about 45 minutes away, because it has a fairly decent Sunday flea market for antiques. Viterbo also gets a less touristy crowd. The best flea market

in Florence proper is held at **Santo Spirito** every second Sunday of the month.

- There's an antiques fair in **Pistoia,** a half-hour away, on the second Saturday and Sunday of each month. The market is covered and houses about 150 stalls. There is no market in July and August. Head for the Via Ciglliegiale.
- There's a market in **Pisa** on the second Sunday of each month and the Saturday that precedes it. This market, which also has about 150 dealers, is known for its furniture, which can be bought at a low price and then restored. The market is not held in July and August. It's located on Via XX Settembre.
- The town of **Siena** has a flea market on the third Sunday of each month. There are only about 60 dealers, but the market does get a lot of "smalls" (the trade term for small objets d'art) and locals selling off estate pieces, so buyers can hope to get lucky here. There's no market in August. Head for the Piazza del Mercato.
- The biggest (and best) antiques fair in Italy is held in **Arezzo,** about an hour south of Florence by train. It takes place the first Sunday of each month and the Saturday that precedes it. There are over 600 dealers at this event, and it does not close in the summer months. Head to the Piazza Vasari and work the area to the Piazza San Francesco.

Bath, Beauty & Erborista

If you can help it, don't buy makeup in Florence—it's expensive, and the choices are pretty average. If you're desperate, go to department stores such as **Coin** or **La Rinascente.** For more beauty products, see "Pharmacies & Soaps" (p. 170).

CHIANTI CASHMERE COMPANY
Siena.

Discover soap made from cashmere goats on a Tuscan farm. For more, see "Hidden Finds in Florence" (p. 134). ✆ **0577/738-080.** www.chianticashmere.com.

De Herbore
Via del Proconsolo 43r.

A local *erboristeria* and source for great-looking (and great-smelling) gift items and cures. This is on the way to Santa Croce. ✆ **055/211-706.**

Erboristeria Palazzo Vecchio
Via Vacchereccia 9r.

This is an herbalist, not a pharmacist—puh-lease! Buy hair tonic, bosom tonics, and much more. It's right in the thick of the shopping in central downtown. The packaging is good and the opportunity for fun gifts is strong. ✆ **055/239-6055.**

Lush
Via del Corso 23r.

This is the British bath firm that makes an effort to produce its Italian products with local ingredients, so they are different from offerings in other Lush shops. While prices are hefty (about 4€/$5.20 for a bath bomb), this is the only international division of Lush that custom-makes products from indigenous ingredients. I am addicted to the limoncello soap and shampoo. ✆ **055/210-265.** www.lush.com.

Books

Art Store
Piazza del Duomo 50r.

This appears to be a museum shop but has a separate entrance from the museum next door, and offers mostly books. You can find art books as well as guides, children's books, and the usual souvenirs and gifts with an artistic bend.

BM Book Shop
Borgo Ognissanti 4r.

This English-language bookshop, right smack in the heart of everything, specializes in American and British books; it's a great place to hang out and ask questions or touch base with the owners. It's located near the Westin Excelsior in a shopping district you will pass every day. ✆ **055/294-575.** bmbookshop@dada.it.

Libreria Edison
Piazza della Repubblica 27r.

This is sort of the local Barnes & Noble. Although most of the books are in Italian, there are also foreign-language books, plus everything from postcards to CDs. It's open on Sunday from 10am to 1:30pm and 3:30 to 8pm. Other days of the week—including Monday—it's open nonstop from 9am to 8pm. ✆ **055/213-110.** www.libreriaedison.it.

Boutiques

Casini
Piazza Pitti 30–31r.

This is a three-part store: One part is more leather goods while the others are designer clothes—some of them made especially for the boutique.

The leather goods include shoes, handbags, briefcases, and accessories, but also the most extraordinary leather clothes for men and women. Prices are quite fair considering the quality and the ability to stitch butter into leather—under $1,000 for a reversible jacket. I saw a black leather doctor's bag for around 500€ ($650) that was killer chic and surely the same quality as Bottega Veneta. Women's shoes are available in large sizes (to U.S. 11); the ballerina slippers are well priced at 75€ ($98).

The owner is American and therefore everyone on hand speaks English and understands the American need to blend

Italian style with real life. Custom work can be ordered and will be sent to you in the U.S. without duties—it will take about 2 weeks for your order to arrive. ✆ **055/210-430.** www.casini firenze.it.

LUISA VIA ROMA
Via Roma 19–21r.

It's one of the best stores in town—maybe the world—when it comes to fashion, style, whimsy, and the look we crave, but usually can't achieve or afford. ✆ **055/217-826.** www.luisavia roma.com.

RASPINI
Via por Santa Maria 72r.

This firm once owned a ton of boutiques carrying designer brands. Now it has cut back its space but still has some of the world's best-known labels—most are Italian but there are also some international makers. Rumor has it the space will become another Prada shop. Film at 11. ✆ **055/215-796.** www.raspini.com.

Cooking Classes

CUCINA TOSCANA (FAITH HELLER WILLINGER)
Every Wednesday Faith Willinger, famous for her books and articles and importance in the world of Italian food and wine, gives a private cooking lesson in her home in the heart of town near the Pitti Palace. I do not give the address because, after all, this is Faith's home and the woman does deserve a little privacy. Once you have booked, you will get directions; her flat is easily reached from all parts of town and is in central Florence.

Technicalities first: The class costs $450 for the day but will be discounted to $400 per day if you mention Born to Shop when you book. Yes, you get more than $450 worth of fun and an excellent goody bag to take away with you.

You'll start with a lesson in making the perfect espresso, and then you're off to the market to pick out lunch. The class makes lunch together, gets a few life lessons from Faith, and then eats the lunch ensemble. Sometimes there is a guest chef at lunch. www.faithwillinger.com.

CULINARY VACATIONS

Chef John Wilson has a business that offers wine tastings and cooking tours; you get a 1-week package tour that includes 5 nights' lodging, all meals and wine, and excursions. The price (without air) is about $2,200 per person. Contact chefjohn wilson@charter.net or call ✆ **770/998-2073.**

LA CUCHINA FIORENTINA

Group classes (in English) are offered for up to eight participants—you get a trip to market and then kitchen and cooking time, all for about $200 per person. This is organized through a private eating club and is booked through Tuscany by Tuscans (www.tuscanybytuscans.it).

VILLA SAN MICHELE SCHOOL OF COOKERY

Via Doccia 4, Fiesole.

That's not Michelle ma belle, it's "mick-*ell*-i," got it? This is one of the most famous, drop-dead-gorgeous villa hotels in the area. In May and September, it conducts cooking classes along with classes in the arts of entertaining, often taught by royalty. ✆ **055/567-8200.** www.villasanmichele.net.

Department Stores

COIN

Via dei Calzaiuoli 56r.

A small department store concentrating on ready-to-wear, Coin exhibits a little of everything for men, women, and children. It's a good place to sniff out next season's fashion direction. Prices aren't at the bargain level, but they are moderate for

Italy. The biggest news here is that the store has totally eliminated makeup and perfume; it now has only a MAC boutique on the ground floor right at the front door. ***Remember:*** When the elevator says T, you are at street level; S stands for second floor. ✆ **055/280-531.** www.coin.it.

LA RINASCENTE
Piazza Repubblica.

La Rinascente is right in the heart of town, obviously put there to compete with the lovely Coin. The store is moderately priced, light, modern, fun to shop, and open on Sunday. It is not a great store, so don't be too hurt. ✆ **055/219-113.** www.rinascente.it.

Designer Boutiques

For details on many of these well-known brand names, check out the "Dictionary of Taste & Design" (p. 55).

CONTINENTAL BIG NAMES

CARTIER
Via dei Tornabuoni 40r.

ESCADA
Via Strozzi 30–36.

HERMÈS
Piazza degli Antinori 6r.

LACOSTE
Via della Vigna Nuova 33r.

LAURÈL
Via della Vigna Nuova 67–69r.

LOUIS VUITTON
Via dei Tornabuoni 2.

YVES SAINT LAURENT
Via dei Tornabuoni 3.

Wolford
Via della Vigna Nuova 93–95r.

Italian Big Names

Benetton
Via por Santa Maria 68r.

Bottega Veneta
Via degli Strozzi 6.

Brioni
Via de Rondinelli 7r.

Emilio Pucci
Via dei Tornabuoni 22.

Emporio Armani
Piazza Strozzi.

Ermenegildo Zegna
Via dei Tornabuoni 3r.

Fendi
Via degli Strozzi 21r.

Frette
Via Cavour 2.

Gianfranco Ferré
Via dei Tosinghi 52r.

Giorgio Armani
Via della Vigna Nuova 51r.

Gucci
Via dei Tornabuoni 73r; Via Roma 32r.

Loro Piana
Via della Vigna Nuova 37r.

Marina Rinaldi
Via Panzani 1.

MAX & CO.
Via de Calzaiuoli 89r.

MAX MARA
Via dei Pecori 23r.

MIU MIU
Via Roma 8.

PRADA
Via dei Tornabuoni 7.

PRATESI
Lungarno Corsini 32/34r–38/40r.

SALVATORE FERRAGAMO
Via dei Tornabuoni 16r.

SAVE THE QUEEN
Via dei Tornabuoni 49.

TRUSSARDI
Via dei Tornabuoni 34–36r.

VERSACE
Via dei Tornabuoni 13r.

Discounters & Stock Shops

See "Outlets" (p. 165) for out-of-town factory outlets.

IL GIGLIO
Via Borgo Ognissanti 64.

This is a stock shop, selling whatever it can get its hands on—and sometimes it's fabulous. There's usually a mix of shoes and clothes for men and women. You'll see some handbags and accessories, but not that many. There is also a store in Prato at Viale del Serraglio 72 (© **0574/317-02**).

I bought a pair of suede Tod's wannabe driving shoes for 39€ ($51). On my last visit, the men's clothing in the rear was exceptional, with designer sports jackets and suits in the $100-to-$200 range. I thought I'd died and gone to heaven. ✆ **055/217-596.**

PIAZZA PITTI CASHMERE
Via della Sprone 13r.

This cashmere outlet, with products from its own factories, is on a street that juts off from the Piazza Pitti. Aside from the usual sweaters and smalls, there are coats and items of clothing for women. ✆ **055/283-516.** www.piazzapitti.it.

Foodstuffs

BARONI
Mercato Centrale, Via Galluzzo.

The entire indoor Mercato Centrale is a fabulous source for foods, souvenirs, and memories. Of the many stalls, this is one of the more famous for 30-year-old cheeses that are not exported, designer olive oils, and much, much more. The staff speaks English. ✆ **055/289-576.** www.baronialimentari.it.

PEGNA
Via dello Studio 8.

Oh boy, have I got a store for you. Despite the fact that this is a few feet from the Duomo, I needed a local friend to find it for me—it is hidden in plain sight and could be the most exciting stop in town (if you're a foodie, anyway). This old-fashioned grocery store sells everything, including English brands of cleaning products. There are foods to take home, foods for picnics, and even gift items of soaps and foodstuffs. Don't miss it. ✆ **055/282-702.**

TOSCANAMIA
Via Guicciardini 57r.

I do know a TT when I see one, but am not above shopping at them, especially one as charming as this one. Although the store sells all sorts of souvenirs, its specialty is food souvenirs—pasta in fashion colors, shrink-wrapped risotto, oil and vinegar sets, excellent quality chocolate (from Stainer), and more. This shop is right near the Pitti. ✆ **055/239-9218.**

Home Style

If you're a freak for fabric and ribbons, don't miss **Antico Setificio Fiorentino,** listed under "Hidden Finds in Florence" (p. 134).

Ditta Luca Della Robbia

Via del Proconsolo 19r, between Piazza della Signoria and Santa Croce.

This place is a little bit off the beaten path (but not enough to count) and is one of the best pottery shops in town. I dare you not to buy. It does shipping—although that may double the price of your goods. It carries plates, tiles, religious souvenirs, and more. ✆ **055/283-532.**

Galleria Machiavelli

Via por Santa Maria 39r.

Despite the stupid name for a shop, this is one of the best resources in town for country wares and ceramics. It's located right in the center of downtown, so you can easily pop in. It ships. ✆ **055/239-8586.** www.machiavelli.it.

Lisa Corti Home Textile Emporium

Via dei Bardi 58.

Lisa Corti is from Milan and sells in the U.S. through Saks Fifth Avenue. Her shop in Milan is off the beaten path, but wonderful; she is also sold in Positano at Emporio Sirenuese, which is where I discovered this brand.

Corti designs fabrics in bright swirls of color with a southern Italian flair and feel. The store sells mostly home style, although there are some clothes and even pieces of pottery.

Because the goods are printed in India, some locals tend to dismiss this brand, which is silly. Very silly.

The shop in Florence is hard to find and takes real patience in order to fully explore the merchandise, which is mostly put away. Best buys are table linens that begin around 68€ ($88); on my last visit, I bought a printed shirtdress for 98€ ($127). To get here, as you exit the Ponte Vecchio on the Pitti side, take an immediate left, and then another one (sort of a big U-turn). The shop is hidden in a tiny courtyard almost under the bridge. ✆ **055/264-5600.** www.lisacorti.com.

PASSAMANERIA TOSCANA
Piazza San Lorenzo 12r.

Maybe you don't plan your travels around your ability to find trim or tassels, but when you luck into a source that makes the best in the world, it's time to celebrate. You'll find pillowcases, embroideries, brocades, assorted trims, and fabrics. Expensive, but chic. ✆ **055/214-670.** www.passamaneria toscana.com.

PASSAMANERIA VALMAR
Via Porta Rossa 53r.

This shop is right in the heart of Florence; just look at your map for easy access to one of the best sources in town for tassels, tie backs, trims, cushions, and more. ✆ **055/284-493.** www.valmar-florence.com.

Jewelry

Make sure you seek out **Alessandro Dari,** described under "Hidden Finds in Florence" (p. 134).

ANGELA CAPUTI
Borgo San Jacopo 82; Borgo Sant Apostoli 48r.

Caputi is famous for her look—sort of an ethnic big-and-bold statement made with enormous style and affordable prices. She serves up dynamite, creative costume jewelry often made with bright-colored plastics and topped with inventive twists and turns. Prices are amazingly low; 100€ ($130) can buy you a stunning piece.

Caputi's original shop is on the Pitti side of the river; the newer, larger shop is on the Trinità side and is right near a cute little hidden courtyard where an olive-oil dealer has a store. © **055/292-993.** www.angelacaputi.com.

Leather Goods

Also see "Shoes" (p. 171) and the listing for **Casini** (p. 149).

Desmo

Piazza del Rucellai 10r.

Desmo is one of my best Italian secrets for reasons of pride and pocketbook—excuse the double entendre. It makes a top-of-the-line, high-quality, equal-to-the-best-of-them handbag at a less than top-of-the-line price. Years ago it made its name as a maker of leather clothing, shoes, and accessories, copying Bottega Veneta creations; now it has its own style and plenty of winners. Colors are always fashionable and up-to-date; the prices are pretty good, too—few items in the house top $200, and you can get much for considerably less.

Now then, don't let the address throw you; Piazza del Rucellai is a little dip in the Via della Vigna Nuova—you can't miss the shop when you're in the thick of the designer stores. © **055/292-395.** www.desmo.it.

Furla

Via della Vigna Nuova 47r.

This Italian chain, with stores all over the world, is known to offer high style and some glamour at realistic prices. Sort of the poor man's Prada, with bags that sell for under 160€ ($208). © **055/282-779.** www.furla.com.

GHERARDINI
Via della Vigna Nuova 57r.

One of the biggest leather-goods names in Italy and Asia but little known otherwise, Gherardini offers a specific look in luggage, shoes for men and women, belts, and accessories. I find its conservative designs drop-dead elegant with old-money style. There are also some tote bags and a printed canvas/vinyl line that is status-y as well as practical. The Florence location is in the heart of the central downtown shopping district. © **055/215-678.** www.gherardini.it.

IL BUSSETTO
Via Palazzuolo 136r.

Il Bussetto features leather desktop boxes, writing portfolios, and other objects unusual enough to bring home with pride. © **055/290-697.** www.ilbussettofirenze.com.

MADOVA GLOVES
Via Guicciardini 1r.

Gloves are back in style, so stock up. I'll take the yellow, cashmere-lined, butter-soft leather ones . . . or should I think pink? Maybe both? Unlined gloves are about $30 and come in a million colors. There's everything here, from the kind of white kid gloves we used to wear in the 1960s to men's driving gloves to very ornately designed, superbly made, high-button gloves. © **055/239-6526.** www.madova.com.

SCUOLA DEL CUOIO (LEATHER SCHOOL)
Monastery of Santa Croce, Piazza Santa Croce 16.

If you insist on shopping in one of the many leather factories in Florence, you may as well go to the best known—it's actually inside the Santa Croce church and is a leather school with a factory on the premises. Open Monday through Saturday year-round, and on Sundays from April 15 to November 15. You enter through the church, except on Sunday, when you enter through the garden. © **055/244-533.** www.leatherschool.com.

Linens & Lace

BRUNETTO PRATESI
Via Montalbano 41, Pistoia.

See "Beyond Florence" (p. 173) for how to visit this factory store, which is just a half-hour outside of Florence in the town of Pistoia.

Brunetto Pratesi founded the firm named after him; his grandson was my friend Athos Pratesi, who passed away a few years before my husband. Now the company is run by Athos's son, Frederico. This is one of the last merchant-prince Italian manufacturing families. © **0573/526-462.** www.pratesi.com.

LORETTA CAPONI
Piazza Antinori 4r.

If you've ever dreamed of being either a Lady Who Lunches or a Lady Who Sleeps Late, this lingerie store is for you. Here you'll find the dreamiest silks in underwear, negligees, and more, as well as some cottons and table linens. This is what having money is all about. © **055/213-668.** www.lorettacaponi.com.

PRATESI
Lungarno Corsini 32/34r–38/40r.

This is a new shop, although old-timers who remember the old store will know this store is nearby. Business has been so great that Pratesi has expanded into the space next door, hence the two street numbers. Once you waltz inside, you'll know why business is so good and swoon from wanting to touch, or snuggle up, into the gorgeous linens. There's nothing old-fashioned here: The store not only has the full line of Pratesi merchandise but also custom-makes whatever you need.

And for the tacky people who want to know the same things I do—yes, there were many (if not most) prints here that were not at the outlet. While the quality is the same, the selection in the store is larger and broader, and they will make anything you need in any size in any prints or fabrics you select.

There's also a beach line, a baby line, and a cashmere collection. Oh Athos, you did good, my friend. © **055/289-488.** www.pratesi.com.

Markets

MERCATO DELLE CASCINE
Piazzale Vittorio Veneto.

Held once a week, on Tuesdays only, this market is famous with locals because it serves them in the same way a department store might. I found the market fabulous from an academic standpoint, but not actually the kind of place with much to buy.

Granted, a lot of that depends on luck and taste, but I just didn't need new pots, pans, dishes, tires, or baby clothes. I was wildly interested in the heap of designer handbags that must have been fake—the prices started at 5€ ($6.50). I liked the local fabrics, tablecloths, and dish towels; I loved the few food vendors. I did work my way through mounds of used clothes and linens in hopes of finding something I had to have.

The market opens at 7am; I got here at 9am and it was just getting going. The hordes had not yet arrived and the vendors were still setting up. Even if you arrive by 11am, you should be just fine. To get here, take a bus to the Jolly Hotel or stroll along the Arno—it's a bit of a walk from the center of town, considering that once you get to the market you are going to walk even more, but you can do it.

MERCATO DELLE PULCI
Piazza dei Ciompi.

This is the local flea market that sells everything from furniture to pictures, coins, and jewelry; it's great fun, especially if

Sarah's Take

I had some initial doubts about the Cascine market, as it takes considerable effort to find and I didn't want to waste a morning in Florence looking at junk or household stuff. I promised myself I would go early, check it out, and then be on the Ponte Vecchio by 10am.

Not so! Suzy and I had only covered about two-thirds of the market when she had to drag me away so we wouldn't be late for our lunch meeting.

Yes, there's lots of cheap clothing and stuff that I didn't need and wouldn't consider hauling home, but then I found the shoes—ballet flats, sandals, kitten heels—all in buttery soft leathers and bright spring colors. And the linen trousers! Did I want the drawstring pair in pale straw or the chocolate tailored crops, or maybe the sage elastic-waist pull-ons? I bought 'em all at $10 a pair. And then there were the cotton and silk hand-knit V-neck tunics. I debated over the hot pink and aqua, and then finally bought basic white. My finds aren't designer goods; in fact, I can't find a label in most of them. But since each piece was under $15, who cares?

—SRL

the weather is fair. It's held the last Sunday of each month. Meanwhile, every week from Tuesday through Saturday, the regular dealers in a small strip of stalls are open (not at all the same as the once-a-month affair); possibly not worth the trip.

The Sunday market is an all-day job beginning around 9am; the daily market closes for lunch and follows more traditional business hours. To get here, walk out the back end of the Duomo onto Via dell Oriuolo, pass the Piazza Salvemini, and hit Via Popolo, which in 1 block takes you to the flea market. It's an easy walk. On Sunday, the nearby Standa is open.

San Lorenzo
Piazza del Mercato Centrale.

I'm sad to report that a visit to San Lorenzo is much like a trip to Hong Kong. Insiders say that more than 80% of the merchandise for sale comes from Asia.

Nonetheless, the market is a popular shopping venue and if you only go for the ties, well—it's worth the visit. But then, wait, the Central Market is part of the market itself, so you can go for the food, too. And Sarah priced a pair of gloves all over town and found the San Lorenzo price to be the best. The market has a few pushcart dealers, and then several rows of stalls that lead around a bend. The stalls are very well organized; this is a legal fair, and stallholders pay taxes to the city. Many of the stalls give you shopping bags with their numbers printed on them. Now, there's class.

With the recent crackdown on phony big-name merchandise, few of the pushcarts sell imitations. ***A word of caution:*** Do not get so excited with the bargains that you don't cast an eagle eye over the goods or, in your haste, think that these are real designer goods. Look for defects; look for details. I have yet to find a faux designer scarf here that really looks good enough to pass as the evil twin sister. What's more, as Sarah entered the market, she saw a large poster with the following message printed in English: "*Warning! In Italy, purchases of counterfeit goods are punished by law with sanctions up to 10,000€.*"

The market is open Tuesday through Saturday from 9am to 7pm. Closed Sunday and Monday. Most stall owners take plastic.

Straw Market
Via por Santa Maria.

The best thing about the Straw Market is that it doesn't close during lunchtime. It's also within walking distance of the Ponte Vecchio, the Duomo, and all the other parts of Florence you want to see, so you can make your day's itinerary and get it all in. Locals call this market *Porcellino,* in honor of the boar statue that stands here.

This market sells far more junk and much more in the way of souvenirs than the other markets. It also gets more crowded than other markets. Still, it's maybe worth a visit, if only to fill a lunch void. The merchandise varies with the season, as it should. It takes a good eye and a steady hand.

The market is open daily, from 9am to 5pm in winter, and from 9am to 7pm in summer. Closed tight on Sunday.

TRAIN STATION
Santa Maria Novella.

Technically speaking, the main train station is a train station and not a market. But it functions as a marketplace. There's a McDonald's, stores, and plenty of people and action. You'll find a mall underneath, with an excellent—although often crowded—Internet cafe.

Multiples

OVIESSE
Via Panzani 31.

While Oviesse is one of my favorite Italian brands, and I buy huge amounts there, my visit to the Florence store was so disappointing that if this was the first Oviesse I'd ever visited, I might shrug, go on my way, and never even tell you about this large chain of low-cost fashion.

There are five stores in Florence and one on the outskirts (the suburban branch is listed on p. 173), but I'm writing about the one that is in the main tourist shopping zone, essentially a block from the train station. This location is so jammed with merchandise and disorganized that it's basically hard to find what's even there.

That said, Oviesse makes a great plus-size line as well as men's, women's, and junior clothes. The average linen dress costs 39€ ($51). This branch has a division of Limoni, a beauty supermarket that's not as good as Sephora, attached to the ground floor. Some Oviesse stores have Limoni branches and others do not. ✆ **055/239-8963.** www.oviesse.it.

ZARA
Piazza della Repubblica 1.

Zara took its time opening in Florence, as there were concerns that the local population would not take to the Spanish brand famous for designer looks at midrange prices. The large store is crammed with locals and visitors alike. While Zara has a wide range of products, this location sells just men's and women's clothing. For more products and kids' clothes, go to the suburban store (see "Beyond Florence" on p. 173). ✆ **055/291-745.** www.zara.com.

Outlets

BARBERINO DESIGNER OUTLET
Via Meucci, Barberino di Mugello.

Be still, my bargain-loving heart. This new mall just about had me reaching for the Epi gun. Handily located between Florence and Bologna (that means north of Florence), the mall is a giant village of cute proportions that sprawls on and on and leaves you (and your dog) panting. The parking lot alone is vast. Luckily I was able to find one of the best Max Mara outlets I have ever visited. After that, breathless over the $50 Marina Rinaldi quilted jacket that didn't fit me, I managed to shop every other major Italian and European designer.

When driving on the A1 from Florence, take the exit marked BARBERINO DI MUGELLO. You may look around and think you're going in the wrong direction. Not so; just loop-de-loop and drive around in a big U. Then follow the OUTLET BARBERINO signs. The mall does not open until 2pm on Mondays, but every other day it is open from 10am to 7pm. ✆ **055/842-161.** www.mcarthurglen.it.

The Mall
Via Europa 8, Leccio.

Take back your Leaning Tower of Pisa and also your pizza pie; in fact, leave me alone when it comes to landmarks, museums, and even palaces and pizzas. Give me the bargains. Show me the designer stuff at a real price. Show me The Mall.

Truly named The Mall, this outlet mall is very chic and modern, stark and well designed, up to the standards of any Gucci store. Ignore the busloads of tourists who are pushing about you.

There are many shops—and new ones come on board each year. I have been given permission to list these names: Armani, Armani Jeans, Balenciaga, Bottega Veneta, Burberry, Emilio Pucci, Ermenegildo Zegna, Fendi, Gucci, Hogan, La Perla, Loro Piana, Marni, Salvatore Ferragamo, Sergio Rossi, Tod's, and Yohji Yamamoto. If that is not enough to get your inner engines revved up, nothing is.

The Mall is about a half-hour from the Prada outlet (see the listing for Space Outlet, below). It is right off the A1 in the Rome direction. It's a pleasant enough drive (once you get out of Florence); you will also pass the D&G outlet, which I now forego. Hotels sell tours to The Mall and the Prada outlet for about 30€ ($39); for information, call © **338/862-3129** or e-mail transfer@centroin.it.

Open Monday through Saturday from 10am to 7pm. Sunday hours are in question, as I have several reliable sources with different information (call ahead). Closed on major holidays, which summer shoppers should note includes August 15. © **055/ 865-7775.** www.outlet-the-mall.com.

Malo (MAC)
Via di Limite 164, Campi Bisenzio.

As soon as I gave away all my cashmeres because they gave me hot flashes, I discovered the Malo outlet, where I almost wept with contempt for the insults of middle age. I was forced to buy cashmeres for others, but did get some suede shoes for myself.

Many Americans are not familiar with the Malo brand because it has only a few stores in the U.S. This is one of the top Italian cashmere lines, and we are talking about sweaters that would retail from $300 to $600—on sale here for a pittance. I could barely breathe, I was having so much fun. You could faint from the glory of all the colors, let alone the stunningly low prices. Two-ply cashmere sweaters were in the $100 price range; four-ply were $150. I don't know if I was there for a sale, or if this is the regular drill, but you take half off the price on the tag. Ask!

By the way, Malo does make a few other things besides sweaters. Years ago, my late husband bought the world's most chic bathing suit at a Malo store. I also saw hats and handbags, fabulous little suede slip-on shoes, and some fashions a la Donna Karan in cotton and silk. I was there in winter, so I would guess seasonal stuff turns up toward summer.

Note: The sign outside not only says MAC but also uses the same type face as MAC Cosmetics, so it's confusing. Cope. This store is right at the edge of Florence, so you do not get on the autostrada unless you are coming from elsewhere. If you are driving and want precise directions, call ✆ **055/894-53-06.**

SPACE OUTLET (I PELLETTIERI D'ITALIA)
Località Levanella, SR 69, Montevarchi.

I have listed the official name of this factory, although everyone just calls this "The Prada Outlet." Yes dear, you heard right.

Montevarchi is an industrial area outside of Arezzo. How far is Arezzo, you ask? Well, about an hour or so by train from Rome and Florence—it's mid-distance between the two, actually, and right on the main train line. It's about a half-hour drive from The Mall.

This situation is a little more formal, and you may feel like you are going to prison. You go behind wire and are given an ID number. The store is large and beautifully arranged and organized. There are other brands here besides Prada and Miu Miu (I found Helmut Lang), and there are shoes as well as sunglasses, clothes, handbags, totes, and so on. It's hit-or-miss, but worth the adventure if you are nearby.

Take the A1 south to the Valdarno exit and then follow signs for Montevarchi; look for the parking lot filled with luxury cars. Hours are Monday through Friday from 10am to 7pm, Saturday from 9:30am to 7pm, and Sunday from 2:30 to 7:30pm. The store now accepts credit cards. © **055/919-6528.**

Paper Goods

Florentine papers are one of Florence's greatest contributions to bookbinding and gift-giving. There are two styles: marbleized and block-printed. The marbleized style is readily found in Venice; neither style is handily found in Milan or Rome.

Scads of stores in Florence sell paper goods; such items are even sold from souvenir stands, in markets, and at the train station. Prices are generally modest, although they can get up there with larger items.

Bottega Artigiana Del Libro
Lungarno Corsini 38–40r.

This small shop next to the Arno has beautiful things that can solve many a gift quandary. Small address books are in the 6€ ($7.80) range; pencils are stunning and inexpensive; picture frames range from 4€ to 12€ ($5.20–$16). (These frames have plastic fronts, not glass.) You'll see photo albums, blank books, and all sorts of other items. Note the business cards printed on the back of marbleized paper swatches. © **055/289-488.**

Cartoleria Parione
Via del Parione 10r.

A few years ago, I got a letter from a reader, a professional photographer, who was looking for marbleized photo albums that she could use to show her work. She said she could find them in the U.S., but they cost about $100, and could I find some in Italy for less? Well, it took me a year, but yes, Virginia, here you go—this store, which sells many of the usual paper goods, also has the photo albums. They come in various sizes, and prices begin at $30! The store accepts fax orders and does shipping. It's located right in the heart of the Tornabuoni shopping district. ✆ **055/215-684.**

FANTASIE FIORENTINE
Borgo San Jacopo 50r.

The owner of this tiny shop in the Oltrarno district handcrafts everything she sells—intricate bookmarks, notebooks, frames, and gift wrap in classic Florentine designs. While you'll find items here similar to those in other shops, Fantasie Fiorentine's quality is far superior to most. This little gem is located next to the Hotel Lungarno.

GIULIO GIANNINI E FIGLIO
Piazza Pitti 37r.

Known for the marbleized type of Florentine paper, this shop has been in business for centuries. It makes bookplates, calling cards, and items for all other paper needs. Several paper-wrapped pencils tied with a bow make a great gift; you can easily put together a beautiful $10 package. Sarah picked up some block-print notebooks with leather ties for $20 each. There are many good paper shops in Florence, but this is the single most famous. ✆ **055/212-621.** www.giuliogiannini.it.

IL PAPIRO
Lungarno Acciaiuoli 112r.

This is the most commercially successful of the marbleized-paper stores, with branches all over Italy and in the U.S. ✆ **055/264-5613.** www.ilpapirofirenze.it.

Johnsons & Relatives
Via Cavour 49r.

This paper store is a little different from the others—there's not as much of the marbleized and more of the old-fashioned printing. You'll find stationery and cards, books, and photo albums. ✆ **055/215-262.**

Pineider
Piazza della Signoria 13–14r.

Do you love to send handwritten notes in the mail? Thick formal note cards that smell of old money and inseparable style? At this shop, you'll find very conservative, old-time stationery as well as some gift items and small leather goods. Prices are steep. This is a serious international status symbol. ✆ **055/284-655.** www.pineider.com.

Perfume

The **Profumeria Inglese** (Via dei Tornabuoni 97r; ✆ **055/289-748;** www.profumeriainglese.it) is a temple to good taste, fine goods, and every imaginable brand, right in the heart of the shopping district. There are no bargains here.

While you're splurging anyway, consider booking a private workshop with the fragrance master **Lorenzo Villoresi,** described under "Hidden Finds in Florence" (p. 134).

For beauty cures and treatments, check "Pharmacies & Soaps," below, or the local *erboristas,* listed under "Bath, Beauty & Erborista" (p. 147).

Pharmacies & Soaps

Not the kind of pharmacy you go to when you need an *aspirina,* these pharmacies seem to be a specialty of Florence—old-fashioned, fancy-dancy places where you can buy creams and goos and various homeopathic treatments as well as European brands and local homemade potions for all sorts of things. There are tons of these places in Florence. One or two will be all you need for great gifts and, possibly, dinner-table conversation.

Also see "Bath, Beauty & Erborista" (p. 147).

FARMACEUTICA DI SANTA MARIA NOVELLA
Via della Scala 16r.

Yep. This is the one—the one you've read about in every American and English fashion and beauty magazine; the one where you buy the almond cream. At least, that's what I buy here. Go nuts. (Almonds are nuts, so go nuts.) Fabulous gift items, fabulous fun. It's located near the train station and downtown—go out of your way to get here. I had to ask three times just to find it; I was even stumped when I was standing outside the front door. Never mind—walk in! It looks unusual because it's a convent, not a storefront. All the more yummy. ✆ **055/216-276.** www.smnovella.it.

FARMACIA MOLTENI
Via Calzaiuoli 7r.

Remember this one because it's open every day of the week, 24 hours a day. It's centrally located, and it's where you go in case of a medical emergency of the pharmaceutical kind. It's also gorgeous. ✆ **055/215-472.** www.farmacia-molteni.com.

Shoes

See "Leather Goods" (p. 158) for more shoe-shopping options.

BONO
Via della Terme 7r.

This is an old-fashioned sandal- and boot-maker. For sandals, you pick the heel and bottom portion you want and then the uppers, and they are custom made—pick them up a few hours later. You can also get bespoke boots or bags. ✆ **055/239-6026.** giannirillio@virgilio.it.

Mantelassi
Piazza della Repubblica 25r.

If made-to-measure shoes are what you have in mind, step this way with your instep. Men and women can design their own, bring a shoe to be copied, or choose from the many styles displayed. ✆ **055/217-521.**

Salvatore Ferragamo
Via dei Tornabuoni 16r.

Yes, there are Ferragamo shops all over Italy and all over the world. But none of them comes near the parent shop in Florence, which is in a building erected in 1215, complete with vaulted ceilings, stained-glass windows, and enough ambience to bring out your camera. The shop has several connecting antechambers with an incredible selection of shoes, boots, and ready-to-wear . . . as well as a library and a kiddie playroom.

Upstairs is the museum, which is *fab-u-lous.* It is not open to the public all day, or every day, so call ahead to ask for hours and to make an appointment. There is also a research library for designers and a small museum gift shop with great merchandise, but very high prices. The postcards cost three times what they should. Save up for shoes instead.

Each January and July there's a clear-it-all-out sale, but I confess that I left brokenhearted last January (there is a limited selection for bigger feet). Clothing provided better deals than the shoes. The sale is held in the basement, which has an entrance at the side door; there are guards and usually lines to get in. ✆ **055/292-123.** www.salvatoreferragamo.it.

Sergio Rossi
Via dei Tornabuoni 35–37r.

Even though this brand is part of one of the French luxury conglomerates, it offers true Italian style in its high heels and luxe leathers. ✆ **055/284-631.** www.sergiorossi.com.

TANINO CRISCI
Via dei Tornabuoni 43–45r.

Tanino Crisci is a big name in Italian shoes and leather goods with an international reputation, but there are not many stores in the U.S., so Americans may not be familiar with the brand. This is a chain of moderate to expensive shoes in sort of sporty, conservative styles. It's a very specific look that is either your style or not—but it wears forever and gets better every year. Very preppy. The quality is well known; prices range from about 100€ to over 150€ ($130–$195).

The product line includes men's and women's shoes, both dress and sports models, plus belts and small leather goods. Logan, my journalist friend who lives in Rome, found the outlet at Via Garibaldi 9, Casteggio, Pavia. © **055/214-692.** www.taninocrisci.it.

BEYOND FLORENCE

CC I Gigli

Huh? You are probably saying to yourself as you read this, whoooaaa, Suze. Gigli is a popular name, and I am now going to tell you about a mall.

If you have a car, you will want to know about this large suburban mall at Via San Quirico 165, in Campi Bisenzio, about 5 miles outside Florence and right off the highway from Florence toward the sea, near the Malo outlet (p. 166) and near the entrance to the autostrada. There's a branch of every big store you may want to shop—take note especially of the good branches of **Oviesse** and **Zara**—plus a large supermarket called PAM.

CC, by the way, stands for Centro Commerciale, which is Italian for mall. You do not come here for charm; you come to load up on groceries or knock off your big-box shopping in record time . . . and eat at McDonald's. © **055/896-250.** www.igigli.it.

Siena

Siena is not very far from Florence, but it takes some advance planning should you decide to go, unless you have your trusty rental car and are totally free and independent. It's a very pleasant day trip, especially nice for a Monday morning, when most of the stores in Florence are closed, or a Wednesday morning, when the market is in full thrall. (Beware—it's mobbed.)

There are prepackaged day trips just to Siena or to Siena and medieval San Gimignano, which is not a shopping town but rather one of those incredible hilltop villages. Do note that if you buy a tour, you will pay about $50 per person for the day trip, whereas if you do it all by yourself, it will cost less than $20.

The train ride, which is free if you have a rail pass, is very long—over 2 hours—and often involves changing trains. It's a better use of your time to pay an additional $15 round-trip and buy a bus ticket via SITA; the *corse rapide* to Siena, which is direct, takes 1 hour and 20 minutes. It drops you on the edge of town, next to the market and within walking distance of everything. There is basically a bus every hour, with more buses running during peak travel times.

The **SITA station,** Via Santa Caterina da Siena 15 (© **055/214-721**), is about a block from the Santa Maria Novella train station. A sign outdoors directs you to where to buy tickets *(biglietteria);* there's an information booth outside the ticket area. After you buy your tickets, you then must find out which lane your bus will be loading from; there is a large sign high up on the wall near the ticket office.

If you take the bus, it may make local stops as you approach Siena. Don't panic: Your stop is the end of the line, San Domenico church. When you get off the bus, note the public bathrooms (very clean, pay toilets) and the tourist information office, which sells a map of the city. If you are standing with your back to the church facing the tourist information office, you'll see that there are two streets to your right. One bears off slightly, and the other turns more dramatically and goes down.

If you are doing this on a Monday morning, most of the stores in downtown Siena will be closed. However, if you take the low road, you'll see many touristy stores that are open, even on Monday. While some open at 9am, many more will open at 11am. In fact, the best time to be in Siena is on a Monday morning between 9 and 11am because you'll have it almost to yourself and you'll still get to go shopping.

The main shopping street is **Via Banchi di Sopra,** which leads right to the Campo and then goes up the hill as the Via di Citta. Take this to the Duomo (well marked) and then follow the signs back down and up the Via della Sapienza, which will bring you back to the bus stop at San Domenico.

Via della Sapienza has a good number of wine (this is chianti country) and tourist shops, especially close to the bus stop, that remain open during lunchtime, too.

As you approach the **Campo,** you'll notice various alleys that lead into the square. Some have steps; others are ramps for horses. Each entryway seems to be named for a saint. Many of the alleyways that lead from the shopping street to the Campo are filled with booths or touristy stands. There are more free-standing booths on the Campo itself.

The Campo is surrounded by shops, many of which specialize in pottery, hand-painted in dusty shades and following centuries-old patterns. Some of them are even branches of other stores you will find up the hill, closer to the Duomo.

The best shops are clustered up the **Via di Citta,** close to the Duomo—you will automatically pass them as you walk around and up.

Pistoia

Okay, okay, so you weren't planning on a side trip to Pistoia, which is about a half-hour from Florence by train. In fact, you've never even heard of it and perhaps think you can survive without it. Wrong.

Pistoia is an adorable little gem worth visiting on its own and doubly worth visiting since it is the home of the **Brunetto Pratesi** factory. At the factory, there is a little shop that sells—you guessed it—seconds. If you show your copy of this book, or say you are a friend of the family, you will be allowed to shop there.

Pratesi, as you probably know, is a family business that makes sheets for the royalty of Europe and the movie stars of Hollywood. They are sticklers for perfection: A computer counts the number of stitches in each quilt. If there are five stitches too many, the quilt is a reject! What do they do with this poor, unfortunate, deformed quilt? It will never see the light of day in Beverly Hills, Manhattan, Palm Beach, or even Rome. No, because it has all of five stitches too many, it will be considered a reject, a defect, a second. It will be sold, at a fraction of its *wholesale* price, in the company shop. It's your lucky day.

The store is in the factory, a low-lying modern building, located at Via Montalbano 41r (© **0573/526-462**). It is set off the street on your left as you come off the highway, and distinguished only by the discreet signs that say BRUNETTO PRATESI. Not to worry—because it's the most famous factory in the area, everyone knows where it is. Show the printed address to anyone at a nearby gas station or inn, and you will get directions. Don't be intimidated; it's not that hard.

If all this truly makes you nervous, ask your concierge to call ahead and get very specific directions for you: He or she can even arrange a person for you to call in case you get lost.

Like all factory outlets, the store sells what it has; you may be lucky or you may not. Last time I was here, the showroom was filled with quilts, nightgowns, and gift items, but low on matched sets. There were blanket covers in various sizes, but you could not put together a whole queen-size bed set. The one total set I priced was no bargain.

The price on an item varies depending on the defect; some items are visibly damaged, some are not. Prices are essentially half of what you would pay at regular retail—a blanket cover that retails for $900 costs $400 here. If you were expecting giveaway prices, think twice. Then look at the beach totes for 15€ ($20) and faint from their chic and your need to own everything in the line.

Pratesi is one of the leading linen makers in the world, and its goods compete with Porthault as the most sought-after by the rich and famous. Considering the quality, these are bargain prices. Do note, however, that Pratesi has sales once a year, in January, at its stores in Italy (and twice a year in some other cities around the world). In January in Italy, the prices are marked down 30% off retail, and you have the whole store to choose from.

Factory store hours are Monday from 2 to 7pm, Tuesday through Friday from 9am to noon and 2 to 7pm, Saturday from 9am to 1pm, and Sunday from 3 to 7pm.

The scenery on the way to Pistoia is not gorgeous, but you drive on a highway (the A11), so you don't need to worry about getting lost on winding country roads. You can also go by rail—get the train to Pistoia at Florence's Santa Maria Novella station. From the Pistoia station, you can catch a taxi to the Pratesi factory; ask the driver to wait for you.

Prato

Prato is almost a suburb of Florence—it's just on the other side of Pistoia or about a half-hour from Florence. It's not on the tourist bill because it is a mostly industrial town and is the home of many fabric mills and *garmento* makers. For those looking for deals and jobbers, this could be your kind of place.

My basic off-pricer here is **Lo Scorpione,** Viale della Repubblica 278 (✆ **0574/572-608**), a jobber offering designer clothing at 50% off regular retail. Yes, big names in sportswear and men's suits. There is another owned by the same company called **Il Giglio,** at Viale del Serraglio 72.

Forte dei Marmi

This is a small beach town, west of Florence on the, uh, coast. It's about an hour from Florence, yet a million miles away in that it is a chic little perfect town with wonderful shopping. Stores are open on Sundays; the crowd is old money. There is a small branch of the **Santa Maria Novella** pharmacy at Via Carducci 59. In fact, all the big stores are on Via Carducci.

Lucca

The good news: Lucca is worth the trouble. The bad news: This is another one of those towns with restricted vehicular traffic so that you have to park outside the walls and walk. Or rent a bike. Lucca is a small town, though, so you can prowl all over by foot easily. It's a well-known food town, so you can buy oil and balsamic, but it's also enough of a real-people town that you can enjoy the local UPIM.

Deruta

This is in Umbria, not Tuscany, and is a bit of a drive (a little over 2 hr. from Florence), but worth it if you are a ceramics freak. The entire town is store after store next to workshop and studio selling nothing but faience, which some locals also call *majolica*.

Among the most famous of the artisans here is Carol LeWitt, an American, who makes large decorative pieces for **Fratelli Mari,** Via Circonvallazione Nord 1 (✆ **075/971-0400**). Her work is also sold in the U.S. through a firm she owns called Ceramica, which has six stores.

Most stores in Deruta will ship. Be sure to check out **Via Tiberina** and **Via Mancini** for some great shops.

When you arrive in Deruta, note that there are two shopping parts: the city center, which is a medieval old town, and on the highway approaching town, the lower-city strip centers. It's easier to walk from place to place in the upper city.

Chapter Seven

VENICE

WELCOME TO VENICE

Venice and shopping are made for each other; you're going to have the time of your life—even in the crowded high season. In winter, the city can be a little chilly or damp, but the town is yours, and you will more than fill your senses—and your shopping bags. Bellini, please. Oh Signor!

Prices here are higher than in other towns; this is not the city for bargains or for fulfilling your dreams of designer clothes. Of course, you can find designer clothes, but you will pay dearly for them. Venice is really for the senses, for smells, for gifts, and for whimsy.

That said, I confess that I found tons to buy in Venice on my last trip and had a much more relaxed spree than in many other better-known shopping towns. Luck has something to do with it, but keeping your eyes open doesn't hurt. Among my discoveries:

- Sarah and I both got costume jewelry in the $60-to-$125 price range that we were delighted with. We went nuts at **Astolfo** (p. 207), but there were many stores and choices.
- You can buy what they sell at Bergdorf Goodman for a fraction of the U.S. prices.

- You pay 36€ ($47) in an ordinary shop in Murano for what would cost 10 times that in an ordinary shop in New York.
- You can load up on tourist junk, take it away from Venice, and turn it into great gifts for your loved ones—it won't even look like tourist junk. Like that box of almond soaps etched with a map of ancient Venice for $10.

Venetian Shopping History

Venice was founded in the 5th century by survivors fleeing from Lombard invaders after the fall of the Roman Empire. The city provided a cultural and political link between Eastern and Western civilizations for many centuries; by the 13th century, it was a leading (and very wealthy) port of trade.

People have been shopping here ever since.

The absence of cars allows leisurely browsing of the shops, churches, piazzas, and palaces. Every area contains boutiques stocked with the lace, fine glass, paper goods, and leather items for which Venice has become famous. The best thing about shopping in Venice is that you are forced to walk just about everywhere—even if you are primarily a museum person, you still pass by the shops and can look in the windows.

Conversely, even the most dedicated shopper is going to get an extra surge of excitement just from walking by the churches and museums. In Venice, culture and clutter, of the retailing sort, are all tied into one very attractive bundle.

Most shopkeepers speak English and are quite accustomed to tourists. All shops are anxious for business. Adjustments in price will reflect just how anxious for business the shopkeepers are. In season (Carnevale–Oct), tourists are plentiful, prices are higher, and bargaining is unheard of. In winter, things are sweeter—and cheaper.

ARRIVING IN VENICE

By Plane

Although the Venice airport is a tad inconvenient, it's not that difficult to use. The airport makes European flight connections a breeze.

Note that if you take a water taxi between Marco Polo International Airport and Venice proper, it will cost about 64€ ($83). I take the public water bus for 10€ ($13). It's crowded but not a problem. Just follow signs from the terminal to the pier.

An ability to handle your luggage will make the difference in whether or not you are in a good mood when you arrive at your hotel. If possible, travel with just one rolling suitcase.

By Train

To ride the regular express trains in Italy, I usually purchase an Italian rail pass or a Eurailpass (see "Getting Around in Italy," in chapter 2), or I simply buy a ticket from Milan and hop on board the fast train to Venice. There are about 20 trains a day between Venice and Milan. Some go faster than others, but the fastest train takes just over 2½ hours.

Sometimes I do second class, but if I'm worried about getting a seat at what might be a peak travel time, I buy a first-class seat as well as a seat reservation so that I have a specific seat assigned to me. First-class seats on Italian trains are not enormously more expensive than second-class seats and may well be worth the difference.

Do learn how to read an Italian rail schedule, and allow yourself plenty of time for the asking of many, many questions. I once found an intercity train (fast train) on my timetable that appeared perfect—it was outbound from Venice and was stopping in Milan but was marked for Geneva. There was no way I could have known that was my train merely from reading the board in the station. If I'd taken the train marked MILANO, I would have wasted 2 hours.

Upon arrival at Venezia Centrale, if you have heavy bags, you may want to avoid the tiered steps at the front of the station. As you're making your way (and pulling your bags) toward the front exit, walk to the far left side of the terminal as soon as you're off the train platform. There's a ramp just outside the station building.

On my last trip, when we were driving across Italy, we left the car in Verona at the hotel we had booked for a few days later. We took the train to Venice and then went back to Verona with just our overnight rolly-rollers and the dog. This was far easier than worrying about luggage left in the trunk of the car or schlepping all that baggage with us. You can also do this from Padua, which is even closer to Venice. (Verona is 1 hr. from Venice; Padua is 30 min. from Venice.)

By Bus

If you are staying in Mestre or Treviso or in the 'burbs, you can take the bus or train into town. The buses do not run that frequently and can be more confusing than you'd like to think.

By Car

Believe it or not, I have driven to Venice. Or, to be more precise, as close to Venice as one can get in a car.

Because I would be leaving my car—with luggage and shopping trophies—in a parking lot for a few days, I decided to leave it at the Venice airport rather than in a parking lot in Mestre, as I thought the airport offered more security and easier connections into Venice.

I can't say it was brilliant because it was a tad confusing and time-consuming, but it worked fine—patience pays off, I kept telling myself—and a 3-night stay in Venice cost me only 20€ ($26) total in parking. Since it costs 20€ ($26) a day in the lots in Mestre, I thought this was worth the trouble.

There was no shuttle bus from the parking lot to the air terminal or to the pier, so I had to roll myself and the bag and the dog some distance. Of course, I was able to leave most of my stuff locked in the car, so this was actually easy. The terminal and adjacent lots were undergoing work, so perhaps the situation will be different when you visit.

By Ship

I don't need to tell you that Venice has been a favored cruise destination for, uh, centuries. Some of the most famous shipyards in the world are outside Venice, and many of today's modern ocean liners are built right there. The number of people who have come to Venice by ship has increased enormously in the last 10 years: Some one million people a year are expected, just from cruises.

Ships disembark at VTP (Venezia Terminal Passeggeri), which is being renovated to handle the mob scene. The terminal has access for both ferries and cruise ships, and each area is color coordinated so that passengers can easily find the right check-in zones. For details, you can always call ✆ **041/533-4860** or check out www.vtp.it.

GETTING AROUND

The most reasonable approach to local transportation is the water bus *(vaporetto)*. The water buses go around town in two different directions: one via the Grand Canal, the other via the Adriatic to San Marco. There are additional routes to various islands and specialty destinations. If you get on (or off) the water bus at the train station, you are at Ferrovia; the bus station is Piazzale Roma. The lines (and routes) are clearly marked; some lines offer express service with fewer stops. The ACTV runs the vaporetto system; you can get a schedule at the Centro Informazioni ACTV at Piazzale Roma.

You are to buy tickets before you board. You can also buy a pass for a timed interval—12 hours for 13€ ($17), 24 hours for 15€ ($20), 36 hours for 20€ ($26), and so on—that is good for your entire stay.

The Venice Card

For a stay of several days, you may want to purchase a Venice Card, available in two colors, for 1, 3, or 7 days. The **Venice Card Blu** offers unlimited transportation on water buses and auto buses. It also provides free use of public toilets (not a perk, believe me; go the nearest hotel and politely find the facilities), free admission to the Casino di Venezia, discounts at some shops and restaurants, and limited medical insurance and legal assistance. In addition, you'll get a parking discount at the Tronchetto Parking Garage. The **Venice Card Orange** includes all of the above, plus free admission to Venice municipal museums and historic churches.

The Venice Card is sold in two versions: Senior, for those over 30, and Junior, for ages 5 to 29. Prices range from 16€ to 103€ ($21–$134), depending on color, age, and duration. If you're between the ages of 14 and 29, you can buy a 3-day Rolling Venice Card for 18€ ($23). For more information and to order discounted cards online, log on to www.venicecard.com.

Prices are (to me) outrageously high. I buy the single-unit tickets for 6€ ($7.80), which are good for 60 minutes, enough time to get to my hotel and then back to the train station. Otherwise, I walk just about everywhere. You're allowed one piece of luggage per person on the water bus. Ha.

The water bus may be a little confusing at first, since there are different little floating stations for the different lines—read the destinations listed. Buy your ticket accordingly and give it to the ticket taker when he comes around to ask for it. Sometimes he doesn't ask.

Then walk. Get lost. Enjoy it. Take the vaporetto (*vaporetti* is plural). And yes, take a ride in a gondola at least once in your life.

Venice Orientation

About Porters

The key to smooth sailing, in all senses of the word, is to pack lightly and know that you can check baggage at the stations—even overnight or over many nights. In these days of international terrorism, it's not easy to find somewhere to leave unaccompanied baggage.

Some hotels will arrange to meet you and will handle luggage for you; many hotels have their own boats to take you back and forth from the airport. Put your Vuitton right here, madame. Fax or e-mail your hotel in advance of your trip to arrange to be met. You'll pay for the service, but it may make your trip a lot more pleasant.

There used to be porters who met the water bus at the train station and then again at San Marco and would help you get to your hotel, but sometimes these guys are nowhere to be seen.

On one of my trips, I was headed to the Luna Hotel Baglioni, about 200m (656 ft.) away from the vaporetto stop, but was curious about the porter when he tried to get me to flag him down for the job. He would be happy to help me roll my single piece of luggage for a mere 30€ ($39). Thank heavens I knew where my hotel was located and was able to avoid this scam.

About Addresses

No city in Italy has a more screwy system for writing addresses; they are virtually impossible to decipher or to use because there is one address for mail and another for the actual building. My advice? Forget addresses. Walk, enjoy.

If you must get to a specific resource and haven't found it in your general lost-and-found, search-and-shop technique, ask your hotel's concierge to mark it for you on a map. Also take business cards that have maps on them so that you can get back to a specific source.

SLEEPING IN VENICE

My best money-saving trick? Don't sleep in Venice. Come in for a day trip. Padua is only 40km (25 miles) from Venice, an easy commute; Verona is about an hour away (see chapter 10).

For something like Carnevale, where you want to be part of the action and then get out as fast as you can before you have a screaming breakdown (some 250,000 people jam San Marco each day on the Carnevale weekends!), this is an ideal ploy. Even Milan is a reasonable place to spend the night during Carnevale.

But since you've probably come to stay for a night or two or three, then just about any hotel will do. Some happen to be a little more magical than others. In Venice, you really pay for location. Since I tend to be here for only a short period of time and since every moment is precious to me, I splurge on the hotel.

Central Venice

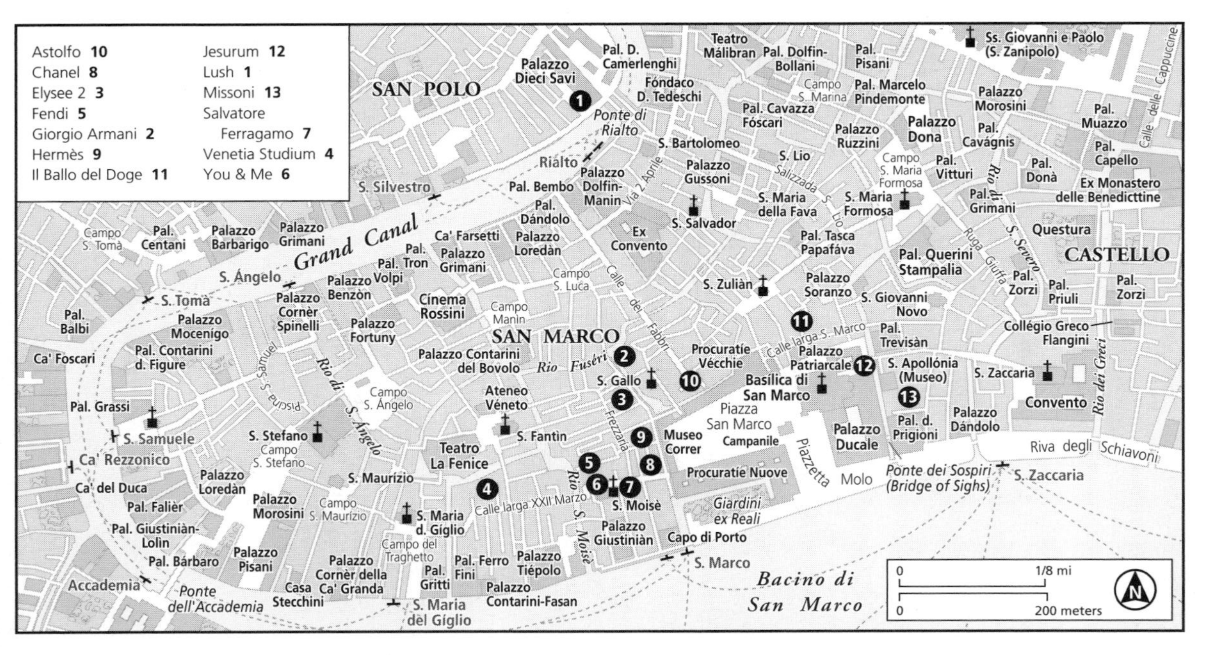

HOTEL BISANZIO
Calle della Pietà, Castello 3651 (ACTV: San Zaccaria).

I was just walking along past the Danieli on the way to my girlfriend's restaurant (Al Covo), and on the sidewalk was a sign for this hotel; so I followed it, and lo, a find. It's set back from Riva degli Schiavoni, but it's brilliantly located and charming and real and funky and affordable.

It's a Best Western hotel with only 40 units; it's air-conditioned and has cable TV with CNN, plus a computer center downstairs. Rates are about $250 if you get a deal online, which we did (and no extra charge for the dog). © **041/520-3100.** www.bisanzio.com.

LUNA HOTEL BAGLIONI
San Marco 1243 (ACTV: San Marco).

This is one of my best finds thanks to the combination of location, luxury, and price. On my last trip to Italy, I stayed mostly in Baglioni hotels, so I was able to do one-stop shopping for room reservations.

Right off San Marco, on the fanciest little retail alley in town, the Luna is an old villa transformed into a palace hotel. You can fall out the door and into a stream of shoppers or sneak out the side door into a waiting gondola or boat and speed off to a shopping rendezvous by water.

It's not inexpensive; expect to pay 350€ to 400€ ($455–$520) in season (lower in winter). This hotel is a member of Leading Hotels of the World (© **800/223-6800** in the U.S.; www.lhw.com). © **041/528-9840.** www.baglionihotels.com.

Sarah's Three-Star Finds

HOTEL ALA
San Marco 2494 (ACTV: San Giglio).

Born to Shop news director Sarah Lahey found this place, and I was mightily impressed with it. A member of the Best Western system, the hotel is just a few feet away from the Gritti

Palace. The style is less formal, but still filled with antiques, beautifully painted walls, high ceilings, and Venetian charm. Rooms start at 140€ ($182). "Ala be praised," I said with delight. ✆ **041/520-8333.** www.hotelala.it.

Hotel Villa Igea

Campo San Zaccaria, Castello 4684 (ACTV: San Zaccaria).

This tiny house, made into an antiques-filled little hotel, is situated in a back corner of San Zaccaria, but it's convenient to everything. Rates, of course, depend on the time of year, but a superior double in high season goes for 256€ ($333), including tax and buffet breakfast, which for Venice is a bargain. There are also less expensive rooms. ✆ **041/241-0956.** www.hotelvilla igea.it.

Snack & Shop

Al Covo

Campiello della Pescaria, Castello (ACTV: Arsenale).

Okay, so this isn't on your ordinary list of legends and landmarks, but it's part of mine because Diane is from Texas and comes to me through my official foodie friends. Also note that this was just named to a list of the 10 best restaurants in Italy.

Diane's husband is the chef, and he is getting increasingly famous and recognized by American authorities, so book now. The restaurant is on the far side of the Danieli, far enough away from the tourists to be pure and family oriented. The food is fabulous (try Diane's *torta nonna*), and you will get the special treatment you crave from a great team.

On the back of your menu, note that there is an order form for all the products. You can take away olive oil, balsamic vinegar, pasta, and polenta. Ask Diane for details.

If you think I'm the only one on to this place, forget it. It came into my family of journalists because Marcella Hazan brought Faith Heller Willinger here, and Faith brought Patricia Schultz, and she told me, and. . . . © 041/52-23-812.

Caffè Florian

Piazza San Marco, San Marco (ACTV: San Marco).

So you sit there at sunset on the Piazza San Marco at a little table, drinking a strawberry version of the Bellini because it's strawberry season and Caffè Florian won't use canned peaches like they do at Harry's (tsk, tsk).

There's a tiny band shell—they play schmaltzy music—and all you want to do is sing and dance and laugh and cry. And that's before you see the bill. Just once before you die. No wonder Napoleon said that San Marco was Europe's most elegant drawing room. Ah, yes, they sell the china, the dishes, and their own house brand of coffee and tea and even Asti Spumante. It's a fabulous gift to bring home for someone who knows Venice. © **041/520-5641.** www.caffeflorian.com.

Harry's Bar

Calle Vallaresso, San Marco 1323 (ACTV: San Marco).

There is a Harry's Bar. There is even a Harry (call him Arrigo). And, no, Harry's Bar is not in the Gritti Palace, as many think. It is where Hemingway and the gang liked to hang out and is located halfway between San Marco and the Gritti.

This is the home of the famous Bellini. I have sipped Bellinis at Harry's—it was swell, and, yes, I saw everyone I knew. I also almost saw stars when the bill came—Bellinis were 15€ ($20) each!

I have wondered just why Harry's is so famous and later discovered that the thing to do is not sip Bellinis (this is for tourists) but to dine upstairs with a chef whom many consider one of the best in the world. Me? I sit downstairs and nibble on the *croque-monsieur,* which is fried to a crisp and makes a super lunch or snack. I also like the *latte macchiato* (milk stained with coffee). © **041/528-7777.** www.cipriani.com.

TERRAZZA DANIELI
Hotel Danieli, Riva degli Schiavoni, Castello 4196 (ACTV: San Marco).

The rooftop of the Hotel Danieli has a wonderful restaurant called the Terrazza (Terrace). The view is spectacular, and the food ain't bad. Ian and I always try to book a lunch here while in Venice, but I have also been known to make this my first stop after I arrive, via train, from Milan in the morning. A mere cup of coffee overlooking the Adriatic is enough to make your heart sing. You can afford coffee here, so don't miss it; lunch may strike you as a very expensive splurge.

Oh, and you don't have to go for the terrace, either. When we were pooped, we just plunked down in the lobby for coffee—$10 a cup, but oh, what a ceiling. ✆ **041/522-6480.** www.luxurycollection.com/danieli.

THE SHOPPING SCENE

Please understand the most basic law of shopping in Venice: Because of transportation, essentially everything is imported. That translates to higher prices than anywhere else in Italy. It means you'll pay top dollar for a Coca-Cola, a roll of film, or a pair of Italian designer shoes. Also, this isn't really a city for designer shopping, although you can buy most everything here.

Your best buys will always be locally made souvenir items, which are quite moderately priced. Also note that the tourist junk here is far more attractive than in any other major Italian city.

There's also more than the usual number of hidden resources because this is the kind of town where the best stuff is definitely put away. Ask.

The Best Buys in Venice

I have been known to go nuts for glass, handbags, paper goods, and local crafts—all can be best buys in Venice. More important: Even if you've seen these items for less money elsewhere, they offer good value as items bought in Venice to be remembered as such and cherished. You don't want to buy your Carnevale mask in Rome just because you might get it cheaper, do you? Marbleized paper goods cost less in Florence, but only slightly less.

Eyeglass Frames Have your prescription put in back at home, but don't miss the chance to buy chic and/or exotic frames in Venice. Note that there are scads of factories in the Veneto nearby, so you can also go discount shopping for glasses frames if you have a car and the time.

Glass Murano is the glass capital of Italy, and Venice is the front door to the glass candy store. Even when it's expensive, glass usually costs less here than if bought in the U.S. Also in the glass category are mirrors and chandeliers. Art glass, a sub category, is very expensive but more available than in any other city. If you buy, be sure you spring for shipping and insurance and know what to do if anything goes wrong. You do not want to hand-carry a one-of-a-kind glass masterpiece, no matter how stable you think your hands are. As for souvenirs and gift items, the hot style of the moment is a Murano glass ring, which costs about 12€ ($16) and is chic as can be. Find them all over town and on the islands, too.

Masks Carnevale has its own rituals—mask-wearing among them. The city now sells scads of masks in every format, from cheap plastic ones to incredibly crafted ones made of leathers or feathers. For the best ones, get to the back streets and alleys and away from the TTs (tourist traps).

Silk When you see the incredibly pleated, teeny-tiny Fortuny silk baggies for jewelry or potpourri for 30€ ($39) at Venetia Studium (written "Venetia Stvdivm," and now expanded to seven branches), you'll know why Marco Polo came home. If you don't want a little baggie, don't pout—just get a look at the silk or velvet flowers to pin on your suit or dress.

The Worst Buys in Venice

If you can help it, don't buy the following:

- **Clothing:** Not a good buy in Venice, unless you need it or hit a sale or bargain.
- **Designer items:** Hermès is more expensive in Venice than in Milan. But wait, to be fair I must say that not all designers raise prices. The Tod's I bought here were the same price as in other cities. I just finally broke down and admitted I couldn't live without them when I got to Venice.
- **Film and prints:** Film is expensive everywhere in Europe; it costs about 12€ ($16) a roll in Venice. Besides, if you don't already have a digital camera, you should buy one instead of another pair of shoes.
- **Fake designer handbags:** Give me a break.

Buying Venetian Glass

I confess that up until the minute I walked into Bergdorf Goodman one fateful day, I thought that only old ladies liked Venetian glass. Then I took one look at a bowl filled with handblown Murano glass in the form of colorful hard candies and flipped out. Such style, such finesse, such color. If this is the passion of little old ladies, sign me up. I've had a sweet tooth ever since. Bergdorf's gets about 12€ ($16) per glass candy. In Venice, you'll pay about 5.20€ ($6.75).

Once you get hooked on glass candies, a whole new world of glass design opens up. *Fazzoletto* (handkerchief vases) will surely be next. While you may not flip out for pink glass goblets with hand-painted roses and baroque gold doodads, you will gasp when you take in the designs made from the early 1920s right through the 1950s—all highly collectible works of art when they are signed by a big-name glass house. Even post-1950s glass is collectible: What you buy today (if you buy wisely) will be happily inherited by your children.

The strings of glass swirled into clear, white, or colored glass are called threads; the value of a piece—aside from the signature—is based on the composition of form, color, and threads or patterns. The way the piece reflects light should also be taken into account, although this is easy to look for in a vase and impossible to consider in a piece of candy. Smoked glass is hot now, as is glass matted with ash, and Deco glass. Crizzled glass is crickly-crackled glass with a nice effect, but it won't last over the centuries and makes a bad investment.

The important names to remember are **Venini, Seguso, Brandolini, Poli, Barovier, Toso,** and **Pauly.** A vase from the 1940s went for $125,000 at auction at Christie's in Geneva; prices continue to rise. New pieces are not inexpensive, as they are considered serious artwork.

Famous designers create styles for glass houses, just as they do for furniture firms. The designer's name associated with a famous glass house can make a piece even more valuable. Do check for signatures, labels, or accompanying materials that uphold the provenance of your piece. If you are buying older pieces of glass—even from the 1950s or so—check the condition carefully.

If you are trading up and browsing for some of the important stuff, here's a quick-fix dictionary to make you sound like a maven:

- *Vetro battute:* Flat beaten glass with a scored surface.
- *Vetro inciso:* Flat beaten glass with scored lines all running in the same direction.
- *Vetro pennelato:* No, it doesn't have pieces of penne pasta in it—this is painted glass with swirly streaks of dancing color that zip across the body of the item inside the glass.
- *Vetro pezzato:* Patchwork made of various pieces of colored glass almost in mosaic form; introduced in the early 1950s.
- *Vetro pulegoso:* This is bubbled glass with the tiny bubbles inside the glass—it will never be confused with sommerso when you see the two in person.

Faking It

Before buying an important (that is, expensive) piece of Murano glass, take time to do your homework (www.promovetro.com is a good place to start) and demand authentication. A number of fakes made in China are sold all the time in foreign markets, on eBay, and even in Venice. What's more, Customs agents in Rome recently intercepted a massive shipment of Chinese glass trinkets, each piece bearing the label MURANO GLASS. And beware of "Murano-style" glass, which isn't made anywhere near the island.

- *Vetro a retorti:* Twisted glass with the threads swirled within the body of the work.
- *Vetro sommerso:* Glass in bubbled, lumpy form is layered over the glass item—the rage in the mid-1930s.
- *Murrina:* Slices of colored glass rods encircled with gold and sold as charms or pendants.

I must take some time here to warn you about the hawkers who offer free trips to Murano and act as guides. They are dangerous, emotionally and physically, and should be avoided. They not only get a percentage of what you buy, but they also make their living by preying off visitors and telling half-truths or lies that may convince you to buy something you weren't certain about.

If you want the free boat ride, ask your hotel's concierge to book it. If you can afford to get there on your own, do so, and buy only from the houses of good repute. If you ship, be prepared to wait a very, very long time for your package to arrive.

While we are into warnings, I got a note from a reader who asked a glass shop about a specific address in Murano and was wrongly told that the shop had closed and was encouraged to do business where she was asking.

The San Marco Rule of Shopping

If you are looking for the best prices on the average tourist items—from souvenirs to snacks—my rule is simple: Avoid San Marco.

San Marco is the center of the tourist universe and, therefore, the center of the highest prices. The farther you go from San Marco, the more the prices drop. Shop on the island where the train station is and you will find the best prices in town.

If you insist on TTs, hit the ones way past San Marco and the Hotel Danieli and on the way to the public gardens. You'll save as much as a euro per item. You'll also avoid the most severe crowds.

The Gondoliers

I don't care how touristy you think it is—riding in a gondola is part of the Venetian experience and something you must do at least once. And please note that Venice now has its first female gondolier.

Tip: Take your gondola ride at high tide—at low tide, you'll have a view of the scummy exposed sides of the canals.

While you can be hustled by a gondolier, there are fixed prices for their services that vary by season. When there aren't as many rich tourists around, prices drop. The winter price can be 75€ ($98); the spring price for the same service is 80€ ($104), but you can try to bargain. Night service, any time of the year, is 100€ ($130) beginning at 7pm. These are the prices for 40 minutes of sailing time with up to six persons in the boat. For each additional 20-minute period after your first 50 minutes, the flat rate is 40€ ($52) during the day, 50€ ($65) at night. You are also expected to tip.

Okay, that was the official line as taught to me by the city. In person, I find that knowing these prices is helpful, as is carrying around a copy of the freebie booklet *Un Ospite di Venezia,* which has a section on gondola prices. You can point to the appropriate page when you bargain and try to be tough.

Either bargain fiercely or else find someone you like and forget the money.

Here's where they really get you—it's the time, not the cash. Gondoliers usually do 30 to 35 minutes, not the 40 minutes you paid for. They also want far more than the guidelines say they should get; they are particularly unfriendly when there are lots of tourists around. Their idea of a great fare is a chump who says yes to the quoted price—and then lays a tip on top.

The gondolier will sing to you—it's part of the deal—but if you ask him to stop the boat en route so that you can get out for a look-see while he waits, or to provide extra services (other than posing in your family snapshot), he will expect more money.

All things are negotiable, but try to have a handle on costs before you get in—nothing spoils the magic more than a fight about money after the fact.

I've seen as many as six people squished into a gondola, so the cost can be amortized into a reasonable expense. You have not seen Venice until you've seen it from a gondola—it is worth the money. If you want an update or an insider tip, call the hot line at ✆ **041/528-5075**.

Shopping Hours

High season is March through October, when shops are open from 9am until 12:30 or 1pm and reopen from about 3 or 3:30pm to 7:30pm. If lunchtime closings bore you, remember that the shops on the nearby island of Murano do not close at midday.

During the off season, most Venice shops are closed on Monday until 3pm. During Carnevale weekends, many things are open no matter what time of the day or day of the week. For Sunday shopping tips, see below.

While Venice does have the most liberal of all the holiday hours, stores do close up early on Christmas Eve and New Year's Eve. Some stores are actually open on New Year's Day—but late in the day, after noon. If there are tourists, some stores will be open.

Sunday Shopping

Si, si, just about all the stores—including designer shops—are open on Sundays. **Emporio Armani, Trussardi, Versace,** and the like are open on Sunday afternoons. Just about everyone is open on Sundays—but closed on Mondays. They may or may not open Monday later in the afternoon, but Sunday is a day of shopping in Venice.

Sunday is also a good day to visit the islands; shops are open on both Murano and Burano. Check with your hotel's concierge for exact opening and closing times, but plan a day trip to Murano as early as you like—the fires are crackling at 9am, and shops are open nonstop until 4 or 5pm. On Burano, Sunday hours tend to be from 10am to 1:30pm.

Also note that stores stay open on Sundays in Verona—a popular Sunday destination for Italians. See chapter 10.

Street Vendors

One of the glories of Venice is the street action—not just the throngs of tourists but the zillions of street vendors who make it possible for you to do very thorough shopping in Venice without ever setting foot inside a store.

The street vendors stay open until the light begins to fade, which in the height of summer can be quite late. There are illegal salespeople hawking wares from blankets all over town—they usually operate during lunch hours and after-hours, as there is less chance they will be arrested then. Louis Vuitton, anyone? Cartier, perhaps?

"This is real Chanel, lady," a vendor tells me with pride. Yeah, sure it is.

Like other retailers, street vendors and cart dealers rig their prices to the needs of the crowd. Therefore, the farther you walk from San Marco, the better the prices at kiosks and carts.

I priced a "Bottega" bag just to do my job; I really wasn't going to buy it, I swear. The asking price went from 125€ ($163) to 20€ ($26) just because I kept saying no. I never did buy it, but I admit I was shocked at how low the vendor would go. "I give you liquidation, lady," he kept shouting at me.

Fairs & Mercatini

San Moisè is the location of many outdoor fairs, from antiques markets to the regular Christmas market. Vendors set up booths and sell from 9am to 8pm.

Sending It Home

Anyone seriously considering glass, or mirrors, or chandeliers is also thinking about shipping. Almost all the stores, even the TTs, will volunteer to ship for you. I am not big on shipping, especially expensive items, but I have noticed that things shipped from Venice do tend to reach their destination—eventually. I have had several nervous letters from readers who have waited many months in a state of panic. My basic advice is simple: Don't fall in love with anything you cannot carry yourself. Always buy from a reputable dealer, and pay with a credit card that has a protection plan on it.

SHOPPING NEIGHBORHOODS

Most of the shops are found in the historic and artistic center, between the **Ponte di Rialto** (Rialto Bridge) and **Piazza San Marco.** A new area of mostly designer shops has been evolving at **San Moisè.**

Looking at a map can be very confusing because of the cobweb of interconnecting streets, bridges, and canals. Finding an address can be equally difficult, as many streets and shops show no numbers—or the numbers are clear, but the street they are on is not clear.

Mercerie One main street will carry you from Piazza San Marco to the Rialto Bridge: Mercerie. It hosts hundreds of shops. Many of the shopping streets branch off this one thoroughfare, or are very close. Mercerie is not a water-bus stop (San Marco is), but if you get yourself to Piazza San Marco and stand at the clock tower with your back to the water, Mercerie will be the little street jutting off the arcade right in front of you. If you still can't find it, walk into any shop and ask. You need not speak Italian.

Piazza San Marco The four rows of arcades that frame Piazza San Marco can be considered a neighborhood unto itself. Three of the arcades create a U shape around the square; the fourth is at a right angle to one of the ends of the U. There are easily a hundred shops here—a few are showrooms for glass firms and a few sell touristy knickknacks, but most are jewelry or glass shops (or cafes). Although many of these shops have been in business for years, and some of them have extremely famous names, this is the high-rent part of Venice and isn't very funky. I was quite shocked at the high turnover I noticed on my last visit: Many old reliable firms have packed up.

Behind San Marco Now, here's the tricky part. "Behind San Marco" is my name for the area that includes **San Moisè** and **San Giglio** (this way to the Hotel Bauer) and is best represented by the big-time shopping drag called **Via XXII Marzo.** This street comes off Piazza San Marco from behind and forms an L with the square and Mercerie. The farther you get from San Marco, the less commercial it becomes.

Frezzeria This is the main shopping street also behind San Marco, but, if your back is to San Marco and you're facing the road to the Hotel Bauer and American Express, it goes off to your right. It's a small alley of a street that twists and turns more than most, and it's packed with small businesses, many of which are artisan or crafts shops. There are also some designer boutiques woven into the landscape.

Giglio This is a secret part of town tucked back and away from the tourist areas. It's also the home of the **Gritti Palace.**

Unless a shop is actually on the piazza, it probably will have a San Moisè address, so you may get confused. Not to worry. Aside from the antiques shops, there's a good paper store and a little market for food for the train ride or a picnic. It's very civilized and quite divine back here.

Rialto Bridge They might just as well have named it the "Retailo" Bridge—not only are there pushcarts and vendors in the walkway before the bridge, but there are also shops going all the way up and down the bridge itself. These are not like the crumbling, charming, old shops that line the Ponte Vecchio in Florence; they are teeny-bopper shops, leather-goods stores, and even sporting-goods stores. Despite the huge number of street vendors from Piazza San Marco to Campo San Zaccaria, the ones here sell things I've never seen before. Most of it is extremely touristy junk.

Over the Bridge Once across the Rialto, you'll hit a two-pronged trading area. In the arcades behind the street vendors to the left are established shops; in the streets and to your right are greengrocers, food vendors, cheese stalls, and, in summer, little men selling little pieces of melon. You can have a walking feast for lunch in any season.

Remember the shopper's basic rule once you cross over to the other side: Prices are usually lower on the far side of the Rialto. Once you make it past the immediate arcades, bear left and follow the shops and crowds toward **San Polo.** The shops here are a little more of the real-people nature and a little less expensive. On the other hand, a fair number of them are smaller branches of the big designer shops found on the big island.

Piazzale Roma This is by no means a hot retailing area, but it is where the bus station is located and where you will get your vaporetto if you come in from the airport, or if you come by bus. (The train station is not here.) Where there are tourists, there are shops. In the case of Venice, or Venice in summer, where there are tourists, there are scads of street vendors selling everything from T-shirts (like the one worn by your favorite gondolier) to plates of the Doge's Palace.

Shopping Murano

Two different experiences are to be had here on the island of glass blowers—so watch out, and don't blame me if you hate it. It can be very touristy or very special—it depends on how you organize your time, as well as what season you visit. Go by vaporetto in high season, and it can be a zoo. Instead, go by private boat, tour a glass factory, wander town, and then take the vaporetto back: It's easy, it's inexpensive, and it's fun. Depending on the weather, the crowds, and your appetite for colored glass, it can even be glorious.

Sunday on Murano can be heaven. Take the no. 5 at San Zaccaria, in front of the Danieli. The visit to Murano can be combined with a trip to Burano (take the no. 12), or you can turn around and come back home. It's a long day if you combine both islands.

Murano is also the perfect lunchtime adventure when stores in Venice might be closed. But do not bring small children or strollers with you.

If you want to take a private boat to the island, call one of the glass factories to come get you. Yes, you are obligated to tour the factory, but you aren't obligated to buy. Besides, the tour is fabulous. It's a perfect Sunday adventure: Sunday is a big day on Murano because they cannot close down the furnaces, as the temperature must stay constant, but the workers don't work. Instead, there are demonstrations and tours.

If you go by public transportation, you will arrive in the heart of Murano. When you get off the boat at Murano, you'll know it by the giant signs that say FORNACE (furnace). You have two choices, really: to work the area, or to realize quickly that this is one of the biggest tourist traps known to humankind. Walk briskly toward the museum, and then head for the lighthouse.

By the way, you can also get a free ride to the island by private boat if you go with a hawker, but you *don't* want to do this! He gets 30% of what you spend in a secret kickback, and you get a lot of pressure to buy (see "Buying Venetian Glass," earlier in this chapter). If you can take the heat, you will be escorted to the *fornace.* But it may be hell, so beware! Hawkers will automatically gravitate to you; you need not even look for them. It's better to ask your hotel's concierge to contact someone from a proper factory for you.

On Sundays, most showrooms, such as those listed below (and their adjoining shops), are open from 9am to 4pm. TTs are open midday.

- **Archimidi Seguso** (Fondamenta Serenella, Murano)
- **Barovier & Toso** (Fondamenta Vetrai 28, Murano)
- **Foscarini** (Fondamenta Serenella, Murano)
- **Manin 56** (Fondamenta Manin 56, Murano)
- **Sent** (Fondamenta Serenella, Murano)

For good, traditional showrooms that have it all, try the resources below. To find these shops, walk from the main drag toward the lighthouse, and you'll wander into a far less touristy world and a hidden street (Viale Garibaldi) of more glass blowers and shops. Once at the lighthouse, round the turn following the water (there's a sidewalk) to find several more glass showrooms, which have boat service and will pick you up at your hotel in town and return you when you are ready to go back.

COLONNA FORNACE
Fondamenta Vetrai 10–11, Murano.

This is a huge firm that picks you up at your hotel and lets you tour its scads of rooms of stuff. I don't mean to give this place short shrift, as I have enjoyed hours of shopping here, but at a certain point, it can be confused with several other competitors (although this one is the first you come to on some approaches). ✆ **041/739-389.**

VETRERIA FOSCARI
Fondamenta dei Battuti 5, Murano.

I asked the concierge at the Bauer-Grünwald to pick a source for me, curious to see what he would suggest, and was pleased to find that this was his choice. They sent a boat for me and picked me up at my hotel, then returned me there when I was ready to go home. I even got a Coke along the way. A true delight. I keep going back, even though the source has passed on to another family member, and I don't always stay at the Bauer anymore.

The showroom is made up of a series of salons, organized by category of goods and by price. One room is devoted to chandeliers, other rooms to glassware. You'll also find beads and just about anything else you can imagine. To arrange a pickup, call at least a day in advance. ✆ **041/739-540.**

VETRERIA GRITTI
Fondamenta Manin 1, Murano.

The Luna Hotel Baglioni concierge chose this glassworks for me; they pick up at the hotel each morning at 9am, so it was easy to get there. They brought me back when I was ready. I asked the concierge to stress that I would not be buying anything, but, of course—I ended up buying something. The showroom was huge, with various styles and prices that seemed fair enough. I paid 52€ ($68) for an etched wine carafe. ✆ **041/739-801.**

Shopping Burano

Although Murano and Burano sound like twin cities, they are not. But if you visit the two in the same afternoon (get the water bus from the lighthouse on Murano to Burano; it runs hourly, but go there for the exact schedule so that you can plan your time accordingly), you can sightsee and do some shopping at the same time. Many stores in Burano are open on Sunday afternoon, so you can combine the two islands for a fabulous Sunday outing.

As touristy and crass as Murano can be, Burano is totally different—I don't happen to like it as much, but I can see the natural, homespun attraction. Certainly, the colors of the houses are divine. The shopping is awfully touristy. I get the feeling that Murano is in the glass business, while Burano is in the tourist business; there's something in the subtext of the air in Burano that lacks wonder. The lace is rarely handmade; there are few really good shops. But if you like to see, to stroll, and to avoid the throngs of pushing people in San Marco, this is a wonderful side trip. Don't think of it as a shopping adventure; rather, take your artistic eye and just enjoy.

You may want to poke into the fish market, **Fondamenta Pescheria,** held daily in the morning only—not that you're going to buy much, but it's fun and picturesque.

The lace-making school is called the **Scuola di Merletti,** Piazza Galuppi (✆ **041/730-034**). The school is open Sunday from 10am to 4pm, Tuesday through Saturday from 9am to 6pm; closed on Mondays.

The boat from Murano to Burano is as big as the ferry that takes you to Nantucket, and you will have the same sense of adventure. Burano is the third stop, so don't have a breakdown wondering when and where to get off (the first stop is Mazzorbo; the second is Torcello). And yes, it's a bit of a schlep, so you'll be on the boat for a while.

When you arrive, you'll see a narrow street lined with shops and think you are in heaven. That's because you haven't been in the shops yet. Pretty soon, you'll think you are in Hong Kong.

Here's the story of the woman in Venice who was buying a lace tablecloth. She had it spread out around her and draped all over—she was oooohing and aaaahing over it, but I knew it was from Hong Kong—like most of the lace in Venice—and I didn't know if I should tell her or not. Well, I didn't say a word because I didn't want to ruin her experience; but readers, you should know the facts.

If you don't like the lace shops, never mind; just take a good look at the colors of the stucco houses and storefronts—they are just fabulous. And the lace school is incredible.

Not all of the shops in the "heart of town" are open on Sundays, but the TTs are. Get the boat schedule before you wander so that you know how long you have—an hour on Burano is probably all you need. Note that when you return to Venice, you will probably end up at a vaporetto stop other than San Marco and will have to buy a new ticket and transfer to get back to your hotel.

VENICE RESOURCES A TO Z

Antiques

If you are the type (like me) who likes flea markets and junk and reasonable prices, Venice is not for you (unless you hit it for one of the triannual flea markets—see below). There are also regular real-people flea markets, but they are on the "land" side of town.

The few antiques shops in Venice are charming and dear and sweet and—should I tell you, or can you guess?—outrageously expensive.

But wait, should you luck into the **Mercatino dell'Antiquariato,** held each April, September, and December, you'll have the giggle of your lifetime. This market is not large, but it's sweet and simple and the kind I like: heaps of stuff on tables laid out in a piazza, the very convenient Campo San Maurizio. The dates are established well in advance and set for each year, so you can call for the exact times (✆ **041/454-176**). This 3-day event is held on a Friday, Saturday, and Sunday; there is no admission charge.

Bath & Beauty

COIN BEAUTY
Campo San Luca.

A free-standing store that's trying to be the local version of Sephora; it's also the beauty department of the department store of the same name, which is several blocks away and has no other beauty department in its regular store. This is not at all a great store nor does it even have a great selection of brands, but if you need something, it is one of the few places to find it. I suffered a nail crisis and turned the town upside down until I found nail-polish remover, glue, and nail polish. © **041/523-8444.**

LUSH

San Polo 89 (Ponte di Rialto, San Polo side); Strada Nuova, Cannaregio 3822 (Santa Felice).

The British cult fave for deli-style cosmetics, bath bombs, and more has set up several stores in Venice, with more expected. The location right near the Rialto Bridge is most convenient for visitors. The goodies are not inexpensive, but they offer high novelty and are not widely available in the U.S. (yet). Many of the products here are specifically Italian—and differ from what's on hand in other countries. © **041/522-1549** for San Polo location; © **041/241-1200** for Cannaregio location. www.lush.com.

Beads & Baubles

ASTOLFO

San Marco 738.

I first discovered Gloria Astolfo in another location—now she is working with her daughter and making even more wonderful things. Note the new address if you are a regular.

Local glass beads are made into jewelry here, but the style is based on the use of tiny beads and charms and fantasy bijoux. You'll pay about 200€ ($260) for a heavily beaded necklace. I got a pair of earrings with an antique feel for 48€ ($62); Sarah got a pin for 112€ ($146). We now consider ourselves stunning. There are also handbags most useful for evening because of the beaded clasps. © **041/296-0640.** www.gloriastolfo.com.

Genninger Studio

Calle del Traghetto (Piazza Contarini-Michel, near Ca'Rezzonico Museum), Dorsoduro 2793a.

Talk about living out your best dreams: Leslie Ann Genninger is American, lives in Venice, makes beads, and sells them from a fabulous little shop where you can buy either ready-made jewelry or individual beads. The beads are made according to medieval (and secret) recipes but are inlaid with silver, which sparkles through. To get here, take vaporetto no. 1 to Ca'Rezzonico, turn right, and *voilà*—it's on the corner. ✆ **041/522-5565.** www.genningerstudio.com.

Le Perle

San Marco 1231; San Marco 706.

It offers new-wave jewelry using the same old glass and beads in totally different ways, so that what you see is very moderne, or trendy, in style. Look for collars of golden glass beads, ropes of charms hanging from gold chains, and more. ✆ **041/528-5614.** www.le-perle.com.

You & Me

Calle XXII Marzo, San Marco 2253.

If I hadn't fallen in love with this store in Milan, I might have passed it by in Venice, which would be my loss. The closet-size shop sells sandals, handbags, and jewelry, all completed with local beadwork. The Birkin-style handbags finished with beaded clasps are to die for—and they're in the 230€-to-300€ ($300-to-$390) range, which is good value considering how stunning they are. I bought a beaded necklace for about 150€ ($195). ✆ **041/277-7825.**

Boutiques

Arbor

Gran Viale Santa Maria Elisabetta 10, Lido.

There are several branches of this boutique on the big island as well as this one at the Lido beach. Arbor carries the hot names, such as Byblos and Genny. The men's shop sells that stylish Italian look that thin men love to wear. © **041/526-1032.**

Elysee

Frezzeria, San Marco 1693.

Elysee 2

Calle Goldoni, Castello 4485.

This is not one but two very sleek boutiques carrying Marni, Maud Frizon, Mario Valentino, and the Giorgio Armani ready-to-wear collection for men and women. Each shop has its own selection, including some shoes. © **041/522-3020** for Frezzeria location; © **041/523-6948** for Calle Goldoni location.

Hibiscus

Calle de l'Ogio, San Polo 1060.

Sarah found this boutique a few years ago; it is nothing like the designer-laden stores that make up the rest of the listings in this section. Instead, it's a small, well-bought store that goes for a funky boho look. There are some designer T-shirts, but I went for the raw-silk shirts that are cut wide and have good drape and are priced at 100€ ($130). © **041/520-8989.**

La Coupole

Via XXII Marzo, San Marco 2366; Frezzeria, San Marco 1674.

Once again, here are two boutiques carrying the same big names and many lines. A few of its makers include Byblos, Alaia, and the sort-of-local Malo cashmere, plus shoes from Moschino and earrings from Sharra Pagano of Milan. Both shops are small and elegant; prices are high. © **041/522-4243.**

Crafts

IL BALLO DEL DOGE
San Marco 1823.

Cooperative of 14 artisans.

LA BOTTEGA DEI MASCARERI
Ponte di Rialto, San Polo 80.

Located at the foot of the Rialto, this shop offers unusual papier-mâché masks that are a notch above the average fare. ✆ **041/522-3857.**

LA VENEXIANA
Ponte Canonica, Castello 4322.

You'll find masks and other Carnevale items here as well as some of the most incredible crafts work I have ever seen. Don't miss it. ✆ **041/523-3558.**

MAX ART SHOP
Frezzeria, San Marco 1232.

This store is right around the corner from the Hotel Bauer and the San Moisè designer shopping area at the start of Frezzeria; it will beckon to you from its velvet-hung windows. Inside, choose from velvet pillows, clothes, Carnevale-inspired wonder, and old-world charm. ✆ **041/523-3851.** www.ballodeldoge.com.

Designer Boutiques

For details on many of these well-known brand names, check out the "Dictionary of Taste & Design" (p. 55).

CONTINENTAL BIG NAMES

CARTIER
San Marco 606.

CHANEL
San Marco 1285.

HERMÈS
San Marco 1255.

LACOSTE
San Marco 218.

LOUIS VUITTON
San Marco 1256.

WOLFORD
Cannaregio 5666.

ITALIAN BIG NAMES

ALBERTA FERRETTI
San Marco 296.

ARMANI JEANS
Calle Goldoni, San Marco 4485.

BULGARI
Calle Larga XXII Marzo, San Marco 2282.

DOLCE & GABBANA
San Marco 223–26.

EMILIO PUCCI
San Marco 1318.

EMPORIO ARMANI
Calle dei Fabbri, San Marco 989.

ERMENEGILDO ZEGNA
San Marco 1241.

ETRO
San Marco 1349.

FENDI
Salizzada San Moisè, San Marco 1474.

Frette
Calle Larga XXII Marzo, San Marco 2070a.

Giorgio Armani
Calle Goldoni, San Marco 4412.

Gianfranco Ferré
Calle Vallaresso 1307.

Gucci
San Marco 1317.

Hogan
San Marco 1461.

Just Cavalli
San Marco 1814.

La Perla
Campo San Salvador, San Marco 4828.

Laura Biagiotti
Via XXII Marzo, San Marco 2400.

Loro Piana
Ascensione, San Marco 1290–1301.

Malo
San Marco 2359.

Marina Rinaldi
San Marco 269a.

Max & Co.
San Marco 5028.

Max Mara
Mercerie, San Marco 268.

Missoni
Calle Vallaresso 1312.

Missoni Sport
Mercerie, San Marco 4918.

PRADA
San Marco 1410.

ROBERTA DI CAMERINO
Piazza San Marco 127.

ROBERTO CAVALLI
Calle Vallaresso 1314.

SALVATORE FERRAGAMO
Calle Larga XXII Marzo, San Marco 2093.

TOD'S
Calle XXII Marzo, San Marco 2251.

TRUSSARDI
Calle Spadaria, San Marco 670 and 695.

VALENTINO
Salizzada San Moisè, San Marco 1473.

Eyeglass Frames

I do not list this under "Optical" because I feel strongly that you want the optics done where you know what's going on and have a handle on the price. Venice and the nearby Veneto area are *the* places to buy the frames, however.

OTTICA CARRARO
Calle della Mandola, San Marco 3706.

They are local makers of chic and fabulous frames that retail for about 80€ to 120€ ($104–$156) per pair, in all sorts of colors and many types of tortoise-y patterns. They also do a hot fashion color for a season and then never do it again. Best of all, they have a website—you can shop online! ✆ **041/520-4258.** www.otticacarraro.it.

OTTICA URBANI
San Marco 1280.

After I had laser treatment (LASIK) so that I no longer wore eyeglasses, I threw away all my scads of pairs of glasses—except the ones from this store in Venice. While it makes myriad styles, the store is most famous for a transparent resin (in fashion colors) in square or round shapes that ensure you look like a cross between a movie star and T. S. Eliot. You'll also find fabulous reading glasses and even some frames that fold. ✆ **041/522-4140.** www.otticaurbani.com.

Fabrics

GAGGIO
San Stefano, San Marco 3441.

Traditional silks, velvets, pleats, block prints, and the to-die-for local look that is part costume and part local treasure. It also has fabrics by the meter, plus clothes and styles for the home. ✆ **041/522-8574.**

RUBELLI
Campo San Gallo, San Marco 3877.

This Italian house is actually a source to the trade for reproductions of stunningly exquisite silken brocades and formal fabrics of museum quality. They have swatches, and they work with individuals, even if your last name is not Rothschild. ✆ **041/523-6110.** www.rubelli.com.

VALLI
San Marco 783.

Valli is a chain of fabric stores with locations in all major cities, and factories in Como; this shop in Venice happens to be right along your path, so it's a good place to stop in. The specialty of the house is designer fabrics, straight from the factory as supplied to the design houses, so you can buy that special fabric in the same season. It's not cheap, but you can save money.

I spent 80€ ($104) on some Gianni Versace silk and made a sarong skirt that I could never afford to buy from Versace ready-made. No phone.

VENETIA STUDIUM
Calle Larga XXII Marzo, San Marco 2403; Mercerie, San Marco 723; and others.

Come to Venetia Studium (written "Venetia Stvdivm") for the Fortuny-style wrinkled fabric (mostly silks) in medieval colors that are pure artistry. The company is expanding, so look for stores wherever you wander. It also does velvets. And a big business in Fortuny chandeliers.

The look is fantasy meets fashion with a Fortuny twist—there are long Isadora Duncan–like scarves and little drawstring purses that make the perfect evening bag. Most prices begin around $200, but there are many accessories in the $40 range.

Note that the main store is near San Moisè, but there are other branches, and each branch promotes a different look. A store around the corner from San Moisè sells just home style. Locations in less-touristy parts of town tend to be more home-decor oriented. © **041/522-9281** or 041/522-9859. www.venetiastudium.com.

Foodstuffs

Also consider a stop at **Al Covo** (see "Snack & Shop" on p. 189), where you can order its products to take away with you.

DROGHERIA MASCARI
San Polo 381.

This is not a drugstore as you might guess from the name, but rather the last remaining spice merchant in Venice. It is located in a real-people part of town, which you can get to by walking over the Rialto Bridge and going on to San Polo. © **041/522-9762.**

GIACOMO RIZZO
Cannaregio 5778.

This is a tiny pasta-maker shop with gourmet pasta in assorted strange colors and tastes—great gift items. Yes, it has blueberry pasta. On the other hand, there are plenty of flavors that you will want to try—I like artichoke. It's right near the Coin department store. Closed Sundays. ✆ **041/522-2824.**

Glass

You'll recognize the difference between quality glass and touristy junk in a matter of seconds. If your eye needs a little training, make a trip to the glass museum on Murano (see "Shopping Murano" on p. 202). These days, just about all the stores have signs in their windows swearing that their product does not come from Asia.

L'ISOLA
Campo San Moisè, San Marco 1468.

There are a few branches of this contemporary gallery around town. It's the best source in Venice for the newer names in big glassworks. This location is across from the Hotel Bauer. ✆ **041/523-1973.**

PAULY & COMPANY
Ponte dei Consorzi, San Marco 4392.

They don't come much more famous than this house, which was established in 1866. Pauly & Company has worked for most of the royal houses of Europe. It will paint your custom-blown glass to match your china (but not while you wait). It ships, too. ✆ **041/520-9899.**

SALVIATI
Campo Sant'Angelo, San Marco 3831.

Salviati is among the most famous master glassmakers in Venice. ✆ **041/522-7074.** www.salviati.com.

Seguso
San Marco 143.

You'll find bright colors and outstanding contemporary works here. © **041/739-048.** www.seguso.it.

Venini
Piazzetta dei Leoncini, San Marco 314.

Credited with beginning the second renaissance of glass blowers in Venice (1920–60), Venini is among the best. Buy anything you can afford, and hang onto it for dear life. © **041/522-4045.** www.venini.it.

Zora
San Marco 2407.

This is the newer guy in town. The shop is very close to the main branch of Venetia Studium, the best store for silks in town, so you will be here anyway. While Zora makes glass, its specialty is glass picture frames, which are sophisticated and stunning and 320€ ($416) each. There are also tassels, beaded flowers, and golden grape clusters. Even if you buy nothing, don't miss it. You go through a little gate into what looks like a private house, so push on. © **041/277-0895.**

Handbags & Leather Goods

Fendi
Salizzada San Moisè, San Marco 1474.

If you have no other chance to shop for Fendi, this store is bigger than the one in Milan, it's modern, and it's right in the heart of your stroll across town. It's even near the American Express office, if you run out of cash. Prices are about the same all over Italy, so your purchase will not cost more here; there are sales, too. The store is located behind San Marco on the way to San Giglio, almost across the lane from the Hotel Bauer. © **041/520-5733.** www.fendi.com.

GUCCI
San Marco 258.

Although I find this Gucci small and rather boring, without the flair of shops in other cities, it still offers the same gorgeous merchandise—sometimes on sale. You'll pass it on the way to the Rialto Bridge, so pop in if you have no other chance for Gucci. ✆ **041/522-9119.** www.gucci.com.

Home Style

ANTICHITÀ E OGGETTI D'ARTE
Frezzeria, San Marco 1691.

Ignore the word *antique* here and concentrate on glam home style, cushions of gilded velvet, velvet devore, painted velvet, and velvet dreams with fringe and beads. Fabrics from centuries past will make you weep with their glory. ✆ **041/523-5666.**

COLORCASA
San Polo 1989–1991.

Sarah reports: "I spotted a gorgeous Fortuny-style velvet picture frame in the window of this tiny shop and, of course, marched right in to check it out. Everything in the store—tapestries, silk velvet pillow shams, curtain panels, tablecloths, tassels, scarves, ties—flaunted the vibrant colors and finesse that other merchants attempt unsuccessfully to copy. Very expensive, though—the frame was 104€ ($135)." ✆ **041/523-6071.** www.colorcasavenezia.it.

MARIO & PEOLA BEVILACQUA
Fondamenta Canonica, San Marco 337b.

The shop is the size of a large closet and is filled with velvets, pillows, tapestries, and tassels. Even if you live in the Sunbelt, you will be tempted to do your home over in dark velvets. ✆ **041/241-0662.**

RIGATTIERI
San Marco 3532–3536.

Located near San Stefano, Rigattieri specializes in faience. It's a two-part shop: One part offers country dishes, and the other more traditional ceramics. A faience plate will cost about 20€ ($26) and can be packed for travel. © **041/523-1081.** www.rigattieri-venice.com.

Linens & Lace

JESURUM
Cannaregio 3219.

Yo—they moved. Jesurum has upheld and continued the tradition of Venetian lace-making, which was all but lost in the early 1800s. Just before the art would have died out, two Venetians undertook to restore it. One of the two was Michelangelo Jesurum, who—along with restoring the industry and putting hundreds of lace makers to work—also started a school so that the art would not die.

When you enter the Jesurum lace factory and showrooms, be prepared to flip your wig. The old church has been left with all its beautiful inlaid arches and its vaulted ceiling. Lace and appliquéd table linens and place mats are displayed on tables throughout the room. © **041/524-2540.** www.jesurum.it.

MARIA MAZZARON
Fondamenta dell'Osmarìn, Castello 4970.

This is a private dealer; you must phone to make an appointment to see her museum-quality treasures. Serious collectors only, please. © **041/522-1392.**

MARTINUZZI
Piazza San Marco, San Marco 67a.

This lace shop is almost as good as Jesurum, and it's located right on the piazza. This is the real thing: embroidered goods, appliquéd linens, very drop-dead-fancy Italian bed gear. The atmosphere is more old-lady lace shop than church-goes-retail, but the goods are high quality. ✆ **041/522-5068.**

Masks

If you saw the movie or play *Amadeus,* you are familiar with the type of mask worn at Carnevale time in Venice. Carnevale here got so out of hand that it was outlawed in 1797. But it's back again, and with it a renewed interest in masks. One of the most popular styles is a mask covered with bookbinding paper that you can find at a *legatoria,* or paper-goods store (see below). But there also are masks made of leather, papier-mâché, fabric, and more.

If all this is more than you had in mind, not to worry—there are masks in plastic for 4.70€ ($6.10) that will satisfy your need to participate. After 3 days in Venice, you'll swear you'll die if you see another mask, so make your selection carefully—many of them seem like trite tourist items.

For a more special item, try any (or all!) of these famous mask makers:

ADRIANO MIANI
Calle Grimani, San Marco 289b.

LABORATORIO ARTIGIANO MASCHIERE
Piazza San Marco, San Marco 282.

LE MASCHIERE DE DARIO USTINO
Ponte dei Dai, San Marco 171.

MA BOUTIQUE
Calle Larga San Marco, San Marco 28.

Paper Goods

Legatoria means bookbindery in Italian, and the famous designs are copies of bookbinding papers from hundreds of years ago. The best makers use the same old-fashioned methods that have been in the house for centuries. Many of the shops will make something to order for you, but ask upfront whether they will mail it for you; most won't. These papers have become so popular in the U.S. that the paper-goods business is now divided between those who are staying old-fashioned and those who are counting the tourist bucks and loving it. When you walk into the various shops, you can feel the difference. There are many 8€ ($10) gift items in these stores. A calendar-diary of the fanciest sort costs 40€ ($52).

Legatoria Piazzesi (Campiello della Feltrina, San Marco 2511; ✆ **041/522-1202**; www.legatoriapiazzesi.it) and **Il Papiro** (Calle del Piovan, San Marco 2764; ✆ **041/522-3055**; www.il papirofirenze.it), the two most famous paper shops in Venice, are almost across the way from each other, right near Campo San Stéfano at Ponte San Maurizio. Legatoria Piazzesi also sells old prints. Don't let the street address throw you; just keep walking and you'll see these two beauties. They are past the main tourist shopping but in a gorgeous part of town not far from the Gritti.

There's a relatively new chain of shops around town called **In Folio** that sells paper goods, books, and gift items as well as sealing wax and wax seals. When I was a teenager, sealing wax was the rage in America; now it's got a nice medieval bend to it that tourists are scarfing up. There are five or six of these shops scattered around town: San Marco 55; San Marco 739; San Marco 2431; San Marco 4852; and Castello 4615.

Shoes

Be sure to check out "Handbags & Leather Goods" (p. 217) for other shoe sources.

Bruno Magli

Calle Frezzeria, San Marco 1583; Calle dell'Ascensione, San Marco 1302; Calle XXII Marzo, San Marco 2288.

As you can tell from the addresses above, Magli has several different shops in Venice, although I swear I saw even more. Not only is there a Magli every place you look, but they display different models, forcing you to visit each if only to drool. © **041/522-7210** or 041/522-3472. www.brunomagli.it.

ROLANDO SEGALIN
Calle dei Fuseri, San Marco 4365.

He is an old-fashioned shoemaker who creates everything by hand and made to measure. Unbelievable stuff—ranging from the type of creative and crazy things you might expect Elton John to wear (shoes shaped like gondolas) to very simple, elegant court shoes. He'll create or copy anything, although the price is about 400€ ($520) a pair. Closed on Saturdays. © **041/522-2115.**

SONNENBLUME
Ponte di Rialto, San Polo 496.

Okay, I am going to put this in perspective—I have big feet and can rarely find shoes that fit, and I am on a tight budget. So excuse me if I rant and rave. This source makes old-fashioned espadrilles, sells them from the Rialto Bridge, and makes a fashion statement to boot—excuse the expression. Sizes go up to 43. Technically speaking, these are not espadrilles (a French shoe) but a creation made by Italians after World War II when supplies were scarce. The original shoe soles were made from tires. The uppers are made in silk, velvet, and linen in the yummiest fashion colors of the rainbow. You can custom order. Prices are about 30€ ($39) per pair. © **041/528-5513.** www.sonnenblume.it.

Chapter Eight

MILAN

WELCOME TO MILAN

Hang on to your spaghetti, guys—the world is close to an end. Get this: Juicy Couture has opened in Milan.

Not only have they opened, but they have a huge showcase right smack in the middle of the otherwise lovely Via della Spiga. And if that's not enough to set you wondering what's going on, then check out the new Dsquared2 store in Milan.

Oh my. Am I getting old or is this global retailing business getting to be too much? The whole point of travel was to see something local, something you couldn't find at home. Now Milan has declared itself to be international territory for all fashion brands.

Ah, Milan: the world's most beautiful ugly city.

First-timers may simply regard Milan as plain old ugly. I understand, really I do. But just you wait. Milan grows on you. Milan worms its way into the soul of a shopper and fills you with promise, even if it's just the promise of a new pair of shoes.

Milan is not a one-night stand. Milan is not the kind of place you fall in love with at a glance (unless you've been driving for days). Milan is not very pretty on the surface. Nonetheless, there's more style per mile here than in just about any other city in the world. And the surrounding area is filled with factories and outlets and bargains galore. Did I mention the trucks?

The more I shop Italy, the more I know that Milan is the center of the universe. You can make day trips from Milan, you can rent cars from the Milan airport, and you can catch trains in Milan. You can go in and out of paradise via Milan. You can also buy a lot of shoes.

Milan's real strength is in the inspiration it provides—not only to the fashion world, but also to visual and creative types of all sorts. Walk down the streets, pressing your nose to the windows, and you'll get *ideas*. There's no doubt that Milan is the real capital of Italian fashion. It's no secret that international *garmentos* comb the streets and markets to find the goods they will tote to Hong Kong to reproduce in inexpensive copies. A day on the prowl in Milan makes my heart beat faster, my pocketbook grow lighter, and my shoulder grow weary from carrying all those shopping bags.

What you see in Milan today will be in style in America in a year. What you adapt for your own lifestyle will compete with the cutting edge. Even if you can't afford to buy, you will feel invigorated by the city's creative energy just by walking its streets and window-shopping. Milan is not a great tourist town; rather, it's a business city, and one of its businesses just happens to be fashion. So what's not to like? There's surely no business like shoe business. Or fur business. Or ready-to-wear.

ARRIVING IN MILAN

By Plane

Because Milan is the hub of the northern Italian area, there are plenty of ways to get in and out of town. But there are a few tricks to learn. There are two big airports, **Malpensa** and **Linate,** so therein lies the need for discovery. Long-haul flights have always used Malpensa; this bit of news regarding the use of both Malpensa and Linate affects those who are traveling into Milan from another E.U. city.

Linate is only 15 minutes and 23€ ($30) away from downtown; in contrast, Malpensa is 1 hour away, and the taxi or limo ride costs around $125 . . . or more. When I fly to Milan from Paris, I usually have my choice of airport depending on the airline and flight. It pays to investigate, especially if your time is limited or you are not on an expense account. Also note that some low-cost carriers use Malpensa, but most use Linate.

One good thing about Malpensa: Malpensa is so far from downtown Milan that you can use this gateway to enjoy the real Italy and never even go into the city. Drive directly to Como (p. 283) or any of the towns in any direction. Do not drive into Milan in your rental car unless you are crazy and/or like paying 58€ ($75) a night for parking. (There's crazy, and then there's insane.) Use Malpensa to see the world, but take public transportation if you are headed into Milan.

If you do arrive at Malpensa International Airport, you'd better have a rich sugar daddy, or be prepared to wait for the bus. Of course, you may want to spring for a car and driver, which will cost about 120€ ($156), including tip.

There is an airport train, the **Malpensa Express** (www.malpensaexpress.it), for those who can manage their luggage. Naturally, I've never taken it. The train takes 40 minutes. Aaron and Jenny—my kids and assistants—were assigned to take this train, but found it required a change of station that was a huge pain, especially after a 10-hour long-haul flight. They took the bus instead.

The **Malpensa Bus Express** pulls up outside the terminal near baggage claim and drops you right at the Centrale train station in the heart of Milan, where you can hop on the Metro or get a taxi to your hotel. The fare is about 10€ ($13); buses run regularly on the half-hour.

Now then, this is a great service, and it's cheap, and it's fine and all that, but hey, you'd better be able to handle your luggage because, *mamma mia,* when they drop you at the train station, they drop you at the side of the building, and the taxi rank is in the *front.* There are no trolleys and no porters and no help whatsoever; go to the front for a trolley.

By Train

If you arrive in Milan by train, you will probably come in to the **Stazione Centrale,** the station in the heart of downtown. Pay attention as you exit because parts of this station have been changed and (if this is a return trip) the layout may not be as you remember it. Most important, there are no longer any porters. Nor is there an elevator. Oy!

They've also taken out the escalators at the front of the station, so if you have a trolley filled with luggage, you could be calling for your mommy.

Arrivals and departures are now from the front of the station. Centrale is connected to the Metro if you can manage your luggage and prefer using public transportation rather than a taxi.

There are free trolleys, but they are usually at the entrances to the station; when you pop off the train, it's unlikely that you'll find a trolley when you need one. If you are traveling alone, good luck. You may want to pack your set of airline wheels with you, or invest in the kind of luggage that has rear wheels and a handle.

Departure Tips

To get the bus to either airport, take a taxi to the Stazione Centrale where the bus pickup is. You do not want to enter the main part of the station to catch the bus. The ticket window is to the side, right where you caught the taxi when you arrived. Beware the beggars and drivers of gypsy cabs who may annoy you while you wait for the next bus.

Last time I took a taxi to Centrale—to catch a train to Venice, actually—the driver asked if I wanted the Pullman for the airport or a train because he will drop you at one of two different places depending on which you want.

GETTING AROUND

Milan happens to be a good walking city. Once you get yourself to a specific neighborhood, most of the shops, museums, and other attractions are in areas that you can easily navigate on foot. This is why it pays to pick a hotel in the center of the action and near a Metro stop.

If you need a taxi, they can be found at stands, hailed in the street, or called. Note that when you call a taxi, the meter starts once the driver heads toward your pickup location. Taxis in Milan are very expensive.

Getting around town on public transportation is not hard. Milan's Metropolitana has three main lines, each color-coded. Visitors will probably find the red line most convenient, as it goes to some of the major shopping areas and also stops at the Duomo. Look for the giant red M that indicates a station. The Metro is great but does not take you everywhere you want to go. However, it does get you to and from your hotel and the best shopping districts. Most of the luxury hotels are within a block of a Metro station.

Metro tickets can be purchased in the station; you will need coins to operate the ticket machines, but there are change machines. Magazine vendors inside stations will not give you change unless you buy something.

Tram and bus systems are also very good. Buy tram or bus tickets at a tobacco stand (marked with a T sign out front) before you get on the vehicle. Enter from the rear, and place your ticket in the little box to get it stamped. Keep it; you can use it again if you reboard within 75 minutes.

You can take a regular train to nearby communities, such as Como or Bergamo, or even to Venice, for a day trip. There's a large commuter population that goes to Turin, mostly for business, but you can go there to shop or to see the Shroud.

If you are using a train pass, do not blow a day of travel on a local commuter ticket. The same ticket can get you all the way to Paris. Save the rail pass for the important stuff. A first-class, round-trip train ticket to Como costs about 16€ ($21).

Metro Milan Area

Milan must be accepted as a total destination. From Milan, you can easily get in and out of Venice and into other northern Italian cities. Milan is less than an hour from Como and not much farther from Turin. From Milan, you can get to Switzerland—or anywhere! Venice is 3 hours away, and Verona . . . well, friends . . . Verona is a miracle unto itself (see chapter 10) and just a 2-hour drive away.

If you are in a car, you must also learn the various suburbs and cities and highways that serve the great metro area. There are truly thousands of small manufacturers, factories, artisans, and showrooms leading from a spider web of highways. Should you be interested in discovering some of these, create a careful assault plan with a map before you attempt to shop.

Car & Driver

If you want to get to seriously out-of-the-way factory outlets, you'll have to rent a car or hire a car and driver. Hiring a car with driver is not outrageously expensive—about 180€ ($234) a day (this includes tip) for 150km (93 miles), although there are half-day options. I've used **Europe Car Service** (© **02/942-5100;** www.ecs-car.com) in the past. If you are going to far-flung outlets, make sure the driver knows where they are. I was very frustrated on one of my outings to be paying by the clock yet to have the driver hopelessly lost.

Another possibility is to hire a taxi driver for a day or half-day rate. No, my driver did not speak much English, and I don't speak much Italian, but we had no problem. He drove me all over, waited for me while I shopped, and it cost about 50€ ($65) for a long half-day.

I have now driven my trusty little Peugeot 306 in and out of Milan and to the nearby outlets. This was made easier by my hotel's concierge, who gave me map printouts. But traffic is fierce; highways can be bumper-to-bumper—make sure you pick an outlet that is worth the trouble. The only outlet I'd really go the distance for is Armani (p. 288).

Milan

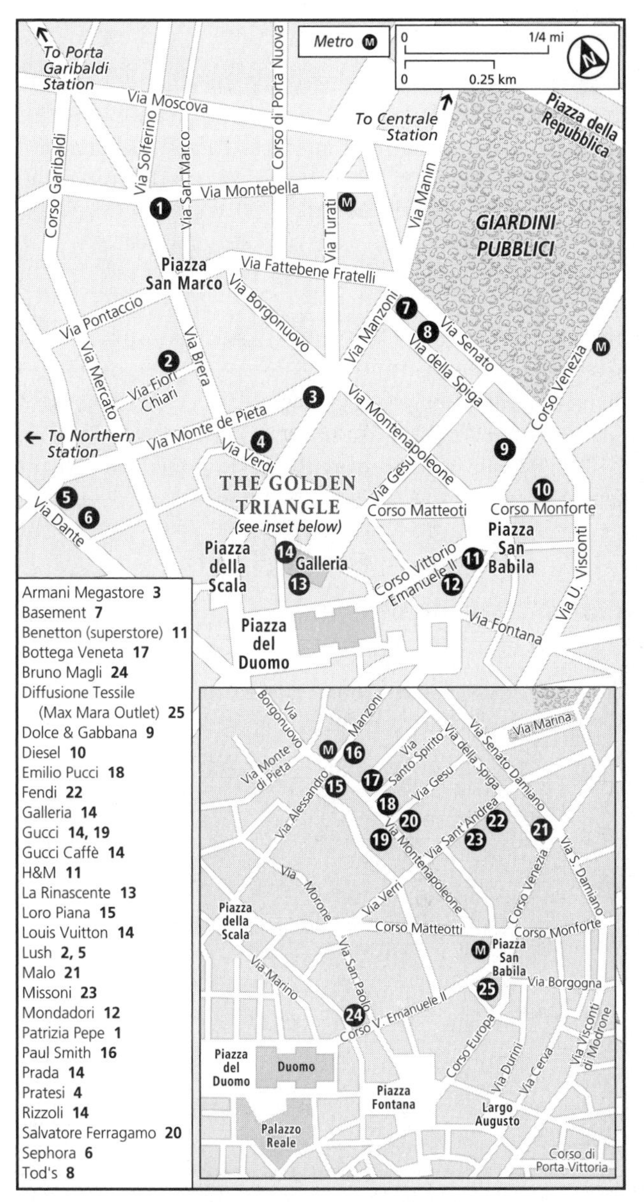

Metro
0
1/4 mi
0
0.25 km
To Porta Garibaldi Station
Via Moscova
To Centrale Station
Piazza della Repubblica
Corso Garibaldi
Via Solferino
Via San Marco
Corso di Porta Nuova
Via Montebella
Via Turati
Via Manin
GIARDINI PUBBLICI
Piazza San Marco
Via Fattebene Fratelli
Via Borgonuovo
Via Pontaccio
Via Mercato
Via Brera
Via Fiori Chiari
Via Manzoni
Via Senato
Via della Spiga
Corso Venezia
Via Montenapoleone
Via Monte de Pieta
To Northern Station
Via Verdi
THE GOLDEN TRIANGLE
(see inset below)
Via Gesu
Corso Matteoti
Corso Monforte
Piazza San Babila
Via Dante
Piazza della Scala
Galleria
Corso Vittorio Emanuele II
Via U. Visconti
Via Fontana
Piazza del Duomo
Armani Megastore 3
Basement 7
Benetton (superstore) 11
Bottega Veneta 17
Bruno Magli 24
Diffusione Tessile (Max Mara Outlet) 25
Dolce & Gabbana 9
Diesel 10
Emilio Pucci 18
Fendi 22
Galleria 14
Gucci 14, 19
Gucci Caffè 14
H&M 11
La Rinascente 13
Loro Piana 15
Louis Vuitton 14
Lush 2, 5
Malo 21
Missoni 23
Mondadori 12
Patrizia Pepe 1
Paul Smith 16
Prada 14
Pratesi 4
Rizzoli 14
Salvatore Ferragamo 20
Sephora 6
Tod's 8
Via Borgonuovo
Manzoni
Via Marina
Via Monte di Pieta
Via Santo Spirito
Via della Spiga
Via Senato Damiano
Via Alessandro
Via Gesu
Via Sant'Andrea
Via Montenapoleone
Via S. Damiano
Via Morone
Via Verri
Corso Venezia
Piazza della Scala
Corso Matteotti
Corso Monforte
Piazza San Babila
Via Marino
Via San Paolo
Via Borgogna
Corso V. Emanuele II
Corso Europa
Via Visconti di Modrone
Piazza del Duomo
Duomo
Via Durini
Via Cerva
Piazza Fontana
Largo Augusto
Palazzo Reale
Corso di Porta Vittoria

More Information

There is a local Time Out guidebook, *Time Out Milan,* that comes in both Italian and English versions. Look for it at news kiosks and bookstores in Milan. The national newspaper, *Repubblica,* has a Milan section toward the rear of the daily paper that includes local listings, weekend happenings, and some flea markets and specialty shopping events.

SLEEPING IN MILAN

In recent years, a number of designers have entered the hotel business—the Versaces in Australia, the Ferragamos in Florence and Rome, one of the Fendi girls also in Rome. Now Milan has a **Bulgari Hotel** (✆ **02/805-8051;** www.bulgarihotels.com).

Luxury Shopping Hotels

CARLTON HOTEL BAGLIONI
Via Senato 5 (Metro: Repubblica).

This is a very small, chic hotel that is a member of Leading Hotels of the World as well as part of the Baglioni chain, giving it a double pedigree. On my most recent research trip to Italy, I did one-stop shopping and booked all Baglioni hotels.

This hotel turned out to be more perfect than I could imagine—yes, I knew it would be fancy and welcoming, but I didn't know there was a private door leading out the rear of the hotel right onto the Via della Spiga, the pedestrian shopping street. The hotel is located in the center of all the stores, offers a shopping program, and has a concierge who will guide you to various venues. (This is the same concierge who also gave me computer printouts for when I was driving to factories and even to Verona and Venice.)

The hotel has several styles of decor to suit its fashion-oriented guests. It's plush but sleek, with an emphasis on dark colors and handcrafted built-ins. Some rooms are all Art Deco with original pieces, while other rooms are done in basic luxury-hotel chic. The restaurant is one of the "in" places in town and good for lunch if you're doing a look-see.

Rates are about $400 to $500, although there are off-season promotions. You can reserve through Leading Hotels of the World (© **800/223-6800** in the U.S.; www.lhw.com). © **02/77-077.** www.baglionihotels.com.

Four Seasons Hotel Milano

Via del Gesù 6–8 (Metro: Montenapoleone).

What would happen if the fashion angel came to Milan and decided to go into the hotel business? The Four Seasons, of course. You'll find this grand hotel discreetly located in the heart of the Montenapo shopping district. With up-to-date amenities and a posh atmosphere, it has a modern feel without seeming too rococo.

For an extra advantage, hit up the concierge desk for its slick magazine on shopping in Milan. Rooms start at 320€ ($416) per night. © **800/332-3442** in the U.S. Local phone © 02/77-088. www.fourseasons.com/milan.

Grand Hotel et de Milan

Via Manzoni 29 (Metro: Montenapoleone).

This is a fancy-schmancy hotel that's romantically small and dark and located on the other side of the luxury shopping district from the Baglioni. The wonderful decorating style takes you back in time and makes you wonder about this century, when the last century had some awfully perfect parts to it. By the way, this is the hotel where Verdi stayed and played. History haunts the hallways.

Yet there's a Metro stop right alongside the hotel, so you get luxury and real life wrapped up in one. Shuttle service is available to airports and the train station. Expect to pay about $400 to $500 per night. You can reserve through Leading Hotels of the World (© **800/223-6800** in the U.S.; www.lhw.com). © **02/723-141.** www.grandhoteletdemilan.it.

Four-Star Biggies

HILTON MILAN
Via Luigi Galvani 12 (Metro: Centrale).

This Hilton is located near the Centrale train station—it's a bit of a schlep to the nearest Metro, but you can walk to many places or hop into taxis. It's not glam, but it does have various promo rates, and the hotel has just been renovated. Watch it, though: The rates are most often per person. Still, a winter deal of 81€ ($105) per person, which includes breakfast, isn't bad. ✆ **800-HILTONS** in the U.S. Local phone ✆ 02/69-831. www.milan.hilton.com.

JOLLY HOTEL PRESIDENT
Largo Augusto 10 (Metro: Duomo).

JOLLY HOTEL TOURING
Via Ugo Tarchetti 2 (Metro: Repubblica).

You'll be jolly, too, when you learn about this hotel chain, with two locations in downtown Milan. The Jolly President (✆ **02/77-461**) is a business traveler's hotel, with small rooms of modern neo-Italian design. It's a great find because of its location. Largo Augusto is next door to Via Durini, and a block from the Duomo, which can be seen from your window.

The Jolly Touring (✆ **02/63-351**) is located near the Principe and the Palace and shares the same Metro with them, but it's a block closer to the shopping action. The rooms are much nicer than at the Jolly President. The hotel does cater to groups, but I was quite happy here.

Rates, if you can get a deal, are in the 200€ ($260) range, including full breakfast—but they do go higher, especially when there are fairs in town. ✆ **800/247-1277** in the U.S. www.jollyhotels.com.

Intimate Finds

THE GRAY
Via San Raffaele 6 (Metro: Duomo).

The Gray is one of those small, newfangled design hotels. It does various shopping promotions and has rates that begin at 218€ ($283), which is considered a bargain for this much luxury in this town. © **02/720-8951.** www.sinahotels.com.

HOTEL MANIN
Via Manin 7 (Metro: Turati).

This is a tiny hotel decorated like an ocean liner from the 1930s. Right near the gardens and the fashion district, it is considered a find by fashion editors and those looking for a good location and an affordable price. Room rates are around 200€ ($260) and can be lower out of season. © **02/659-6511.** www.hotelmanin.it.

HOTEL MANZONI
Via Santo Spirito 20 (Metro: Montenapoleone).

I found this three-star hotel by accident—it's small and well priced and in a great location near all the most expensive stores. There are only about 50 rooms, and they rent for between 150€ and 190€ ($195–$247) per night. With breakfast! © **02/7600-5700.** www.hotelmanzoni.com.

SNACK & SHOP

BREK
Piazza Cavour, Via dell'Annunciata 2, at Via Manzoni (Metro: Turati).

This is a chain of cafeterias, with branches in key shopping districts. Now that euros are so dear, you may be delighted to have a nice meal or two for not much money. For lunch, there's a special of pasta, dessert, and drink for 5€ ($6.50)—you can't beat that. Midday is busy with worker bees and the selection of foods seems to be greater; dinner sometimes feels like leftovers. Still, you can eat like a king for not much money. ✆ **02/653-319.** www.brek.com.

COVA

Via Montenapoleone 8 (Metro: Montenapoleone).

A lot like Sant Ambroeus (see below), but more formal and touristy. It's a local legend and an "in" place for tea—come at 5pm if you want to make the scene. The chocolates are a status-symbol hostess gift in fall, the jellied fruit squares in summer. Note that there's the old, Russian system for paying if you buy food to go: Make your choice at the counter, pay at the front desk, and return to the counter to pick up your choice. There's a rumor going around town that the real estate that Cova sits on is worth about $25 million, so if they've sold out by the time you get there, well, you can't blame them! ✆ **02/7600-0578.**

EMPORIO ARMANI CAFFÈ

Armani Megastore, Via Manzoni 31 (Metro: Montenapoleone).

Because I frequently eat at the Emporio Armani Caffè in Paris, I thought this would be a good place to test in Milan. It's also located near my regular hotel choices, in the heart of the truly great shopping district, and a few steps from a Metro stop—plus it's part of the Armani Megastore. All that said, the food was good and the prices fair, but the portions were so small I wanted to cry. Also note that Sarah and I went here on our last visit and they were very snotty to us. We weren't wearing Armani. ✆ **02/7231-8680.** www.armani-viamanzoni31.it.

GUCCI CAFFÈ
Galleria Vittorio Emanuele II.

Yes, friends, Gucci has a cafe and it's right in the Galleria, so you can't miss it and won't want to—even if you just stop for a coffee and a Gucci chocolate. It serves mostly sweets and snacks, but the crowd is to die for. Also open Sundays from 2 to 7pm. ✆ **02/859-7991.** www.gucci.com.

PECK
Via Spadari 9 (Metro: Duomo).

This is possibly the most famous food store in Milan. The main shop is on a side street on the far side of the Duomo, away from the Montenapo area but still convenient enough to be worthwhile. I always buy a picnic to take back on the plane. ✆ **02/802-3161.** www.peck.it.

SANT AMBROEUS
Corso Matteotti 7 (Metro: San Babila).

I've fallen in love with this fancy space right off Montenapoleone. It has a bakery and candy shop for takeout, or you can stand at the bar or grab a table. Sort of the Italian version of tea at the Ritz. It opens at 8am if you prefer to breakfast here. I can eat the little *prosciutto crudo* sandwiches all day long. ✆ **02/7600-0540.** www.santambroeus.org.

10 CORSO COMO CAFFÈ
10 Corso Como (Metro: Garibaldi).

It's pricey (about 58€/$75 per person) but much fun to be part of the scene at 10 Corso Como. And after you've blown your wad on the meal, you can walk it off by going around the corner to the store's outlet, where markdowns offer a savings. ✆ **02/2901-3581.** www.10corsocomo.com.

THE SHOPPING SCENE

Because Milan is the home of the fashion, fur, and furnishings industries, you'll quickly find that it's a city that sells style and image. Milan is a city of big business: The souvenir stands are overflowing with an abundance of international magazines, not kitschy plastics. The big toy sold by street vendors? Plastic telephones for kids!

Although Milan was a medieval trading city, in its modern, post–World War II incarnation, Milan has sizzled and made its mark. The city hosts the international furniture salon every other year. There are fashion shows twice a year, bringing a cadre of fashion reporters from all over the world to tell the fashion mavens just what Italy has to offer. Besides these, there are a zillion fairs and conventions and other business happenings, meaning Milan is always happening. Hmmmm, except in August.

Even if you aren't a fashion editor and don't plan your life around what comes trotting down the catwalk, you'll find that Milan's high-fashion stores offer a peek at what's to come. You'll also find that the markets and real-people shopping reflect the proximity of nearby factories. You'd be amazed at what can fall off a truck.

The best shopping in Milan is at these designer shops and showrooms, or at the discount houses, jobbers, and factory-outlet stores that sell designer clothing, overruns, and samples. If you really care about high fashion at an affordable price, you'll plan to spend January of each year prowling the sales in Milan—not London.

The Best Buys in Milan

Alternative Retail Mavens will give me the evil eye for mentioning this, but Milan is a good place for a bargain. There are good flea markets and street markets, and the buys in Como cannot be underestimated. It's more than just a resort town; it's heaven for bargain shoppers who want high-quality silks and outlet deals—Armani, anyone? Have the words "Factory Store" written over a door ever been more beautiful?

Designer Home Design Again, maybe not a best buy in terms of price, but a best in terms of selection and unique opportunity. The hottest trend in Milan of late has been that all the big designers are doing home furnishings, from dishes and ashtrays to sheets and then some. **Dolce & Gabbana, Missoni,** and **Ferragamo** are all into home design now. It's luxe, it's expensive, and it's gorgeous. Just press your nose to the **D&G Home** store, take one look at the dark-red silk brocade, leopard prints, and majolica, and know that when it works, it works! But wait, I now also shop for home design in the outlet store that **Lisa Corti** has in her workrooms—fabulous stuff at half the price of Saks.

Designer Selections While designer merchandise is expensive, the selection and the possibilities of a markdown or discovery of a small, reasonably priced item are greater in Milan. **Etro** isn't a bargain resource and is available in other Italian cities, but it will please you to no end to buy here and to soak up the atmosphere of class, elegance, and northern Italian chic. The Etro outlet, right in town, will also please you to no end.

Young Fashions Aaron and Jenny—our 20-something reporters—had a wonderful time exploring shoe, vintage, and fashion shops and found prices often fair. Some items were too high for them but fun to stare at; others were affordable and sensational. There are specific parts of town that cater to the young look and the young wallet (see "Shopping Neighborhoods," later in this chapter). And don't forget my fave: **Oviesse** (p. 259).

The Five Best Stores in Milan

In alphabetical order:

DIFFUSIONE TESSILE (MAX MARA OUTLET)
Galleria San Carlo 6 (Metro: San Babila).

Yes, the official name of this store is Diffusione Tessile, but it is indeed the Max Mara outlet, and it's smack-dab in the center of everything, easy to get to, and easy to shop. Because Max Mara makes the best wool coats in the world, the store offers better shopping when fall and winter merchandise is in stock. Summer pickings can be slim, although I did get some accessories, sleeveless silk tops, and other smalls on my last springtime visit. See p. 275 for more info. © **02/7600-0829.** www.diffusionetessile.it.

LISA CORTI HOME TEXTILE EMPORIUM
Via Conchetta 6 (Tram: 15).

You will spend a lot on the taxi ride here, but to me it's worth it. Corti has shops in other Italian cities, but this is also the showroom and has the best prices. She makes home style and women's clothing in colorful prints; they're sold for double the price at Saks Fifth Avenue. For fans, this will be the highlight of your trip to Milan. See p. 270 for details. © **02/5810-0031.** www.lisacorti.com.

SPACCIO ETRO
Via Spartaco 3 (no nearby Metro).

This store offers great prices on quality items—accessories, yard goods, and clothes for men and women. You will go mad. See p. 276 for the scoop. © **02/5502-0216.** www.etro.it.

10 CORSO COMO
Corso Como 10 (Metro: Garibaldi).

This is one of the best stores in the world because of the way the product is bought and the way it constantly changes. It's owned by a woman who is a member of one of the most important fashion families in Italy and sells a little of everything, but all of it seemingly unique. See p. 276 for the outlet and p. 235 for the cafe. © **02/2900-2674.** www.10corsocomo.com.

You & Me
Via della Spiga 50 (Metro: Montenapoleone).

This is what we travel for—ideas and color and energy and something you've never seen before but is just plain brilliant. You & Me sells handbags, shoes, and costume jewelry, all of it very jingle-jangly and bejeweled. See p. 271 to find out my favorite item in the store. © **02/7600-6039.** www.youandme.it.

A Fun Afterthought

Lush
Via Fiori Chiari 6 (Metro: Duomo).

If you haven't been to a Lush store in Italy, this is your chance. The store is on the way to the Brera district and offers the famous British bath products with an Italian twist. I find Lush expensive and am very much over it as a trend—but I am still impressed by the Italian branches because of their use of Italian ingredients. See p. 253 for more. © **02/7201-1442.** www.lush.com.

Milanese Style

In terms of clothing, Milanese style is much more conservative, chic, and sophisticated than the more flamboyant southern Italian look. In Milan, if you don't buy from a trendy designer, you can actually load up on basics—good cashmere sweaters and shawls, knits, shoes, handbags, and furs. That's right: furs! Northern Italy is one of the few places in the world where it's not only politically correct to wear fur but also part of the fashion scene. In Milan, attitude is part of fashion, so you can wear all black and be chic; it need not be expensive or laden with labels—you just need the look and a pair of great sunglasses.

Much of what's for sale in Milan is of the same design school as the English country look; this will interest Europeans far more than Americans looking for hot looks, not tweeds and V-necks. Also note that a large influence in Italian fashion these

The Look

When I travel for Born to Shop, one of the first things I do is pay attention to what everyone's wearing and what shopping bags they're carrying. This not only gives me a sense of local style, but it also leads me to shops I might miss otherwise.

In Milan, I immediately spotted many women (of all ages) wearing variations on a single fab look. The common factors were their jeans and shoes: dark, pencil-leg denim with sparkly gold ballet slippers. The tops varied from cropped and slim (on the tiny teens and tweens) to oversize linen tunics on those who needed more coverage. Like me.

I couldn't wait to put my Milan look together. I already had the jeans (denim "leggings" from Wal-Mart), so the search was on for sparkly slippers and the perfect top. No problem. I saw the same basic gold ballet flats in every shoe shop in Milan. Some were priced as high as $250, so I was quite proud of myself for discovering a $25 pair in the Centrale Metro station. The linen tunic was also a great buy; I found a long, slim, white linen shirt for $16 at the Diffusione Seta outlet in Como.

—SRL

days is the American mail-order catalog look—Levi's, J. Crew, L.L.Bean, and so on. I didn't come to Italy to buy things like this; you probably didn't either, and will someone spare me the Gap wannabes? Still, there's plenty of trendy stuff for the Ferrari in your soul.

Milan is a great place for spotting color trends. Yes, fashionistas always dress in black because it's easy, but Italian fashion highlights a few new, key colors each season. Even if you just window-shop, you'll soon see that almost all clothing in any given season, no matter which designer is presenting it, falls into a few color families. Each season will have one or two hot colors that define the times; each season will also have a wide selection of items in black because black is the staple of every Italian (and French) wardrobe. The best thing about these colors is that other designers and even mass retailers in America will pick up on the same shades, so what you buy in Italy will carry smoothly into the fashion front for several years.

Another aspect of Milanese style comes in furnishings, home decor, tabletop, and interior design. No matter what size you are or what age you are, you will see things to light your fire in this city of desire.

Shopping Hours

The big news in Milan is that shopping hours are not as strict as elsewhere; nor are they as strict as they used to be. Furthermore, Milan now has stores that are open on Sunday!

Many of the big-name designer shops are open "nonstop," which means that they do not close for lunch. If you don't want to take a lunch break, shop the Montenapo area. Dime stores such as **Standa** and **UPIM** have always been open nonstop; **La Rinascente,** Milan's most complete department store, has always been open during lunch as well. During the week, stores usually close between 7:30 and 8pm.

Most stores in Milan are closed on Monday through the lunch hour (they open around 3:30 or 4pm). Note that La Rinascente does not open until 1:45pm on Monday. Most of Italy is dead from a retail perspective on Monday morning. But wait! Food shops are open, and factory stores are frequently open, too. If you are heading out to a certain factory or two, call ahead. Make no assumptions.

Sunday Shopping

Laws have changed, and all of Italy's big cities have Sunday shopping now; mostly it's the big department stores that are open. If you want to shop on a Sunday, try for a flea market. Or go to Venice, which is wide, wide, wide open on Sunday.

Milan is far more dead on Sunday than other communities, but you can get lucky—at certain times of the year, things are popping on Sunday, and yes, **La Rina** (the department store, La Rinascente) is open. In fact, you can even have your hair done there on a Sunday—**Aldo Coppola** (© **02/8905-9712**) is the only hairdresser in town that's open on Sundays.

The regular Sunday stores are **10 Corso Como** and **Virgin Megastore.** Sunday hours are most often noon to 5pm, but I am seeing a trend of big-name designers opening their doors from 3 or 4pm until 8pm.

During fashion weeks, stores in the Montenapo district often open on Sunday; they're also open on specific Sundays from October until Christmas. Some stores in the Navigli area stay open on Sunday as well.

Personal Needs

The **American Express** travel office is at Via Brera 3, at the corner of Via dell'Orso. This is in the thick of the shopping district, so you need not go out of your way to get here. If you use traveler's checks, cash them in your hotel—even if they are in euros, they are hard to use in normal stores. ATMs are easy to find and are your best bet.

To find a pharmacy, look for the neon-green cross. Should you need an all-night pharmacy, there is one at Piazza Duomo. There's also a very good all-night pharmacy, where the staff speaks English, at the Centrale train station. In fact, the train station has an excellent selection of shops selling basic items you may have left at home: Try **Free Shop,** an enormous grocery store that sells everything from food and souvenirs to health and beauty aids—even condoms.

SHOPPING NEIGHBORHOODS

Golden Triangle/Montenapo All the big designers have gorgeous and prestigious shops here. You can easily explore it in a day or two, or even an hour or two, depending on how much money and how much curiosity you have. Although the main shopping street is **Via Montenapoleone,** sometimes this area is referred to as Montenapo.

This is the chic part of town, where traditional European design flourishes along with Euro-Japanese styles and wild, hot Italian New Wave looks. It includes a couple of smaller streets that veer off the Via Montenapoleone in a beautiful little web of shopping heaven; note that Via della Spiga is just plain yummy with charm. This area is where you'll find **Armani, Fendi, Ferragamo, Gucci, Tod's, Viktor & Rolf,** the many **D&G** shops, and more.

The outermost borders of the neighborhood are **Via Manzoni** and **Corso Venezia,** two major commercial streets. Use them mostly for finding your way (although in the past year, Corso Venezia has become a hot address for designer bridge lines). Your real shopping streets will be **Via della Spiga, Via Sant'Andrea,** and, of course, **Via Montenapoleone.** But don't miss the back streets of this little enclave—streets like Via Gesù, Via Borgospesso, and also Via Manzoni (which is not a back street).

For anyone with limited time who wants to absorb a lot of the scene in just a few hours, this is the top-priority shopping district for looking around. You may not buy your souvenirs here, but you'll see the stuff that dreams are made of.

Duomo The Duomo is the main landmark of Milan. It's an incredibly detailed and gorgeous cathedral, not a store. It is on the Piazza del Duomo and is happily surrounded by stores, however. You guessed it—there is even a **Virgin Megastore** to one side and the country's leading department store, **La Rinascente,** to another side.

Via Montenapoleone angles away from Corso Vittorio Emanuele II as you move away from the Duomo, so the Golden Triangle and Duomo neighborhoods sort of back up to each other. This makes it very easy to shop these two areas in the same afternoon. When you are finished with them, there are two other shopping neighborhoods, Brera and Largo Augusto, which you can connect with on the other side of the Duomo. You did come to Milan to shop, didn't you?

Corso Vittorio Emanuele II This neighborhood is filled with big stores, little stores, and half a dozen galleries and minimalls that house even more stores. The most maddening part about this area is that you can hardly find an address. Just wander in and out and around from the Duomo to **Piazza San Babila,** which is only 2 or 3 blocks.

At San Babila, turn left and you'll end up at Via Montenapoleone for entry into the Golden Triangle. Or you can do this in the reverse, of course. But don't forget to check out this intersection. Because the San Babila area is very important, you'll find everything from the new **Benetton** superstore to **UPIM** to plastics-mongers and fashion mavens.

At the front end of the Duomo, off the piazza, is a shopping center of historic and architectural-landmark proportions, the **Galleria.** This is one of the most famous landmarks in Milan, and some tout it as the first mall in Europe. Other galleries in Europe also make the same claim, but who cares? Take one look at the ceiling and you'll marvel. Then visit the **Prada** store.

The Galleria has a vaulted ceiling and looks like a train station from another, grander, era. Inside, there are restaurants and bistros where you can get coffee and sit and watch the parade of passersby. Several big-time shops are here besides Prada—don't miss **Rizzoli** for books in English, the **Diffusione Tessile** outlet for all of the **Max Mara** lines, and the newish **Gucci** and **Louis Vuitton,** too. If you go out the back end, you will be at La Scala, the famous opera house. Behind La Scala is the Brera area.

If you are at the piazza with the Duomo to your back and have not turned right to enter the Galleria, you can walk straight ahead toward the Virgin Megastore and yet more retail. The arcade across from the Duomo is filled with many old names of Milanese retailing and some newer shops, too, including a **Missoni** jeans store that sells the sports line. **Galtruco** is a very famous fabric firm where you can buy every imaginable type of yard goods, including designer fabrics from local mills.

Durini The Via Durini is only 2 blocks long and runs parallel to the Corso Vittorio Emanuele II, ending right at the far side of the Duomo. Because of its perfect location, this should be a strong street for retail, but because it's also hidden in plain sight, the street has had many personalities. These days, there are some home-style showrooms and some interesting new stores that use the location as a jumping-off point to test the retail waters. Look at **Nava Store** (no. 23) for carry-on and rolly-rolly bags made by big names in Italian design.

Brera Brera is one of the most famous shopping districts in Milan thanks to its slightly less expensive rents. It's the part of town where young designers can break into retailing and high style, and it has both designer shops and up-and-coming trendsetters.

Brera is a fair (but not difficult) walk from the Duomo. The main stretch is rather commercial, with shops oriented toward teens, quite a few jeans stores, and very obvious branches of famous international retailers such as **Laura Ashley, Shu Uemura**, and **Patrizia Pepe.** Behind all this, there are narrow and bewitching back streets, closed to vehicular traffic, that call out to you to explore them. Many host the most expensive antiques dealers in the city; some have the ateliers of new, hot designers.

Designer boutiques here include **Il Bisonte** (Via Madonnina 10) and **Angela Caputi** (Via Madonnina 11). Don't miss **Etro,** Via Pontaccio 17, at the corner of Vicolo Fiori, and **Babele** (Via Brera 11) for classic women's clothing. And while you're in this neck of the woods, don't forget that London's **Lush**—that adorable deli of bath bombs, face masks, and homemade soaps and suds first created in England—has opened up here at Via Fiori Chiari 6.

The best way to see the area is during the Brera antiques street fair, on the third Saturday of each month, when vendors put out tables in the narrow streets and a well-heeled crowd browses. But any day is a good day. Carry on from Brera to Solferino (the street just changes names) and then over one to Garibaldi.

Largo Augusto/Durini Another option is to move from the other side of the Duomo to Corso Vittorio Emanuele II, and then over to Via Durini. Via Durini is only a block long, but it's a good-size block that is crammed with fabulous stores. It veers off at an angle from San Babila and runs straight to Largo Augusto.

Please note that you can catch a bus to **Il Salvagente,** the discounter, at Largo Augusto, or walk via the **Corso Porta Vittoria,** and be there in 10 minutes. I usually walk because I enjoy window-shopping along the way.

Train Station/Ingrosso In the area between the Centrale train station and the Repubblica Metro station, there's a grid system of flat streets that makes up the *garmento* wholesale *(ingrosso)* and discount district of Milan. You can browse the scads of stores here and just go in and out—about half of them are closed for lunch, and all of them are closed on Saturday and Sunday. The area is trying to fashion itself as a fashion destination, calling itself **CMM,** or **Centro Moda Milano** (fax **02/9357-2218;** www.centromodamilano.it); it now has a printed brochure of the showrooms and keeps special hours for holiday shopping and during fashion weeks. Pick up the free brochure at any showroom.

If your time is limited and you crave high style and multiple marvels, this is not your destination. If you like a bargain and don't mind hit-or-miss shopping, step this way. I had a ball here last time I visited because I got lucky. For E.U. visitors who specifically come to Milan to beat the high prices in other parts of Europe, this is your cup of tea.

Buenos Aires Don't cry for me, Buenos Aires; I've got my credit cards. This street is more for teens and tweens and may not appeal to designer shoppers at all. The street is almost a mile long and features more than 300 shops: It is one of the most concentrated shopping areas in continental Europe. The best stores are located around the Lima station of the Metro. Did I mention there is an **Oviesse** store here? In case you haven't been reading that carefully, I am having a love affair with Oviesse and its low-cost fashions. See "About Oviesse" (p. 64) for details.

Avoid shopping on Buenos Aires on a Saturday—it's always mobbed. Remember, this is where the real people shop, so few people will speak English. The clientele is not always chic; the scenery is neither cute nor charming.

Many of the shops have no numbers; often the number by a store represents the block rather than the store address (so many shops may be called "3"), but it's all easy once you're here. Just wander and enjoy—you can't miss the good stuff.

You can get here easily by taking the no. 65 streetcar from the Centrale train station and getting off at Corso Buenos Aires (about three stops). Or take the Metro to Loreto and walk toward Venezia or vice versa.

Magenta For the opposite type of experience, get to the Corso Magenta, a rich residential thoroughfare where the best bakeries, cafes, and shopping brands are located to serve those who live in this area; it's the equal to Paris's 16th or 17th arrondissement. From October to May, do remember to wear your fur.

Dante As an extension of the Magenta neighborhood (it is adjacent) but accessible for tourists visiting the castle or using the red-line Metro, this area is heaven, not hell. It is a wide avenue made pedestrian area that stretches from the Piazza Cairoli (take the Metro to Cairoli), filled with branches of many big names—but they're international big names like **Sephora, Kiko** (Italian makeup brand), and **Lush,** so it's not exactly like the same old mall back home. In good weather, scads of people eat or sip coffee at outdoor cafes.

Navigli South of the Porta Ticinese is the canal area of Milan. The canals have been mostly built over, so don't spend too much time looking for a lot of water (wait for Venice): There's just the one canal. Yet the Navigli is becoming a funky shopping neighborhood. Wander here for an hour or two if you like colorful junk, secondhand shops, artists' studios, and the feel of getting in on the ground floor of up-and-coming Italian style. Cash only; no one speaks English.

The two streets running along the canal are called **Alzaia Naviglio Grande** and **Ripa di Porta Ticinese.** You can walk down one, cross a bridge, and walk back on the other side. There are some cute restaurants, and you can make an afternoon out of it if this is your kind of thing.

An antiques market is held on the last Sunday of each month on both sides of the Naviglio Grande. Tell your taxi driver that you want either *"mercatone dell antiquariato"* or the name of the street, Ripa Ticinese, which is one of two streets hosting the market along the canal.

Papiniano Every Tuesday and Saturday, there is a regular street market along the Viale Papiniano. This is a great place for designer clothing that fell off trucks and all sorts of fun fashions and accessories. Plan to be here early—9 to 10am is fine. In addition to two lanes of stalls selling clothing and dry goods, part of the market is fruit and food. To save money, so you can spend more at the market, forget the taxi and hop on the red line of the Metro; get off at San Agostino.

Porta Vittoria The Corso di Porta Vittoria begins shortly after the Duomo and changes its name to Corso XXII Marzo; it stretches from the side of the Duomo that is opposite to the La Scala side (look for Largo Augusto on your map) and turns into a nice residential area. Just use your feet. I like this walk because it takes you to a famous discount store and enables you to see something of upper-middle-class Milan along the way.

You'll pass many favorites, such as **Max Mara** and **Bassetti,** plus a nice branch of the department store **Coin.** This is where well-off locals shop and it's very non-touristy, not unlike the Corso Vercelli. After the street name changes to Corso XXII Marzo, turn left on Via Fratelli Bronzetti to get to **Il Salvagente,** the discounter. Hail a taxi to get back to your hotel if you have too much loot.

Tortona Take the green line to Porta Genova and get out for a walk around what is becoming a hot new design district called Tortona. Via Tortona is parallel to Via Savona and is filling up with showrooms and design studios. This is more for those

Navigli

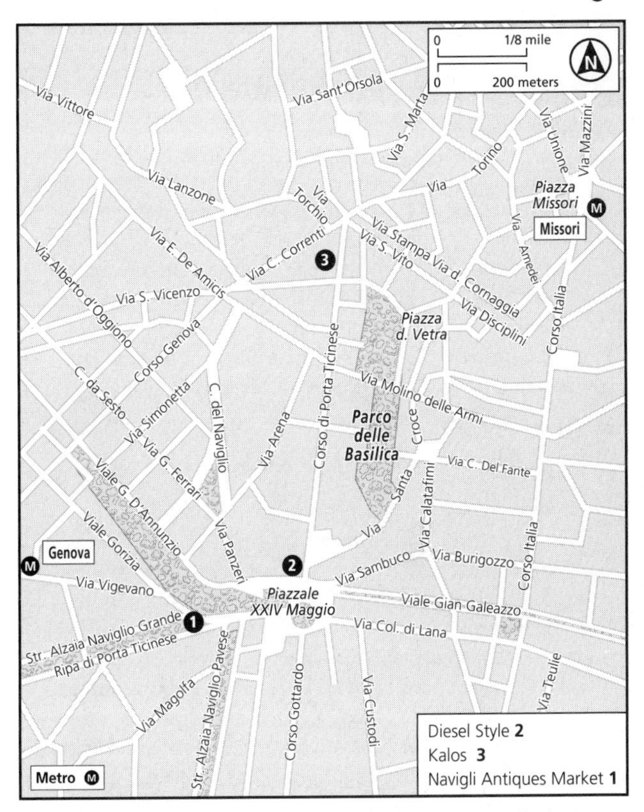

in the trade than the average consumer. See the map for Navigli, above.

Aprile & Beyond Not for the average visitor, Aprile stands for the piazza of the same name: XXV Aprile. It is an up-and-coming neighborhood that attracts design mavens and fashion editors thanks to a handful of important shops, including **High Tech** and **10 Corso Como.** The few retailers who have set up shop here are inventive, creative, and exciting, so take a look if you want to be in with the in-crowd. If you are more interested in sightseeing, and don't have much time in Milan,

Jenny's Turn: My Finds Milanese

CARPE DIEM

Viale Tunisia 1 (Metro: Porta Venezia).

Need a toaster/CD player and don't know where to go? Just off the main shopping street of Corso Buenos Aires lies this cute, kitschy shop where the colors and odd interpretations of normal household items are as vivid as the imagination will allow. Stop in and pick up a much-needed monkey-shaped lighter or just look at the marvels of modern nonsensicality. ✆ **02/2951-7833.** www.carpediem-milano.it.

KALOS

Corso di Porta Ticinese 50 (Metro: Porta Genova).

I stumbled upon this funky jewelry shop among the vintage-clothing stores on Porta Ticinese. Innocently enough, I started gazing longingly at the handmade pieces, as I often do when walking past a jewelry store. Then I noticed them. The prices. These gorgeous and unique pieces were priced very generously—what an invitation to shop!

I walked away with two necklaces and a pair of earrings for under 40€ ($52)—that's my kind of budget. The saleswoman (and designer) was very friendly, although she spoke little English, and gift-wrapped each box uniquely.

The jewelry items make perfect gifts for those who want a piece of Italian glamour—and they're perfect for your wallet at the same time. ✆ **02/8940-4329.** www.kalos-snc.it.

this area may not be for you. Piazza XXV Aprile is between the Moscova and Garibaldi stops on the green line. After this plaza, Corso Garibaldi changes its name and becomes Corso Como.

MILAN RESOURCES A TO Z

Antiques

Milan's antiques markets are great fun, but don't be afraid to get out of town to explore a few more. In Pavia and Brescia, there are antiques markets on the second Sunday of each month. On the third Sunday, there's a flea market in Carimate (Como). Begamo Alta also celebrates on the third Sunday, in Piazza Angelini. Many villages have antiques markets on certain Sundays in April and October only; ask your hotel's concierge for details. For markets in Milan proper, see "Flea Markets," later in this chapter.

Antiques stores are mostly located in the Brera area, on or off Via Madonnina, with a few fancier ones in the Montenapo area. The Montenapo shops do not offer affordable items for mere mortals.

Serious dealers include **Legatoria Conti Borboni** (Corso Magenta 31), for antique books; **Amabile** (Via Brera 16), for carpets; and **Mauro Brucoli** (Via della Spiga 46), for furniture. There's a tiny gallery of about eight or nine shops right near a couple of luxury hotels, the Westin Palace and the Principe di Savoia (and the Jolly Hotel Touring). Take the Repubblica Metro and walk or taxi to **La Piazzetta degli Antiquari** (Via Turati 6).

Bath & Beauty

Don't look now, but there is a color war in Italy, centered in Milan where everyone is suddenly doing makeup. This was probably instigated by the success of the Versace cosmetics line, which was actually launched a few months after the Versace murder and was obviously created before he died. That line didn't survive, but do get a look at the Armani makeup.

Diego Dalla Palma

Via Madonnina 15 (Metro: Duomo).

This is embarrassing, but here goes: I am forever getting Diego Dalla Palma, a well-known local makeup artist, and Diego Della Valle, the creator of Tod's shoes, mixed up. That said, Dalla Palma is an artist with connections to the Italian couture houses; he has a small shop where you can purchase his line or make an appointment for lessons and a makeover. The location is adjacent to the Brera district on a great shopping street. © **02/876-818.** www.diegodallapalma.it.

Giorgio Armani

Armani Megastore, Via Manzoni 31 (Metro: Montenapoleone).

As we go to press, Giorgio Armani cosmetics does not have very much distribution in Italy or elsewhere in the world. This could be because the line is so new, and the intent is to keep it very exclusive. Regardless, you can see it all and play with it all at the Armani flagship; the line is also sold in Milan's La Rinascente. I have tested many of the products and adore the pearlized liquid foundation that really does add light to the face. The last time I bought a blush, it was presented to me in its own little Armani canvas tote bag. © **02/7231-8600.** www.armani-viamanzoni31.it.

Kiko

Corso Buenos Aires 43 (Metro: Loreto).

By the time I got to Kiko, a cute little shop in the best part of the trendy shopping on Buenos Aires, I could no longer tell one brand from the next. I can't quite tell how this line differs from Madina, although it is not as sophisticated in the packaging and marketing. Still, the products are well priced and getting raves from local fashion editors. © **02/2024-0502.** www.kiko.it.

L'OCCITANE
Via Solferino 12 (Metro: Duomo).

A branch of the French mass-market bath and well-being line. The prices are probably the same as in the U.S. ✆ **02/655-4389.** www.loccitane.com.

LUSH
Via Fiori Chiari 6 (Metro: Duomo).

I am assuming that most readers already know the Lush chain, from visits in the U.K., U.S., or Canada. If you have no idea what I am talking about, then this is going to be a must-do experience. For those who already know and may even be bored with the gimmick, snap out of it—what's brilliant here is that the concept has been adapted to local specialties, so you'll find things such as limoncello shampoo, not sold in stores outside of Italy. This street is right off the Via Brera; there are now Lush stores all over Italy, so if you miss this one, you may still find another in your travels. ✆ **02/7201-1442.** www.lush.com.

MAC
Via Fiori Chiari 12 (Metro: Duomo).

MAC, the professional color line from Canada that's now owned by Estée Lauder, has gone global and has a free-standing store in Milan in the Brera area. Aside from the products, you can get a makeup lesson or just play with the colors. ✆ **02/8699-5506.** www.maccosmetics.com.

PERLIER/KELEMATA (ARMONIE NATURALI)
Corso Buenos Aires 25 (Metro: Loreto).

You may remember Perlier as a French bath line; it was bought by the Italian Kelemata family that now has a chain of very spiffy stores all over Italy (and several other shops around Milan). Recently the company joined the color wars and added a makeup line under the Perlier name; it is sold only in its own stores, which are named Armonie Naturali. © **02/2951-8261.** www.perlier.com.

SHU UEMURA
Via Brera 2 (Metro: Duomo).

Uemura is the king of color, and the man who started it all over 20 years ago in Japan, where he brought professional makeup to the public. His products have a cult following, and he is clearly in a league above all others; so are his prices. © **02/875-371.** www.shuuemura.com.

Books

There's a small international bookstore upstairs at the **Armani Megastore** (Via Manzoni 31) and another, larger one upstairs at **10 Corso Como.**

MONDADORI
Corso Vittorio Emanuele II (Metro: Duomo or San Babila).

Mondadori is a big, modern bookstore with an enormous selection in every category and a very good travel department. It offers some books in foreign languages, including English, and some gift items. © **02/7600-5832.**

RIZZOLI
Galleria Vittorio Emanuele II 79 (Metro: Duomo).

A large bookstore with books in several languages; the travel department is toward the front of the store, although it may not have the latest editions of guides. Open evenings and on Sundays, too. © **02/8646-1071.** www.libreriarizzoli.it.

Boutiques

ALBERTO ASPESI
Via Montenapoleone 13 (Metro: Montenapoleone).

This is a large gallery/boutique with the same concept as Colette in Paris and Dover Street Market in London. It is so large, in fact, that you can enter from Montenapo or from Via Bigli. © **02/861-792.** www.albertoaspesi.com.

FONTANA
Via della Spiga 33 (Metro: Montenapoleone).

This is modern Italian design of the most expensive and highest order. The interior is swank and very Milan, with lots of marble and sleek woods. The counters are suspended from thin wires and seem to hang in midair. © **02/7600-5372.**

GIO MORETTI
Via della Spiga 4 and 6 (Metro: Montenapoleone).

There are three different Gio Moretti stores: one for men, one for women, and one for children (across the street). You'll see all the big names here. For women, stock up on Sonia Rykiel, Complice, and those designers who don't have their own freestanding shops. © **02/7600-3186.**

LUISA CEVESE
Via San Maurilio 7 (Metro: Duomo).

This textile designer does works of art that are often sold through museum stores around the world—for example, the MoMA in NYC. She does some clothes and handbags and whatever amuses her—all bold and exciting and very individual. © **02/8699-7099.**

MARISA

Via della Spiga 52 (Metro: Montenapoleone).

This is one of those absolutely quiet, chic, drop-dead spaces that sells simple clothes that tell the world you are a simple soul who wears $1,000 linen dresses. It's all about the cut here, where several designer lines are chosen to demonstrate that philosophy—among them, Eskandar. © **02/7600-2082.**

10 CORSO COMO

Corso Como 10 (Metro: Garibaldi).

Like I said in chapter 1 and earlier in this chapter under "The Five Best Stores in Milan," I'll repeat myself: 10 Corso Como is one of the best stores in the world. Please also see p. 276 for the outlet and p. 235 for the cafe. © **02/2900-2674.** www.10corsocomo.com.

Cashmere

One of the things I am most frequently asked about is cashmere. Italian cashmere is of the highest quality because of the way it is combed and milled. With so many factories in northern Italy, there's the chance to buy at outlets or to check out what may have fallen off a truck and is being sold at markets. I saw the best buys at the Tuesday and Saturday markets.

DORIANI

Via Sant'Andrea 2 (Metro: Montenapoleone).

It's more of a men's than women's source, more of an English than a cutting-edge look—but luxe beyond belief. © **02/7600-3030.**

LORO PIANA

Via Montenapoleone 27 (Metro: Montenapoleone).

A three-story temple to cashmere and luxe, selling not only men's and women's things but also items for the home. Interactive displays here include videos and tests you can perform to see how the fabrics hold up, proving this is an art *and* a science. ✆ **02/7600-6027.** www.loropiana.com.

MALO
Via della Spiga 7 (Metro: Montenapoleone).

One of the most famous names in Italian quality cashmere, Malo has opened a shop that sells both men's and women's lines; in summer, there are non-cashmere items, too. The factory outlet is located outside of Florence; see p. 166 for details. ✆ **02/7601-6109.** www.malo.it.

MANRICO
Via della Spiga 29 (Metro: Montenapoleone).

The address says it all—this is a local source for those with money who are in the know. There's also a store in Aspen, so you get the idea. ✆ **02/782-155.** www.manrico.com.

MYSELF
Via Giuseppe Verdi 2 (Metro: Duomo).

I am well aware that two of my favorite new stores are named You & Me and Myself. But if you can get past me, note this small cashmere shop, right across from La Scala, that specializes in lightweight cashmeres. There's another branch at Corso Magenta 29, if you're in that neighborhood. ✆ **02/8050-6712.**

Department Stores

ARMANI MEGASTORE
Via Manzoni 31 (Metro: Montenapoleone).

I don't know what to call this except a department store, although the word "showroom" comes to mind, as does "showcase" . . . as does "ohmigod." I am both horrified and delighted with the store and think all students of retail, marketing, and merchandising should rush here for a look-see. Everyone else: Well, you are on your own.

The store is almost a city block long and has three levels, some of which bleed through from one to the next to add height and drama. The giant video screen says it all—this is a store for people who don't know how to read (although there is a small bookstore upstairs).

You'll also find a cafe, a branch of Nobu, a florist, and several of the Armani lines (many of which have goods that are not sold elsewhere, such as the home furnishings, which look like something designed by Terence Conran). Casa Armani is going fancy on that look, so stay tuned—bespoke furniture will be next.

I am partial to the denim line because the logo is AJ, which are my son's initials. To me, the best part of the store is the large makeup bar because the Giorgio Armani makeup is great and relatively hard to find, even in Italy.

Note that the more prestigious Armani lines are not sold here. Giorgio Armani (Black Label) is located at Via Sant' Andrea 9, while the Armani Collezioni boutique is at Via Montenapoleone 2. ✆ **02/7231-8600.** www.armani-viamanzoni31.it.

Coin

Piazza Giornate 5; Corso Vercelli 30–32; Piazzale Cantore; Piazzale Loreta.

Pronounced "co-*een,*" this department store is not as convenient or as much fun as La Rinascente. But if you find yourself near one of the four locations, by all means check it out. I feel like Coin has more energy than La Rinascente and is more likely to have hot styles and designer copies. In fact, Coin specializes in designer-inspired looks at moderate prices; it has completely re-created itself in the last couple years and is far more upscale than ever before. ✆ **02/5519-2083** for the Piazza Giornate location. www.coin.it.

La Rinascente

Piazza del Duomo (Metro: Duomo).

The mother of all Milanese department stores has shed its chrysalis and emerged a social butterfly.

There's a ton of merchandise here, making it a good place to see a lot and absorb trends and makers quickly. The style of the store is in the American-Anglo model, so don't expect all goods to be Italian, and don't expect to feel very Italian while shopping here. Things are organized by brand; there's also a mezzanine level of big-name accessories.

Note that this is a full-service department store; along with the cafe, there are hairdresser and beauty facilities, free alterations (except on sale goods), banking facilities with an ATM, customer service, and more.

The store does not close for lunch during the week. The hours are extraordinary, especially for Italy: Monday to Saturday from 9am to 10pm, Sunday from 10am to 8pm. You can go to church at the Duomo and then go shopping! © **02/88-521.** www.rinascente.it.

OVIESSE

Corso Buenos Aires 35 (Metro: Porta Venezia).

Technically, this might be a lifestyle store, not a department store; it is the antithesis of the Armani Megastore. It is a temple to cheap thrills—the most exciting copies of fashions for the least amount of money you have ever seen. It is the Italian version of H&M and then some. I went nuts here and dream of going to all the other branches. Skirts for 16€ ($21). Knit polo shirts for 12€ ($16). You get my drift. Sizes up to 52, although the sizes do run a little small. © **02/2040-4801.** www.oviesse.it.

UPIM

Corso Buenos Aires 21 (Metro: Porta Venezia); many other locations in town.

UPIM, sort of a dime store for fashion and real people, is not as cutting edge as it used to be. Still, this store is useful partly because it doesn't close for lunch, and partly because it has a supermarket in the basement. It's worth exploring; look for inexpensive cashmere sweaters (if you come in the winter). ✆ 800/824-040 in Italy. www.upim.it.

Designer Boutiques

American Big Names

Obviously you didn't go to Italy to buy American designs. And it's obvious that I am quite shaken by that **Juicy Couture** store on the Via della Spiga. No question, there is a Yank invasion taking place in many different financial brackets. **Timberland** has three stores in town; **Foot Locker** is everywhere; and **Guess** has opened quite a temple to teens, its second store in Italy, at Piazza San Babila. (The other is in Florence.) **Tiffany & Co.,** I welcome to the Via della Spiga, but Juicy? Give me a break. **Dsquared2** (in the Brera district) is more interesting, I guess; hmmm, let me think about that.

Among the foreign-based arrivals is the makeup guru from Canada by way of Estée Lauder, **MAC** (Via Fiori Chiari 12), which has already moved off Via della Spiga to a very spiffy shop in the Brera district. **Brooks Brothers** has opened up all over Italy; there's even a small store in Como. And **Ralph Lauren** is at Via Montenapoleone 4.

Keep in mind that American brands (and by that I mean North American—from both the U.S. and Canada) are always going to cost more in Europe than they do back home.

Continental & U.K. Big Names

Use the Montenapoleone Metro stop for all listings unless otherwise noted.

Burberry
Via Pietro Verri 7.

Celine
Via Montenapoleone 25.

CHANEL
Via Sant'Andrea 10.

CHRISTIAN DIOR
Via Montenapoleone 12.

ESCADA
Corso Matteotti 22 (Metro: San Babila).

FOGAL
Via Montenapoleone 1.

GAULTIER
Via della Spiga 20.

GIEVES & HAWKES
Via Manzoni 12.

HERMÈS
Via Sant'Andrea 21.

HUGO BOSS
Corso Matteotti 11 (Metro: San Babila).

KENZO
Via Sant'Andrea 11.

LAURA ASHLEY
Via Brera 4 (Metro: Duomo).

LOUIS VUITTON
Galleria Vittorio Emanuele II.

PAUL SMITH
Via Manzoni 30.

RENA LANGE
Via della Spiga 7.

SONIA RYKIEL
Corso Matteotti 3 (Metro: San Babila).

VENTILO
Via Manzoni 25.

VIKTOR & ROLF
Via Sant'Andrea 14.

WOLFORD
Via Manzoni 16b.

ITALIAN BIG NAMES

Use the Montenapoleone Metro stop for all listings unless otherwise noted. For details on many of these well-known brand names, check out the "Dictionary of Taste & Design" (p. 55).

ALBERTA FERRETTI
Via Montenapoleone 21.

ANTONIO FUSCO
Via Sant'Andrea 11.

ARMANI COLLEZIONI
Via Montenapoleone 2.

BOTTEGA VENETA
Via Montenapoleone 5.

BRIONI
Via Gesù 4.

D&G UOMO
Corso Venezia 7 (Metro: San Babila).

DIESEL
Galleria San Carlo (Metro: San Babila).

DOLCE & GABBANA
Via della Spiga 2.

EMILIO PUCCI
Via Montenapoleone 14.

ERMENEGILDO ZEGNA
Via Pietro Verri 3.

ETRO
Via Montenapoleone 5.

FENDI
Via Sant'Andrea 16.

GIANFRANCO FERRÉ
Via Sant'Andrea 15.

GIORGIO ARMANI
Armani Megastore, Via Manzoni 31.

GIORGIO ARMANI (BLACK LABEL)
Via Sant'Andrea 9.

GUCCI
Via Montenapoleone 7.

JUST CAVALLI
Via della Spiga 42.

KITON
Via Gesù 11.

KRIZIA
Via della Spiga 23.

LA PERLA
Via Montenapoleone 1.

LA PERLA UOMO
Via Manzoni 17.

LAURA BIAGIOTTI
Via Borgospesso 19.

LES COPAINS
Via Manzoni 21.

MARIELLA BURANI
Via Montenapoleone 3.

MARINA RINALDI
Corso Vittorio Emanuele II at Galleria Passarella 2 (Metro: San Babila).

MAX & CO.
Via Victor Hugo 1 (Metro: Duomo).

MAX MARA
Corso Vittorio Emanuele II (Metro: San Babila).

MISSONI
Via Sant'Andrea 2.

MIU MIU
Via Sant'Andrea 21.

MOSCHINO
Via della Spiga 30.

NAZARENO GABRIELLI
Via Montenapoleone 23.

PHILOSOPHY DI ALBERTA FERRETTI
Via Montenapoleone 19.

PRADA
Via Montenapoleone 18.

ROBERTO CAVALLI
Via della Spiga 42.

SALVATORE FERRAGAMO
Via Montenapoleone 3.

TOD'S
Via della Spiga 22.

Discounters

See "Outlets (In Town)" (p. 275) for more good deals.

BASEMENT
Via Senato 15 (Metro: San Babila).

True to its name, this store is in a basement. You must be looking for it in order to spot the stairs that lead to the door. The small space contains neat racks of designer clothes, plus a few accessories. The selection wasn't great when we visited, but because the location is so handy, you might want to stop in. Yes, Armani. ✆ **02/7631-7913.**

DMAGAZINE
Via Montenapoleone 26 (Metro: Montenapoleone).

Considering the address and convenience factor, this one is a must-do: a discount store selling high-end fashion names right in the heart of the biggest fashion stores in town and not far from a Metro stop. Most of the time, I see a few items of note but am soon yawning. This visit, I was drooling over the racks of Dries Van Noten and didn't want to let go. There were Lagerfeld shoes, Miu Miu clothes, and some Helmut Lang items. The names were in place; the prices were fair. I diet tomorrow. ✆ **02/7600-6027.**

IL SALVAGENTE
Via Fratelli Bronzetti 16 (no nearby Metro).

Il Salvagente is a famous off-price shop located in a tony residential area. There is no sign out front and no indication that you are to enter through the gate, walk down the driveway, and continue toward the courtyard, where you will eventually find a sign that marks the entrance. This place looks like a prison; you will be asked to use a locker for your shopping bags and maybe even your purse (though dogs and baby strollers are allowed inside).

American and European styles from big-name designers, even in larger sizes, are sold from two floors of retail space. While the labels are still in the clothes, the merchandise is not well organized, so you must be feeling very strong to go through it all. There's so much here that you have a good chance of finding something worthwhile, but you could strike out. Some items have been seen on runways or are over a season old; not everything is new or in perfect condition.

On various visits, however, I've spotted Krizia, Armani, Valentino, Guy Laroche, Trussardi, made-in-Italy Lacroix handbags, and designer sunglasses for 50€ ($65) each. On my most recent visit, I was truly dizzy from all the choices. I once happened on the January sale, when prices at the register were 30% lower than the lowest ticketed price.

Remember: The atmosphere is drab; the display is zero. This place is for the strong and the hungry. Dressing rooms are available, however. Pay attention to the hours: The store is closed Monday until 3pm. On Wednesday and Saturday, it does not close for lunch and is open nonstop from 10am to 7pm. Tuesday through Friday, it's open from 10am to 12:40pm and 3 to 7pm. ✆ **02/7611-0328.** www.salvagentemilano.it.

Il Salvagente Bimbi
Via Balzaretti 28 (no nearby Metro).

This is a separate shop from Il Salvagente, specifically for children's clothing, but it's harder to find—ask for a map at Il Salvagente and you can walk from there. It's hard to find a taxi to get home, so you may want to ask an employee to call you a cab. "Taxi" in Italian is *taxi.*

Note: I used a car and driver to get here, and my Milanese driver got lost. Still, if you're looking for expensive kids' clothing at affordable prices, this is the place. ✆ **02/2668-0764.** www.salvagentemilano.it.

Vestistock
Viale Romagna 19; Via Boscovich 17; and others (no nearby Metro).

Vestistock is a chain of discount shops in various neighborhoods, including the very convenient Buenos Aires for Viale Romagna and the train-station district for Via Boscovich. If you hit it lucky, you can choose from labels such as Les Copains, Moschino, Versace, Montana, and more. There are men's, women's, and kids' clothes as well as accessories, so go and have a ball. Take bus no. 60, 90, or 91 for the Buenos Aires area shop, or call for more specific directions.

If you prefer the store between the train station and many major hotels, it's open nonstop from 9:30am to 6:30pm Monday through Friday. When I visited, I saw Tod's boots and plenty of men's clothing in large sizes. ✆ **02/749-0502.** www.vestistock.it.

Flea Markets

The following markets sell all manner of old and/or used things—what we Americans consider a flea market. The words the Italians use to describe such a market are *mercato di pulci.* Note that more and more flea markets are opening all over Italy, so ask your hotel's concierge if there is a new market near you, and check the pages of the monthly magazine *Dove* (pronounced "do-*vay*"; Italian for "where") for fairs and flea markets in nearby communities.

BOLLATE ANTIQUES MARKET
Piazza Vittorio Veneto, Bollate.

Take the train or a taxi to this suburb on the north side of Milan, where there is a Sunday *mercato dell'usato,* or antiques market. Unlike most Sunday markets, which are held once a month, this one is held weekly. Most of the 300 dealers sell English antiques, if you can believe that; silver is especially hot, as are old prints. There's not much in the way of bed linens, but there are some old hats and a fair amount of furniture.

Consider renting a car for this day in the country, or hop the bus: Take the no. 90 or 91 to the Piazza della Libertà in Bollate. Open from 8am to 6pm.

BRERA ANTIQUES MARKET (MERCATONE DELL'ANTIQUARIATO)
Via Brera (Metro: Duomo).

This flea market, held on the third Saturday of each month, is a local favorite. Because it takes place right in the heart of downtown Milan (in the shadow of La Scala, in fact), this is a drop-dead-chic market to be seen prowling. About 50 antiques dealers set up stalls, and many artists and designers turn out. To find it, just head for Via Brera. Do wear your fur and walk your dog if at all possible.

NAVIGLI ANTIQUES MARKET
Grand Navigli (Metro: Porta Genova).

If flea markets are your thing, be in Milan on the last Sunday of the month. Then you can spend midmorning at this fabulous flea market, which stretches all the way from Porta Ticinese to Porta Genova and the Viale Papiniano. With approximately 400 dealers, some say it's the most stylish flea market in all of Europe. You'll find the usual antiques and wonderful junk, and the crowd is one of Milan's top see-and-be-seen.

While the market is open from 8am to 2pm, do remember this is Italy, not New York—things are most lively from 10am to noon. The area has lots of cafes, so you shop until 2pm and then eat lunch—one perfect Sunday in Milano. To get here, take the no. 19 tram to Ripa di Porta Ticinese or the green line to the Porta Genova Metro stop. See the map on p. 249.

Foodstuffs

ARMANDOLA
Via della Spiga 50 (Metro: Montenapoleone).

This is a teeny-weeny, itty-bitty deli with fresh foods, dried mushrooms, tuna in jars, and all sorts of fancy, expensive, and yummy things. I paid 12€ ($16) for a jar of tuna fish; the recipient said it was worth the price. Sometimes I buy a ready-made picnic here; you can't beat the location for convenience. © **02/7602-1657**. www.armandola.com.

ENOTECA COTTI
Via Solferino 42 (Metro: Duomo).

Considered one of the best wine stores in Milano, it also has serious olive oil, as is the custom at a good *enoteca.* ✆ **02/657-2995.** www.enotecacotti.it.

FREE SHOP
Centrale train station (Metro: Centrale).

Don't snicker. I do a lot of my gourmet-food shopping here because it's convenient. Pick up some Italian specialty food items for gifts and home use. ✆ **02/669-1273.**

Home Style/Showrooms

B&B ITALIA
Via Durini 14 (Metro: San Babila).

Almost a supermarket of design stuff, this showroom is new to the area and another in a string of important style shops. Some smalls and accessories are sold, too. ✆ **02/764-441.** www.bebitalia.it.

CASSINA
Via Durini 16 (Metro: San Babila or Duomo).

One of the long-standing big names in post–World War II design, Cassina makes mostly office furniture, but all of its pieces are quite avant-garde. Colors are vibrant; lines are beyond clean. I popped into this showroom recently to look at the leather chairs designed by Mario Bellini, which are the prototype for the plastic Bellini chairs that my friend Alan makes with Bellini (at a Target store near you). Even though I was just snooping, the people in the showroom could not have been more gracious. ✆ **02/7602-0745.** www.cassina.com.

Lisa Corti Home Textile Emporium

Via Conchetta 6 (Tram: 15).

I don't even know how to describe this space or shopping experience. First off, you should understand who Lisa Corti is—an artist and magician with color and textiles, whose work is sold at Saks Fifth Avenue. She is best known for her home design for table and bed and sofa, but she also makes clothes for women and children, accessories, and, at one time, dishes and ceramics. She is an artist and does it all; her work is her signature. Even her postcards are glorious (and free).

The showroom is a real workroom; the shopping op is sort of like being in the factory outlet. The prices are not low, but they're still just a fraction of what you'd see in the U.S. I paid about 120€ ($156) for a quilt that cost 200€ ($260) in the south of Italy, and 280€ ($364) at Saks.

The store does tax refunds, and someone there does speak English. You might want to call ahead before you make the trek. The showroom is in the middle of nowhere—if you take a taxi, have the driver wait for you. There is a front door on the street, but I didn't find it and went in through the courtyard. I also called from my mobile phone, as I thought I was lost. © **02/5810-0031.** www.lisacorti.com.

Jewelry

Angela Pintaldi

Piazza Sant'Erasmo 9 (Metro: Duomo).

This is very serious costume jewelry. Pintaldi's work is similar to Bulgari, but funkier. For the last decade, she has ruled as the "in" creator of creative and expressive jewels, frequently made with semiprecious stones. She also works with ivory and other materials, based on color and texture—pure magic meets pure art. © **02/781-778.**

You & Me
Via della Spiga 50 (Metro: Montenapoleone).

This is one of my new favorite stores in town—it sells costume jewelry in the form of accessories, meaning there's necklaces but also jeweled sandals and handbags. The store is tiny, but the look is big. While everything here is stellar, the most remarkable effect is the Birkin-style faux-croc handbag with the jewel-encrusted clasp that will make you faint dead away. Everything is very creative and fairly priced; sandals are about $100, necklaces $200, and bags $300 to $400. There's also a store in Venice. © **02/7600-6039**. www.youandme.it.

Linens & Lace

Bassetti
Corso Vercelli 25; Corso Garibaldi 20; Corso Vittorio Emanuele II 15 (Metro: Duomo).

A famous name for years, Bassetti makes the kind of linens that fall between ready-to-wear and couture—they're more affordable than the big-time expensive stuff and far nicer than anything you'd find at the low end. Although it does sell colors, its hot look is paisley fabrics in the Etro vein. There are branch stores in every major Italian city. © **800/820-129** in Italy. www.bassetti.com.

Bellora
Via Manzoni 43 (Metro: Montenapoleone).

This more-than-a-century-old Italian firm is famous for its bed linens and pajamas. It does nursery sets for infants and a kids' line of sheets as well. Styles vary between old-fashioned solid linens (which you must have embroidered, *cara*) to lively colors in the current mode. There's also a made-to-measure department. © **02/659-6361**. www.bellora.it.

FRETTE

Via Montenapoleone 21 (Metro: Montenapoleone).

This line has gone so far upscale that it now calls itself "home couture," with items such as pajamas and robes and leisure clothing, as well as bedding. Naturally there is a business in custom-created bed linens as well. There is an outlet store near the Jolly Hotel President at Largo Augusto. ✆ **02/783-950.** www.frette.com.

JESURUM

Via Pietro Verri 4 (Metro: Duomo).

A branch of the Venetian linen house, famous for old lace brocades—really swank stuff, with prices to match. ✆ **02/7601-5045.** www.jesurum.it.

PRATESI

Via Verdi 6 (Metro: Duomo).

This is a new address, somewhat hidden in the courtyard of a palazzo. It's the Milan retail shop for this family-held linen and luxe group. Pratesi is most famous for bed linens, but you'll also find baby- and beachwear, and bathrobes, and quality like you've never seen; prices are 25% to 40% lower than in the U.S. The store is long and narrow and fits around one side of a light-filled courtyard, with various parts of the showroom devoted to pajamas, toiletries, towels, and so on.

By mentioning this, I am assuming you can't make it to the outlet store (p. 176). If it makes you feel any better, sheets sold at regular retail go for about $1,000 each, but they will last for well over 25 years. ✆ **02/8058-3058.** www.pratesi.com.

TEZEMIS

Corso Vittorio Emanuele II (Metro: Duomo).

Find pajamas and underwear for young women, in solids or cutie-pie prints, from this fast-growing Italian chain with stores all over Italy. It's a good source for gifts to bring home, as the line is virtually unknown outside of Italy.

Markets

To a local, there's a big difference between a market and a flea market. A market sells fruits and vegetables and dry goods, while a flea market sells old junk. See "Flea Markets" (p. 267) for more about the other kind of market.

MERCATO DI VIALE PAPINIANO (SAN AGOSTINO MARKET)
Viale Papiniano (Metro: San Agostino).

First, I must admit that no other guidebook calls this the San Agostino Market. I call it that because San Agostino is the name of the closest Metro stop, and it helps me remember where this market is located on the Viale Papiniano.

This is a T-shaped market. The cross of the T is the fruit, food, and vegetable market; the long stroke is the dry-goods market. The dry-goods portion goes on for 2 blocks, so don't quit after the first block. Everything in the world is sold here, including a few designer items that seem to have fallen off the backs of trucks (but are carefully mixed in with less valuable items). For example, one dealer in the dry-goods market seems to specialize in bath articles but also has a small selection of Missoni bathrobes.

You'll find everything from the latest teen fashions to CDs, kitchen supplies, car supplies, pet supplies, aprons, and housedresses. There are also socks, towels, batteries, luggage, underwear, sewing thread, running shoes, designer shoes, lace curtains, and fabrics by the bolt. I saw the best cashmeres at the best prices here.

The market is open on Tuesday and Saturday.

Menswear

Boggi
Piazza San Babila 3 (Metro: San Babila).

Boggi specializes in the English look, the preppy look; whatever you call it, you'll find cable-knit sweaters and plaid hunting trousers. There are several shops, but the main store is near Via Montenapoleone. It's not cheap here, but the quality is very high. © **02/7600-0366.** www.boggi.it.

Cashmere Cotton and Silk
Via Madonnina 19 (Metro: Duomo).

This is one of those fancy stores on the little side streets of Brera that is worth looking at, if only for its charm. It's modern with an old-fashioned feel. Inside, you'll find Milanese yuppies scurrying around, choosing among the shirts, sweaters, and suits made only of the three fibers in the store's name. Prices are very, very high, but the shopping experience makes you feel like royalty. © **02/805-7426.**

Dior Homme
Via Montenapoleone 14 (Metro: Montenapoleone).

I am not sure which is more gorgeous, the architecture or the slim young things who shop here. All worth staring at in this new store, one of several created specifically to sell the work of Hedi Slimane. It's very stainless-steel and art-gallery minimal; the dressing rooms have mirrors created by sensors that relay your image onto the wall. © **02/7631-8822.** www.dior homme.com.

Eddy Monetti
Piazza San Babila 4 (Metro: San Babila).

One of the leading sources for Anglo style in Milan, Monetti deals with rich gentlemen who want to look even richer. It hand-stitches suits and shirts but also sells off the rack. The Monetti customer likes special service and hates to shop; he wants to come here and be pampered and know that he'll walk out looking like a million dollars. ✆ **02/7600-0940.** www.eddy monetti.it.

Ermenegildo Zegna
Via Pietro Verri 3 (Metro: Duomo).

For centuries, the family has excelled in the quality wool business. Until recently, the ready-to-wear was a small sideline, but now, in a smattering of free-standing boutiques, the world's richest men can buy the best suits ready-made in Italy. There's one in Paris, one in Florence, and this shop in Milan, which is the closest to the mill in Biella, and serves as the family flagship. The shop is large and modern and sells classic tailoring to discriminating men. ✆ **02/7600-6437.** www.zegna.com.

Tincati
Piazza Oberdan 2 (Metro: Porta Venezia); many other locations.

Tincati is an old-fashioned men's store, or haberdashery (as they used to be called), with a very good old-world reputation—not for hotshots who want the Euro-Japanese look. Its shirts are famous because they come with a tab that passes between the legs (trust me on this) and an extra collar and two cuffs. ✆ **02/2940-4326.** www.tincati.mi.it.

Outlets (In Town)

Diffusione Tessile (Max Mara Outlet)
Galleria San Carlo 6 (Metro: San Babila).

I can't stop to sing about this outlet, as I am too busy getting there. It's large, it's clean, it looks like a normal store, it has two levels, it takes plastic, it carries all of the Max Mara lines—including Marina Rinaldi (large sizes)—and it has coats for 36€ ($47). Note that this location is in a mall. You will easily find the mall but may have trouble finding the actual store, as the mall has alleys. Ask. ✆ **02/7600-0829.** www.diffusionetessile.it.

OUTLET
Via San Spirito 14 (Metro: San Babila).

Sarah writes: "This tiny shop, located off Via della Spiga, had just opened when we last visited Milan. In fact, it was so new, a permanent name was still under consideration; for the time being, it's to be called simply 'Outlet.' The owner is obviously concentrating on stock rather than titles, as the boutique is full of gorgeous dresses and separates. There are no labels in most of the garments, and I didn't recognize any top designers. However, most items are priced under $100 and the selection is impressive, especially in larger sizes. Everything is new and seasonal, with most styles mimicking those of Eileen Fisher and CP Shades. The displays are arranged by color; I found summer linens in a rainbow of sherbet shades, with evening wear mostly in black (this *is* Milan . . .)." ✆ **02/783-600.**

SPACCIO ETRO
Via Spartaco 3 (no nearby Metro).

This began life as an employee store in the firm's offices, but it's open to the public and is the kind of a secret that every smart shopper in Milan knows about. Now then, did I have fun? I get sweaty just reminiscing. The tiny shop has two levels; the clothes are downstairs. There are bins filled with things: I got men's pocket squares for 20€ ($26) each, silk suspenders for 12€ ($16). You'll also find fabric by the meter and everything else. Ask your hotel's concierge for bus directions. ✆ **02/5502-0216.** www.etro.it.

10 CORSO COMO OUTLET
Via Tazzoli 3 (Metro: Garibaldi).

With the fashion-forward fashion sold at 10 Corso Como (see "The Five Best Stores in Milan" on p. 237), it's not a surprise that it might not all sell or be too far ahead of its time. When the clothes go off the floor in the main store, they are taken around the corner to the outlet. Prices range from reasonable to low; in many cases, the marked-down price is what you would have wanted to pay in the first place (240€/$312 instead of 480€/$624), so it doesn't seem like a real bargain. There are some accessories, as well as menswear.

The outlet is a little hard to find, though it's not much more than a block from the main store. Turn right from the store, then left at the corner, pass the ATA Hotel, and turn onto Via Tazzoli—which is an oblique left, so pay attention. ✆ **02/2900-2674.** www.10corsocomo.com.

Outlets (Out of Town)

FRANCIACORTA OUTLET VILLAGE
Piazza Cascina Moie, Rodengo Saiano.

This is probably the closest outlet mall to Milan, situated between Milan and Verona. There are two different outlet villages in the Brescia area; the other is on the way to Mantua, which is in a different direction. Of the two, I like this one better. Stores include everything from Benetton and Boggi to Frette and Mariella Burani. The mall is located 5km off the A4 and is easy to find—take the Ospitaletto exit and follow the brown OUTLET VILLAGE signs. ✆ **030/681-0364.** www.franciacortaoutlet.it.

SERRAVALLE DESIGNER OUTLET
Via della Moda 1, Serravalle Scrivia.

This is the oldest of the American-style outlet malls in Italy, meaning it's about 8 years old. It's closer to Genoa than Milan, although it's only a 90-minute drive from Milan. It has a village atmosphere and just about every store—and designer boutique—you can imagine, including Brioni, Bruno Magli, Bulgari, Diesel, Diesel Kids, Dolce & Gabbana, Etro, Frette, La Perla, Moncler, Roberto Cavalli, Salvatore Ferragamo, Versace, and more.

Don't try to do this on public transportation from Milan. I spent over an hour with my hotel's concierge and his computer trying to route this, and with changing trains and all that stuff, it was a nightmare not worth attempting. © **0143/609-000.** www.mcarthurglen.it.

Paper Goods

FABRIANO
Via Verri 3 (Metro: Montenapoleone).

This Milan firm sells everything from bound notebooks to pens and papers. You can pick up some fabulous gift items for not much money. © **02/7631-8754.** www.fabrianoboutique.com.

PINEIDER
Corso Europa 13 (Metro: Montenapoleone).

Italy's most famous name in old-fashioned, heavy-duty, richer-than-thou stationery is Pineider, with stores in every major city (and a few locations in Milan). The real news is that this old-time brand has decided to perk itself up, as other companies have done. Accordingly, it has hired the American designer Rebecca Moses, who lives in Milan, and has expanded beyond paper goods to gift items that are chic, sublime, and very expensive. © **02/7602-2353.** www.pineider.com.

Perfume

For the most part, perfume is expensive in Italy, and you must be smart to catch a bargain, so buy at the airport duty-free shop or in **La Rinascente,** where you get a 10% discount at the checkout counter if you show your passport.

There are several branches of the enormous German chain **Douglas** dotted around the main shopping districts. You may want to ask about its Douglas Card, which will bring you extra perks and which you can use in any of its stores worldwide.

If you are a fan of the scent **Acqua di Parma,** note there is a free-standing store at Via Gesù 3. **Etro** also sells its line of perfumes from its shops.

If money is no object, pop into **Profumo** (Via Brera 6), where American and English imports are sold at higher prices than you are used to.

Shoes & Leather Goods

Shoe shops obviously abound, with shoes in just about all price ranges. The greatest problem with cheap shoes is that they wear out more quickly than well-made shoes. You can stick to brand-name shoes in Milan, or explore some of the low-cost no-names—it's all here. No-name shoes start at about 24€ ($31) a pair. Better no-name shoes cost 40€ ($52) a pair. Just wander the middle-class neighborhoods where real people shop.

In expensive shoes, there are two completely different schools of thought: English-style, conservative, country classics that you wear for 20 years, and high-fashion fluff bundles that will last only a season or two but will signal the world that you are a major player.

Please note that I have listed several of the big-name leather-goods firms under "Designer Boutiques: Italian Big Names" (p. 262) because they are more or less icons in the business and most of them also have clothing lines. The following brands are not as famous in the U.S., but they deserve attention while you are studying the scene in Milan.

BOTTEGA VENETA
Via Montenapoleone 5 (Metro: Montenapoleone).

BRUNO MAGLI
Corso Vittorio Emanuele II (Metro: Duomo).

CASADEI
Via Sant'Andrea 15b (Metro: San Babila).

COCCINELLE
Via Manzoni at Via Bigli (Metro: San Babila).

HOGAN
Via Montenaploeone 23 (Metro: Montenapoleone).

VALEXTRA
Piazza San Babila 1 (Metro: San Babila).

Tabletop & Gifts

Don't miss **Lisa Corti** under "Home Style/Showrooms" (p. 269).

HIGH TECH
Piazza XXV Aprile 12 (Metro: Garibaldi).

By Milan standards, High Tech is an enormous place. The second floor is completely devoted to home furnishings, all with the look we've come to associate with the city of Milan. Begun by Aldo Cibic, formerly of Memphis Milano fame. © **02/624-1101.** www.high-techmilano.com.

LORENZI
Via Montenapoleone 9 (Metro: Montenapoleone).

Milan's leading cutlery store, where you can buy all kinds of knives—not just for the table—as well as pipes and other gifts and gadgets for men. © **02/7602-2848.** www.lorenzi.it.

MORONIGOMMA
Corso Matteotti 14 (Metro: San Babila).

This store has plastics from all over the world, so don't buy any of the expensive American stuff. Instead, get a load of the Italian designer vinyl, the car products, and the household items. With its affordable prices, this may be the only store in Milan where you can go wild and not be sorry the next day. It's conveniently located at the start of Via Montenapoleone, on the far side of the Piazza San Babila; there are many other wonderful design hangouts in the area, too. © **02/796-220.** www.moronigomma.it.

Teens & Tweens

Teens need no specific addresses; just plop them onto Corso Buenos Aires. Or try these specialty-label stops:

DIESEL STORE
Galleria San Carlo (Metro: San Babila).

All the Diesel products (way beyond jeans) as well as a Diesel Style Lab; teen heaven. © **02/7639-0583.** www.diesel.com.

H&M
Corso Vittorio Emanuele II (Metro: San Babila).

The Swedish low-cost retailer has taken space once occupied by Benetton, which shows that it's the newest international brand to move in on Italian expertise in low-cost fashion. © **02/7601-7222.** www.hm.com.

ONYX
Corso Vittorio Emanuele II 24 (Metro: San Babila or Duomo).

Cheap thrills and an amazing scene filled with technology and great clothes at great prices—sort of the local version of H&M, but much younger and less sophisticated than Oviesse. © **02/7601-6261.**

ZARA
Corso Vittorio Emanuele II (Metro: San Babila or Duomo).

The Spanish retailer has come to town and is making a big dent on Italian fashions, which it somewhat emulates. © **02/7639-0606.** www.zara.com.

BEYOND MILAN

Past Milan: Parabiago

Parabiago is an industrial suburb of Milan, where many of the shoe factories and leather-accessories people have offices. Many consider it within the metro Milano area and not a day trip; however, no public transportation goes here, and when I asked my driving service about getting here, they made it clear they considered it out of town. Whether you take a car, a taxi, or drive yourself, do remember that even factory stores close for lunch.

CLAUDIO MORLACCHI
Via Castelnuovo 24, Parabiago.

The factory looks like a house, but don't be alarmed. Push the large wooden door and enter into a light, airy courtyard. To the right is a room with a small but wonderful display of all the shoes the Morlacchi people make—among Morlacchi's clients are Lanvin and Guy Laroche. ✆ **0331/555-411.**

FRATELLI ROSSETTI FACTORY
Via Cantù 24, Parabiago.

There is a Fratelli Rossetti boutique in Milan (Via Montenapoleone 1), but why shop there when you can go to the factory in Parabiago? It has no ads and no markings; it kind of looks like a prison from the outside. The shop, in a separate building from the factory, houses a large selection of men's and women's shoes and boots in a big open room with blue rubber flooring. The help does not speak English, but is very friendly. Men's shoes in traditional styles cost 52€ ($68); more elaborate slip-ons cost 100€ ($130); boots start around 80€ ($104); and pumps begin at 64€ ($83). ✆ **0331/55-22-26.** www.rossetti.it.

Lake Como Area

Once upon a time, silk was made in Como and the area around the lakes. There were wonderful outlet stores that you could visit on a Monday morning, when stores in Milan were closed, and you could shop your heart out. Those days are gone.

I won't get into an economic or geopolitical discussion, but as you know, most everything we buy these days is made in Asia. As a result, most of the factory stores in Como and surrounds have closed. Some of the outlets that do exist are professionally in the outlet business or even sell goods from Asia.

If you have a car, you will want to explore this entire area. If you want a fun adventure, you'll come to Como for a taste of the real Italy by way of much luxury and delight.

Getting There

If you have a rail pass, don't use it: It's a waste of money to use one of your travel days on the trip to Como. I got myself a round-trip, first-class ticket for about 15€ ($20). I bought it at the ticket counter in Milan's Centrale rain station; the transaction was in Italian, so I didn't get too much of what was happening. The ticket was marked "via Monza," and I panicked that I would have to make a connection in Monza—but I did not. The ride was a simple 20 minutes on a commuter train, nothing to it.

On another trip, I booked a car and driver from Milan for a half-day and 150km (93 miles). The cost was about 160€ ($208), which I thought was okay except the driver kept getting lost and I was paying by the hour. Instead, consider arriving by train and then hiring a local taxi to drive and wait for you.

Last trip, I drove. Driving to Como is wonderful and easy, especially if you don't go in or out of Milan. Driving to the Armani outlet, however, was a nightmare—basically because the road was not properly marked, the woman I kept calling at Armani got annoyed with me, and I quit after 3 very frustrating hours. Once I drove into town, got directions, and headed out again, everything was very simple. (Specific directions below.)

Arriving in Como

The train station, **Como San Giovanni,** has a tourist office window, many free brochures, a newsstand, and a bar. Out front, you'll find a line of taxis and vans with, finally, some English-speaking help. You can hire a taxi for the morning to take you around and wait while you shop.

The town proper is located below the train station, within walking distance. However, if you've come on a Monday, most of the town will be closed in the morning, so you might as well head first to your hotel (if you are staying for a while) or the outlets.

Sleeping in Como

Hotel Metropole Suisse

Piazza Cavour 19, Como.

I kind of hate to tell you about this hotel because I'd like it to remain my personal secret and hideaway. Born to Shop news director Sarah Lahey found this place online; it seemed like a good price and a good location, so we booked it. It turns out to be the dream three-star you've always wanted, right on the main square at the lakefront. You can walk everywhere in town or take ferries; you will need a car (which the hotel will garage for you) to get to outlets or other villages without ferry service. Rates vary with the season but start at $200. ✆ **031/269-444.** www.hotelmetropolesuisse.com.

Hotel Miralago

Piazza Risorgimento, Cernobbio.

If you love the area but can't handle the landmark Villa d'Este (see below), this small, *intime* hotel is right in downtown Cernobbio (which is all of 2 blocks long) and also faces the lake. You can walk to the Villa d'Este from here for a look-see, or vice versa. This is not the Ritz, or anything like the Villa d'Este, but if you want charm on a three-star level and this location, you will thank me forever. The rooms have been recently renovated and, best of all, prices are reasonable. A double room ranges from $140 out of season to $200 in high season. © **031/510-125.** www.hotelmiralago.it.

VILLA D'ESTE
Via Regina 40, Cernobbio.

This is the dream hotel of a lifetime: the wedding hotel, the honeymoon hotel, the romantic hotel, the escape-from-reality hotel, the George-Clooney-is-your-neighbor hotel. Set in park-like surroundings, the grand hotel has gardens, some stores, fine dining, and long halls where your dachshund can run at full speed with his ears flopping. (Well, mine did.) The so-called villa is really more of a palace (and was once a private home). You can sit outside on the terrace overlooking the lake, sip a coffee, and feel royal. Indeed, the hotel has royal connections going back to Caroline, Princess of Wales, and it publishes a guide to the history of the villa so you can get all the glam first-hand. There's a spa, nearby golf, cooking classes—it's a world of luxury that removes you from the world of cares, woes, worries, and realities. Rates vary but start at around 450€ ($585). You can book through Leading Hotels of the World (© **800/223-6800;** www.lhw.com) or contact the hotel directly. © **031/3481.** www.villadeste.it.

THE SHOPPING SCENE

Como lies at the southern end of Lake Como, about 50km (31 miles) north of Milan, and offers all the charm you want in a teeny, old-fashioned village on the edge of a lake surrounded by forest and Switzerland.

The town caters to the wealthy landowners who live in the villas surrounding the lake, as well as to the merely rich and/or fashionable who stop by for the weekend (as Gianni Versace used to do). There are also loads of day-trippers and visitors, many of whom are coming from Switzerland.

Best buys in the village shops include clothes, silk scarves, and leather goods. While you'll find lots of antiques, most of them are fakes or reproductions. The downtown also has few big designer names, which is part of its charm. One of my favorite stores is the local branch of **Standa,** because I love dime stores and because there is a supermarket in the lower level. You come to Como and the area to absorb a piece of the real Italy, to shop like a local, to look out at the lake and be spirited away to romance and cashmere, with the last remaining rustle of silk. You come here because if you don't, you will have missed one of the most magical places on earth. Sarah came looking for George Clooney. No luck. The shopping is just part of the magic.

If you are making a return to this area after a few years, note that the most wonderful stores are all closed now. Yes, even Ratti. While **La Tessitura** (p. 287) is owned by Mantero, it is nothing like the old Mantero shop in downtown Como. RIP. There is fun shopping, but the serious shopping is out of town and only accessible to those with a car.

Okay, wait a second—there is still a **Ratti** outlet, which I have written about below. But the gorgeous outlet in the palazzo overlooking the lake that was easy to get to and had incredible designer goods—that one is gone forever. Just like my waist.

About Monday

While several outlets are open on Monday morning, most of the stores in Como are not. And the **Silk Museum** (Via Castelnuovo 1; © **031/303-180;** www.museosetacomo.com) is only open Tuesday through Friday, from 9am to noon and 3 to 6pm.

The Last of the Como Outlets

Diffusione Seta

Via Pasquale Paoli 3, Como.

This is one of the oddest outlets I have ever been to. It's large, it's easy to shop, and it has designer merchandise at half price. It also has a lot of silks from Asia. Sarah bought a white linen shirt here for 12€ ($16) that was one of the best buys of our trip. Go figure. ✆ **031/523-800.**

EMPORIO DELLA SETTA
Via Canturina 190, Como.

The Emporium of Silk sounds pretty good, huh? Many big designer names are represented in this clearinghouse for silk from the local mills. Discounts are in the 40% range. To add to your savings, there are seasonal sales in January and July. ✆ **031/591-420.**

LA TESSITURA
Viale Franklin Delano Roosevelt 2a, Como.

This is a large warehouse-cum-showroom that is so chic it even has a cafe. Better still—it has its own parking lot. And the parking is free. The space is filled with merchandise; note that the home style toward the rear is much better than the fashion here. ✆ **031/321-666.** www.latessitura.com.

SETERIE MARTINETTI
Via Torriani 41, Como.

By now you surely know that *seterie* means silk maker in Italian. This is rumored to be one of the best silk resources in the area, although there are so many good ones that it is hard to quantify them all. You'll find the usual scarves, ties, robes, and yummy items from the usual cast of international big-name designers. Closed on Monday morning. ✆ **031/269-053.**

AROUND COMO

Let me now mention the words Fino Mornasco and Lomazzo, which are names of towns where there are zillions of factories and some outlets. Etro is located here (no outlet, though). I could drive this area blindfolded because of the number of streets I have been up and down while looking for the Armani outlet. If you are on your honeymoon, I do not suggest this adventure.

But if you can afford the gas, like the spirit of the chase more than the actual bargain, and think this sort of thing is fun—off you go. And don't tell me about the Loris Abate outlet store. I know it's there. Believe me, I've passed it about a hundred times and each time I always say "the best bathrobe my husband ever owned was from Loris Abate."

Suggestion: Have your hotel's concierge do a Michelin printout for each address, with directions in Italian, so when you are lost (as you will be, I promise) you can ask people for help.

Diesel Outlet

Via Odescalchi 2, Vertemate (exit Fino Mornasco).

This outlet is not far from Armani on the SS35 highway; together they could be the shopping spree of your life. Prices are basically half of regular retail. It's open Monday to Saturday from 10am to 12:30pm and 3 to 7:30pm. © **031/901-573.** www.diesel.com.

Emporio Lario

Via Vittorio Veneta 52, Cirimido (exit Lomazzo).

Lario is a very exclusive brand of fancy and expensive shoes that most Americans do not know about. Never mind. This factory also makes shoes for many designers—I think it made the best shoes of my life, bought at Bob Elliot in Charleston. Open Monday through Friday from 9:30am to 7pm. © **031/ 352-3255.**

Factory Store (Giorgio Armani)

Vertemate (exit Fino Mornasco).

For those with cars and a spirit of adventure, head over to the new Armani outlet at the Intai factory, near Bregnano (which is between Milan and Como and no, I don't mean Bregamo and this isn't a typo).

Take the A9 north from Milan to the Fino Mornasco exit, and head for Bregnano (which isn't marked and will make you screaming crazy). Turn right at this unmarked junction; keep driving and driving and praying; look for the factory at the crossroad of SS35. Final tip—the outlet is only marked with the words FACTORY STORE on the front. Honest. For more specific directions, call ✆ **031/887-373.**

Once you've gotten there, you can do more than celebrate. This is a large, two-level outlet that sells everything from lingerie to kids' clothing to home style. I find the men's selection better than the women's, but it does depend how you hit it. I bought the most wonderful trouser suit here for about 400€ ($520). That was a size ago. This trip, nothing fit me.

The store is open Monday through Saturday from 10am to 1pm and 2 to 7pm. Credit cards are accepted.

RATTI
Via Vivaldi 6, Cadorago.

Perhaps my feelings about this outlet are colored by the fact that we were really looking for the Armani outlet; or the fact that when we drove in and were asked to surrender our passports, I discovered I'd lost my passport. Either way, the old Ratti will always have a space in my heart. This one is hit-or-miss, if you can find it. Open Tuesday through Friday from 9:30am to 6:30pm, Monday from 3 to 7pm. ✆ **031/886-6280.**

Past Como: Biella

Biella is a mill town in northern Italy, famous because it is the headquarters of the **Zegna** woolen mills. It's also known for the **Fila** outlet store and other nearby outlets. Paola, from the Delta flight, gave me this info.

ERMENEGILDO ZEGNA
Via Roma 99, Trivero.

This is the one you've been looking for. This is the really big time of the big time. Of course, price tags—even at discount—can also be big time, but there is no finer or more famous name in Italian wool and cashmere. The store takes credit cards and is used to tourists and visitors. Trivero is near Biella; follow signs to Centro Zegna. ✆ **015/756-541.** www.zegna.com.

FILA
Via Cesare Battisti 28, Biella.

Here's an exception to factory stores being open on Monday morning—this factory store does open on Monday, but only at 3pm. It closes at noon, not 1pm, for lunch daily and reopens at 3pm. Needless to say, Fila is an enormously famous name internationally. It is most famous in the U.S. for tennis gear, but it makes clothing and gear for all sports; the ski stuff is sublime. There are bargains for all members of the family, and the store is conveniently located near the cute part of the old city. ✆ **015/34-141.**

FRATELLI PIACENZA LANIFICIO
Biella.

This place is a mill for cashmere, wools, and mohair, which is big this year. There are bargains, but you are still looking at price tags over 520€ ($676) for a cashmere coat. Rumor has it that Escada gets its goods here. Call for an appointment and directions. ✆ **015/61-461.** www.piacenza1733.it.

MAGLIFICIO DELLA ARTEMA
Strada Trossi 31, Verrone-Biella.

Located right outside Biella, this is yet another cashmere resource from the famous mills; watch for ARTEMA signs. It sells the Zegna line as well as other Italian labels, including some designers from the big-name circuit—rotating according to availability, of course. It stocks everything from underwear to outerwear. ✆ **015/255-8382.**

Vercelli (Beyond Biella)

Vercelli is actually a province that includes the city of Biella. It also includes a zillion mills, more known for their wool and cashmere than for silk, but some silken luxuries can be found. Vercelli is about a 2-hour drive (one-way) from Milan, so I didn't go. Let me know how it is if you get there. I did have the concierge call from Milan; he also said that the Loro Piana cashmere factory is nearby, though it has moved recently.

SAMBONET
Via XXVI Aprile 62–64, Vercelli.

When I told Logan, my insider source, the saga of my enthusiasm for the cashmere mill and my reluctance to go on a blind trek, she threw in another nearby resource. From the sublime to the ridiculous, guys, this one sells pots and pans—big-name pots and pans—and stainless, flatware, and silver plate, including seconds from the Cordon Bleu line. ✆ **0161/597-219.**

Switzerland

Not far from Como, you find yourself in Switzerland, headed toward Lugano. But don't panic; you're also on the way to **FoxTown** (www.foxtown.ch), which is a 5-minute drive into Switzerland across the Italian border.

FoxTown is an outlet village with around 130 stores (200 brands), a casino (for husbands, no doubt), and a cafe. There's quite a large number of big-name designer outlets here, including Bruno Magli, Loro Piana, Valentino, and Yves Saint Laurent.

Remember, Switzerland is not in the euro zone, so prices are not in euros but in Swiss Francs. If the U.S. dollar is weak, you may save money by shopping with CHF.

For specific directions, call ✆ **410/848-828-888.** The mall is open 7 days a week, from 11am to 7pm nonstop. If you are driving, you want the Mendriso exit, which is 7km (4⅓ miles) from the Swiss-Italian border.

Chapter Nine

THE RIVIERA

MEDITERRANEAN DREAMS

While most American tourists think of the Riviera as the French Riviera and even call it the Côte d'Azur, the Mediterranean does not stop at the French-Italian border and thus provides many more miles of beach, cute cities, fresh seafood, and shopping days. Yes, this is sort of an extension of the Côte d'Azur, but it's very Italian and amazingly different for real estate that is so close to the glitzy French towns.

Technically speaking, the Italian Riviera is divided into two parts. The first part, called the Riviera di Ponente, begins at the French border and stretches east to Genoa. The second part, the Riviera di Levante, reaches from Genoa to La Spezia. (Note that the Amalfi Coast—much farther south—is covered in chapter 5 and is in no way part of the Italian Riviera.)

If you are driving this route as a way to get to Florence, shortly after La Spezia you will get to Livorno, the port city for Florence. Note that directional signs are marked to Livorno and not Firenze. You don't really see the signs for Florence until you take a turnoff *before* you get to Livorno.

Combining the Italian Riviera with the Tuscan hill towns is a great way to taste a lot of olive oil and see a lot of Italy. Did someone say "road trip"? We packed up the Peugeot, the bags, and the dog and began in Nice, then sped into the hills—the foothills of the Alps (which make up the Italian Riviera) and then the hills of Tuscany. *Mamma mia,* what a trip. Having a car, of course, meant we could get to more outlets and schlep more stuff.

Just as northern and southern Italy have their own personalities, just as big cities differ dramatically from country towns and villages, so the Riviera offers a totally different style and way of life. Most of the time in your visit here, you will be in the state of Liguria (this comes before bliss and after France), which because of its shape and its coastal layout is very unique. Even the olive oil has a specific taste to it.

Forget your experiences in St. Tropez or Cannes; there's no hustle here—except maybe in Portofino. There's just sunshine, boats, and lunch. The pace of life is slow; the people are friendly. You can stay in glam palace hotels overlooking the sea or tiny little three-stars right next to the sea. You can drive the hills or walk out at night and just prowl the piazza. The lights twinkle, the gas is less expensive, and you can shop at night. This part of Italy is known for its flowers, its olive oil, its seafood, and, to me, the very casual chic and warmth of the lifestyle, the people, and the things you will buy.

Andiamo.

GETTING THERE

This part of Italy is readily accessible and is served by a number of autostrada highways. Like many jet-set locations, this one takes a little organization to get to. It also doesn't hurt to study a map when you make your plans. I had a lot of trouble figuring out whether towns I wanted to see were before or after Genoa; this happens to make a big difference in your routing.

By Plane

This region is accessible via several airports. To make our Riviera explorations complete, we started at one end by flying to

Nice, in France. It has the largest international airport in the area, with service to most parts of the globe. It also welcomes some 22 low-cost carriers such as easyJet and Ryanair. You are only a half-hour from Monte Carlo and about an hour from the Italian border. It's 2 hours to Genoa (without traffic) if you drive like an Italian.

If you choose to fly into **Genoa**—the next largest international airport in the area—then you will either be backtracking toward France and then coming back, or up and around and then down, or just going forward through the second part of the Italian Riviera. Again, you need that map!

The other way to do this is the reverse of what we did: Fly into **Pisa** or **Florence,** pursue your dreams there, and then drive up, up, and away across the Riviera in the western direction toward France. In this case, you might want to return the car in Genoa or Nice depending on drop-off charges.

Alternatively, if you want to fly round-trip to **Milan,** you can rent your car at the Malpensa International Airport and never even go into the city of Milan (which you don't want to do with a car, anyway). Just head down the highway south, cut over toward La Spezia, work your way up the Riviera to Genoa, and then circle back up north from Genoa, eventually getting back to Milan and making a very nice tour through the center of Italy. You'll hit several outlet malls if you take this route, by the way. There are two routes of the autostrada that can serve you well, since most roads in Italy lead north-south. With that map in hand, check the Milan-Genoa route and the Milan-Parma route that brings you to La Spezia.

By Train

Again, you have more or less the same approaches as above. If you have a rail pass, you can easily hop on and off the train in various cities. Or you can take the train to where you want to be, rent a car, and then head toward the beaches and the buys.

By Ship

Cruises of the Mediterranean often have ports of call on the Italian Riviera. This is perhaps the best ever way to see Genoa, because driving in Genoa is a nightmare. Ships often anchor off the coast and tender to Portofino; from there you can take a public bus to Santa Margherita Ligure. Ships may also come into ports that allow you to tour the Cinque Terre—far easier by boat than by car. If you are not familiar with **easyCruise** (www.easycruise.com), take a look at the website—this is a casual, low-cost cruise line by the same folks who brought you easyJet; it serves several Italian Riviera ports.

By Car

Italy is not as big as it looks. Italian drivers are aggressive, and the roads—yes, even the highways—are often curvy and dark (you go through hundreds of tunnels), but a car gives you the freedom to pop on or off the highway, to drive through small villages, to look at houses, to check out hotels, and to be part of the passing parade. Note that the parade is often at a standstill in July and August, when traffic jams may make you curse the choice to drive. We did this trip in May—it was gorgeous weather and there were no traffic problems.

Using Nice as your port of entry, figure on 5 to 6 hours to get to Florence. If you've been on a long-haul flight, lay over in Nice or Monte Carlo for a few days to cut the jet lag and then head out. You just may want to do your car rentals from France rather than Italy for price and insurance reasons.

Note that even in low season and even on the autostrada, you will hit congestion around Genoa. Pretend you are Italian: Wave your arms and shout a lot.

GETTING AROUND

I'd say the basic purpose of this trip is to be in a car and be free to drive around by day and to walk around at night. However,

Stopping for Wine & Outlets

Don't drink and drive, but if you are driving a roundabout route and not sticking strictly to the coast, in nearby Piedmont you can pop into vineyards, wine shops, and the vinotherapy spa **Caudalíe** (www.caudalie.com) at the **Relais San Maurizio** (© 0141/841-900; www.relaissanmaurizio.it).

If you'd prefer to take your side trip to an outlet mall, you can leave the autostrada at Genoa and head north toward Milan. The **Serravalle Designer Outlet** (© 0143/609-000; www.mcarthurglen.it), a village-style outlet mall that might be the largest in Italy, is less than an hour's drive from that junction; see p. 277 for details.

you can do the trip rather easily by staying in one city as your base camp and using trains, buses, and ferries to visit all the towns. Once in the towns, having a car is more of a pain than a pleasure—especially if you don't have a hotel with parking.

Parking in July and August can be so impossible that it will ruin your vacation. Parking in the off season is usually not too bad, although do know the local rules, since in most cases you must park, go to the little P machine, buy a ticket for the amount of time you want, go back to the car and put the ticket inside the car by the windshield on the driver's side, lock the car, and do your thing. (You know not to leave any luggage or attractive packages in the car.)

If you are driving, remember that you will pay 20€ to 30€ ($26–$39) per night in garage fees at your hotel, so budget accordingly.

SLEEPING IN THE RIVIERA

We first stayed over in Monte Carlo and then based ourselves in Santa Margherita Ligure. The Italian Riviera is small enough that you can stay in one city and go all about on day trips.

The only city that requires a whole other kind of planning is Genoa, which is huge (population almost one million) and has all the big-city hang-ups (traffic, traffic, traffic). But if you want to get a feel for the whole area, you could spend a few nights in Genoa and then move on to a smaller town. For Genoa you don't want a car; for the rest of the Riviera you do.

Tip: **Leading Hotels of the World** (www.lhw.com) has several hotels in this area, and most of the Riviera towns are served by **Best Western** (www.bestwestern.com) as well. There is usually a three- or four-star Best Western in the heart of town, often overlooking the sea, just where you want to be. We did not stay in any of these hotels, but the ones we inspected looked just fine, thank you.

GRAND HOTEL MIRAMARE

Via Milite Ignoto, Santa Margherita Ligure.

This is one of those grand old hotels, overlooking the sea, with gardens in the rear and the entire town stretched out below. The rooms are large and very grandmother's resorty Palm Beachy in style—this is neither a palace nor a modern high-rise. Rates are usually $300 to $400 (but can be lower), depending on the time of year. You can book through Leading Hotels of the World (✆ **800/223-6800** in the U.S.; www.lhw.com) or call the hotel directly. ✆ **0185/287-013.** www.grandhotelmiramare.it.

THE SHOPPING SCENE

Except for Portofino and the outlet malls, the retail emphasis in this area is neither designer shopping nor status names. Many towns have a few designer shops (Portofino has only designer shops), but the more likely retail style is the local boutique that carries several designer lines, which will probably be touted in the window of the store. There's also an emphasis on beachwear, resort clothing, board shorts, swimming gear, and boating needs. Beach and sand toys can easily be found everywhere.

This is also a food area. Wines and olives are grown on the hillside, and you can spend much time buying specialty oils and assorted wines. Genoa is the home of pesto—and while it's illegal to bring fresh basil back to the U.S., you can purchase prepared pesto or buy a mortar and pestle to make your own once you get back home.

If you really want to do heavy-duty, big-name designer shopping, head to Monte Carlo, described below.

To me, the charm of the shopping here is the small shops, the chance to browse merchandise you haven't seen at the mall back home, the food and fish markets—it's the pace of life, the way back to the earth and the sea and the Tod's.

MONACO

Monaco is a very strange, glam, and unique beast. It is a principality currently surrounded by France, but throughout time has been part of Italy. It's as good a place as any to start your trip to Italy, especially if you arrive at the Nice airport.

Most Americans only got hip to Monaco in the 1950s, when Grace Kelly married Prince Rainier. Yet a hundred years before then, Monaco was part of Italy. As a result, this tiny principality is trilingual (French, Italian, English) and HQ for the quietly rich who like to watch fast cars zoom through town or plunk down the dice in the casinos or their credit cards at Chanel.

Still, you'll also find affordable eats, real-people grocery stores, and plenty to buy. The villages that make up the principality mostly rest atop cliffs overlooking the sea (Monte Carlo is just one of the towns within Monaco), and the people are as well dressed as their dogs. Often called a sunny place for shady people, Monaco is a delightful mix of charm and sophistication—and fine dining. Don't forget the cultural scene and the tourist treasures—like a museum of vintage autos and a world-class aquarium. The city is famous for its relationship with the circus, too; the circus comes here regularly. Numerous international sporting events are held here as well as musical and rock concerts. Rock at "The Rock," man.

Getting There

There is no international airport in Monaco, but you are a mere half-hour from the airport in Nice, France, which is the gateway to the region. From Nice, you can take a bus, train, or taxi to Monaco, or do what I do: fly. I used to be terrified of helicopters until I became a regular on this route—it's a treat. Call **Heli Air Monaco** (✆ **377/92-050-050**; www.heliair monaco.com). This firm can transfer you between airports and also take you to other places—it even has programs coordinated with all the famous chefs in the area, so you can fly and dine and return to Monte Carlo on your own sked.

Sleeping in Monaco

When assessing hotels here, it's sometimes hard to know if you are in France or Monaco—unless you are in downtown Monte Carlo or on the beach portion of Monte Carlo, right below the town. A wide range of hotels is represented, from the big chains to the many luxe resorts up the hill, down the hill, and around the bend. But if you've come for the shopping, as I have, you want to be right in the heart of Monte Carlo.

Note that Monte Carlo has a number of sporting and glam events—ranging from the circus to the Red Cross Ball to the Grand Prix and more. These events cause rooms to be scarce and rates to be high.

SBM (Société des Bains de Mer), the group held by the Grimaldi family (as in Prince Albert, Princess Caroline, and so on), owns hotels and casinos as well as **Les Thermes Marins de Monte-Carlo**—one of the best spas in the world. There are several hotels in the SBM group, with a slight variety in style and price. I sometimes stay at the **Hôtel Hermitage,** which is a little more relaxed than the **Hôtel de Paris,** the crown jewel of the group and the fanciest (it's where I bumped into Prince Albert in the lobby). Many of the SBM hotels are also members of Leading Hotels of the World. For info, check out www.montecarloresort.com.

HÔTEL MÉTROPOLE
4 av. de la Madone 4, Monte Carlo.

How can you not book a hotel that is drop-dead chic, gorgeous, overlooks the sea, was designed by my hero Jacques Garcia, has one of the best tables on the Riviera right in the lobby, and stands atop a shopping mall? Be still my heart, I feel a swoon coming on.

This deluxe hotel offers rooms and suites that come with state-of-the-art amenities, plus Joël Robuchon, plus ESPA with individual treatment rooms and private spa suites, open 7/7.

Prices vary with the season; you can ask for a Born to Shop rate, which includes breakfast. Expect to pay $400 and up. You can book through Leading Hotels of the World (© **800/223-6800** in the U.S.; www.lhw.com) or call the hotel directly. © **377/93-151-515.** www.metropole.com.

Snack & Shop

I don't need to tell you that this is a major foodie town. It's home base for Alain Ducasse, who has two restaurants here (**Louis XV, Bar & Boeuf**); the famous Joël Robuchon now has a restaurant in Monaco as well.

If you're not doing the stars-on-your-plate thing, consider **Le Train Bleu,** at the Casino de Monte-Carlo (© **377/98-062-424**). This is touristy and hokey (and expensive), but great fun if you want to get dressed up, go into the casino itself, eat Italian, and pretend that James Bond is over yonder.

Also note that famed Parisian pâtisserie **Ladurée** (© **377/97-703-913;** www.laduree.fr) has just come to town—the macaroons alone are worth a hike up the hill to place des Moulins.

Shopping Neighborhoods

As small as the principality of Monaco is, it has various towns and parts, so Monte Carlo is merely one part of the whole.

Since Monte Carlo gets most of the press, you have probably been confused about the difference between Monaco and Monte Carlo. I am therefore dividing this up into two sections, Monaco neighborhoods and downtown Monte Carlo neighborhoods.

In Monaco

Fontvieille Home to the Columbus Hotel and also the CC de Fontvieille (Centre Commercial de Fontvieille, as in shopping mall), which has a very good French supermarket named **Carrefour.**

La Condamine This is the port, where if you arrive by cruise ship you will come right up alongside some palm trees and a giant staircase that leads into downtown. There's not too much shopping down here, but it's a nice place to stroll at night.

Beachy Monte Carlo Located below the area I call Métropole—and (sort of) within walking distance of it—is the beachside, which is mostly hotels, resorts, and restaurants. There are a number of art galleries along the way. The Fairmont Hotel Monte Carlo has a lot of retail spread throughout its lobby.

Old City Welcome to "The Rock," Le Rocher, where the palace is located and assorted TTs still sell postcards of Princess Grace.

In Downtown Monte Carlo

Métropole The center of downtown alongside the main park. With the casino to your right (if you are facing the Hôtel Métropole) and the Hôtel de Paris behind you, the Métropole comprises a swank hotel and a spa and a mall—who could want for anything more? The Métropole shopping center has 80 boutiques as well as a tiny grocery store hidden in the basement (ask someone how to get there as you will never find it on your own). I will not list all the stores, but trust me, there's everything from big-name designer boutiques to mass-market chains (like **FNAC** and **Sephora**) to gourmet-food shops (this is not counting the grocery store I mentioned) to places for hair and nails.

Avenue des Beaux Arts This small street, on the other side of the park from Métropole, is home to major names in design and jewelry such as **Bulgari, Chaumet, Fred, Louis Vuitton,** and more. **Hermès** is around the corner at avenue de Monte Carlo. **Chanel** is at the place du Casino. Other designer boutiques dot hotel lobbies in this part of town.

Park Place This is a building at the top of the park, a residence with a mall on the street level where you'll see several fancy designer shops such as **Escada.** Note that there is also a resale shop for designer clothing at this little mall.

Boulevard des Moulins This is the real-people shopping part, where multiples that aren't in the Métropole mall can be found. These include **Benetton, Blanc Bleu, Façonnable,** and the like. It is a little higher up the hill, but within walking distance from the heart of downtown Monte Carlo.

SAN REMO

San Remo has a yummy fall-of-the-Russian-aristocracy, shabby-chic-gone-to-hell-in-a-Gucci-handbag air that makes it a nice place for lunch, a stroll, or a short visit. It has a casino, a Russian Orthodox church, and a main street just meant for shoppers. Corso Matteotti is the main shopping drag. Visitors to France sometimes like to hop across into Italy (there is no official border; you don't even show a passport), since gas and sometimes clothes are slightly less expensive in Italy. But don't expect any bargains.

GENOA

Beyond the high-rises that look a lot like those in Beijing, and the traffic that looks a lot like that in Shanghai, beyond the arena of real people and closer down near the sea, lies the Genoa you want to see. Named European City of Culture in 2004 and protected as a UNESCO world treasure, Genoa has been going after the cruise and tourism business since 1992, the 500th anniversary of you-know-what. Much has been rebuilt; much has been left untouched over several centuries. The Slow Food movement was begun here; the city functions on Mediterranean time—everything goes slowly. Nonetheless, there's more pesto than you can imagine, the old harbor that was revitalized by the wonderful architect Renzo Piano, and an aquarium, an antiques district, markets, winding streets that are more like alleys, and all sorts of coffee shops that sell sweets to make you swoon. Just why was it that Columbus was so anxious to leave town?

Getting There

You may arrive in Genoa by cruise ship—obviously one of the most famous cruise ports in the world—or by train, plane, or car. The international airport is not as large as Nice's, but it is served by both mainstream (BA, Air France, Alitalia) and low-cost (Ryanair) carriers. Should you drive, you are about 2 hours from the French border.

Note: Getting *to* Genoa by car is no big deal; but getting *into* Genoa is a nightmare. I strongly advise you not to drive in Genoa itself. Walk, take a bus, or try the limited but new subway instead. Do not drive. Repeat: Do not drive.

The Lay of the Land

Via Garibaldi is where the rich folks lived, the home of palazzos to visit and museums galore . . . and from there you can wander to historic quarters, see the famous cathedral, and ponder the Holy Grail, which may or may not be located there.

The Columbus family (you remember their boy Chris) lived nearby—that's the really old part of town, dating from the 12th century, that leads to the water's edge. The harbor has been renovated by none other than Renzo Piano. If you brought along the kids, check out the famous aquarium.

The main shopping parts of town radiate from the **Piazza de Ferrari** and include **Via XX Settembre** and **Via Roma.** Via

Roma is the main street for big names; then you hit **Via Garibaldi.** Note that by big names, I mean you will recognize some of the names but not all, since, after all, this is a town that has an H&M but no Gucci.

If you like hunting for old junk, **Piazza Campetto** has antiques shops housed in palazzos.

If you consider the Bay of Naples as the center of the world (many once did), then the western part of the bay (toward France) is called **Sampierdarena,** while the eastern portion is **Sottoripa,** which includes the old port and all of the spice shops, crooked alleys, and medieval streets you've dreamed of.

Because the city climbs away from the sea, there are assorted elevators and routes up, up, and away.

Finds

Coin
Via XX Settembre 16a.

It's the big department store, less designer-oriented than La Rina (see below). ✆ **010/570-5821.** www.coin.it.

Galleria Mazzini
Piazza Ferrari.

This may remind you of the Galleria Vittorio Emanuele in Milan; it's one of those large, glass-and-metal covered shopping malls with stunning arcades and much charm.

La Rinascente
Via Vernazza 1.

The leading department-store chain in Italy; it carries designer clothing and big beauty brands. ✆ **010/586-995.** www.rinascente.it.

MERCATO ORIENTALE
Via Galata and Via XX Settembre.

This covered market is open Monday through Saturday. It's odd that anything in Italy stays open on a Monday, so you are in luck here. ***Note:*** It's closed on Wednesday afternoons.

STANDA
Via Cesarea 2.

A dime store/department store for real people, it has a grocery store, affordable clothes, home style, and everyday needs. ✆ **010/583-625.** www.standa.it.

UPIM
Via XX Settembre 2.

Similar to Standa, but without the grocery store. ✆ **010/580-696.** www.upim.it.

SANTA MARGHERITA LIGURE & RAPALLO

Few places in the world are as seductive as this small piece of real estate on the far side of Genoa, nestled into Italy right where the shape of the land begins to dip down into the boot. Santa Margherita and Rapallo are almost twin cities, like Buda and Pest. Rapallo is a mere 3km (2 miles) beyond Santa Margherita, so if the weather isn't too hot you can actually walk. But then, why walk when you can take the local bus?

Santa Margherita does have a Dolce & Gabbana shop and a few other designer boutiques, but that's not what we came for. This is where you just walk around and look and shop and stare and enjoy. We found Kérastase shampoo here for 13€ ($17)—it's 14€ to 18€ ($16–$23) in France and $30 in the U.S.—and we bought bottles of Ligurian olive oil (a little more bitter and tart than Umbrian); Sarah even spied a leopard-print motorcycle helmet for me. It's that kind of place: low-key and yummy.

Like all the cities here, this one also reaches around a bay. At the farthest end is a point where Portofino is located, while at the easternmost part of the bay is the city of Rapallo. In between lies Santa Margherita, more casual than San Remo and more exciting and real than Portofino. Santa Margherita strings along the beach, so you get a nice walk into town as you pass various shops and stalls, licking your ice-cream cone and wishing you had a Starbucks franchise. At night, the day-trippers have left and you'll feel very elegant, sophisticated, and, uh, Italian.

THE CINQUE TERRE

This portion of Italy is high on the cliffs and so hard to get to that it's considered easier to walk from town to town. La Spezia is the main transportation gateway—this is the big town in the center of the little bay, the city that also connects to highways in the north-south or east-west directions. Most of the towns are separated by a 2- to 3-hour walk. This is more difficult if you are carrying a lot of shopping bags, so consider the train—you can get to all of the towns by rail. Note that Monterosso is the most touristy of the towns but has the best shopping.

Sleeping in the Cinque Terre

GRAND HOTEL
Via Garibaldi 5, Portovenere.

Stay in a 17th-century convent turned hotel. Portovenere is the main hub of the Cinque Terre (although not one of the five towns) . . . but very hard to get to. By car it's fearsome, so take a boat or even a bus. I like buses around here. Just wear deodorant and pray others do, too. This hotel has a total of 54 rooms; 10 of those are suites. Remember that since this was once a convent, rooms are spare. Prices are about $200 a night. © 0187/792-610.

Jolly Hotel La Spezia
Via XX Settembre 2, La Spezia.

Jolly is a great chain to know about for several reasons: It's Italian, it has a hotel in every city you want to visit, it has four- and five-star properties, and few Americans know about it. Jolly has "the" hotel in La Spezia, so if you require the best address and the fanciest hotel, this is the one. In low season, a double room starts at around $175 a night. ✆ **800/247-1277** in the U.S. Local phone ✆ 0187/739-555. www.jollyhotels.com.

SARZANA

I have a weakness for Sarzana since my real name is Susanna. If I married Tarzan, surely this would be my new name. But never mind. Sarzana is along the coast but not on the beach; you will pass it from the highway if you are driving. It has a number of ancient sights to see. But let's get serious, folks. We came to shop. There is a legendary resource right here.

Victoria
Via Variante Aurelia 96.

The real reason you came to Sarzana is for Victoria, a big discount store that sells Prada, Miu Miu, and more. This is far from your average outlet store or jobber—it's a fancy boutique with excellent service and prices equal to the second markdown at a department-store sale.

To get here, exit from the A12 highway at Sarzana and then drive in the Carrera direction for less than 2 miles. The store is open 7/7, but watch the odd hours: Saturday from 10am to 1pm and 3 to 8:30pm, all other days from 2 to 7:30pm. ✆ **081/762-7197.**

Chapter Ten

HIDDEN ITALY

SEEK & YE SHALL FIND

I was deep in travel talk with my friend Ruth. She was talking about how Rome, Florence, and Milan are among her favorite places in the world. I asked if she'd ever been to Bologna or Verona. She had not.

I explained that the well-known cities are nice enough, and everyone should go there a few times, but the delights of Italy—especially if the euro is strong—are the smaller cities, where you can get away from some of the tour buses and find the real Italy.

"Bologna," sighed Ruth. "I've never even thought about it."

I am not dissing the old faithfuls. I stand to paraphrase that chestnut about London . . . when a man is tired of Venice, he is tired of living. But I dream of taking my kids, my partner, my tour groups, my beloved ones to Bologna, Parma, Verona, and beyond. What I have seen has awakened new places in my heart and my wanderlust and, yes, my suitcase. And next time, we cross over to Croatia and Slovenia.

While we're talking about my dreams, I think it's only fair to throw in some information about nightmares. I thought that driving around northern Italy and popping into real factories and factory stores would be a dream come true; I thought that Turin, as the host of the 2006 Winter Olympic Games, would be a dream to revisit since I hadn't been in years. I figured Olympic endeavors must have left behind improved shopping. I thought it would be fun to return to San Remo and maybe even see what changes are afoot or afloat in Genoa. In my mind, it was all perfect. It wasn't even going to be fattening.

If endless driving behind trucks on a single lane of road is fabulous, that too escaped me.

Having a car and driving around Italy can be wonderful, but also remember that you can get to most of the gems of Hidden Italy by train or even low-cost carrier (Bologna has a very good airport), allowing you to leave the driving to someone else. Then you get more cheese.

RULES OF THE ROAD

I have now driven across Italy several times and learned a lot. Technology has also come a long way. These days, you can get your hotel's concierge to print out the directions for you in the language of your choice, or you can do a MapQuest search before you even leave home, or you can use a GPS device. Or all of the above.

Nonetheless, I must warn you that the driving can be stressful. Italian drivers are very aggressive. The French are angels compared to the Italians; French roads are 1,000% better than Italian. Italian *highways* are not even moderately well marked, and country roads are so hopeless that you may want to weep. Some days there were no restaurants when it was lunchtime or when we wanted to eat. Grocery stores where we thought we could grab picnic supplies may or may not have been open during the lunch break.

Factories—or their stores—were often not marked. Directions given in outlet guides seemed easy to follow in the bookstore, but were impossible to match to existing roads. Road conditions were often deplorable, especially on superhighways where all lanes, save one, were closed and you had to drive single file behind a convoy of trucks while a madman on a Moto Guzzi motorcycle wove in and out of traffic.

Just keep this in mind: The reason you want to go to northern Italy and drive all around to the factory outlets is that the area is filled with factories. So far, so good. But wait. Remember this part: Where there are factories, there are trucks. Why didn't I think of that before I booked this trek?

In my most desperate moments, I prayed that I was in Manhattan with the ability to walk into Bergdorf Goodman and pay full retail price for any desired goods. The notion of a bargain hardly seemed worth the trouble it took for the excursion.

With the same breath, may I say that the driving in the south—actually the middle of Italy—was a pleasure, possibly because there were neither as many factories nor as many trucks.

Hidden Italy is somewhat hidden from the crazies as well, so I suggest that this chapter might be your guide and your bible if you want to get out there and hit the road, Lorenzo.

If your trip is planned as a romantic getaway or on the basis of relaxation, I'd reconsider an extended driving tour to outlets and outlet malls. If you are doing some of the Hidden Cities and driving a little in between and hitting a favorite outlet or two, you should be fine. But if you are in a new relationship or on your honeymoon, think twice about how much driving you commit to. Just remember this last warning: A French driver will tell you that you're beautiful before he screws you. Not so an Italian driver.

BOLOGNA

Located about 1 hour north of Florence, and about 2 hours south of Milan, Bologna is the most perfect Italian city—not just in Italy, but in the world—because it has the infrastructure to work as a tourist town, but is not so overwhelmed with visitors that the charm has been choked away. Hmmm, well, maybe Verona is the most perfect city in Italy. Let me think about that for a little bit. (See p. 323 for more on Verona.)

Bologna

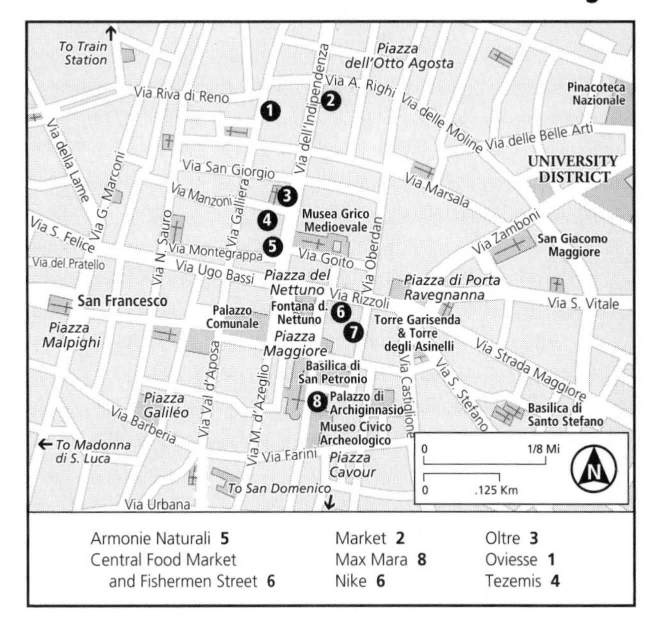

Bologna is far larger than Verona; even the historic part of the city is larger than Verona's. Bologna has good shopping in terms of all the big brands you may want to buy. It has a good market (Fri–Sat only) and enough well-located luxury hotels to offer choice at a price, as well as delights for those who need them. There's food forever. And shoes, did you know that shoes are made in the nearby villages?

Bologna is also a huge university town. As such, there's plenty in the stores for teens and tweens and those on a low budget. The number of accessible mass-market stores offering low-cost fashion is staggering. There are plenty of stores that sell to plus sizes as well. After all, Bologna is one of the most famous food towns in all of Italy. Think little rustic restaurants all over and gelato to die for.

Getting There

This part of Italy is called Emilia-Romagna. Foodies know it as the center of Italian eats. Shoppers know it as the home of various shoe factories and outlet malls. It is pretty much in the center of the country and easy to reach, as roads and transportation in Italy tend to run north-south. Bologna is located right on the main rail line between Milan and Florence.

The Bologna Marconi Airport is served by several low-cost carriers from the U.K. and continental Europe.

By car, the drive north from Florence is relatively easy—slightly more than an hour of good highway. Note, however, that this highway becomes one big parking lot on certain travel days and during rush hour. If you plan to drive, do so with much organization.

This was one of the few big cities where we actually slipped right into town and parked in front of the hotel with a minimum of stress. The printout from our previous hotel was good; the streets were well marked—we got lucky. We also knew to call ahead and give our license-plate number to the hotel (see "Getting Around," below).

Getting Around

You really can walk just about everywhere in the historic center. The train station is not far from the heart of town, but you will probably need a taxi between there and your hotel.

If you have a car, note that you are not allowed to drive in the city center without a pass from your hotel. If you are stopped by a policeman, tell him (or mime) which hotel you are headed to and ask the best directions. Once you arrive at the hotel, have the staff call the police with your license-plate number so that you are not given a ticket. Even if police do not stop you on entering the city center, still ask the hotel desk to give the police your plate number.

Should you need a taxi, call © **051/372-727.** This is a radio taxi service, so the meter will start when the driver heads out to fetch you.

Booking It in Bologna

Any good tour operator or travel agent will advise you of the fair dates in Bologna. The city has a very active trade-fair schedule, during which times the best hotel rooms (sometimes *all* the hotel rooms) are taken. The fairs are booked years in advance and can be discovered in various ways, including contacting **Bologna Fiere** (✆ **05/128-2111**; www.bolognafiere.it).

There's also the **CST,** or **Centro Servizi per Turisti** (✆ **800/856-065** in Italy, or 051/648-7607; www.cst.bo.it), a visitor organization that helps with dates, hotels, and so on.

If you are out at the fairgrounds or merely in town for a day but with a car, you can park and ride—there is a shuttle bus that will get you into the historic center of town in 8 minutes. The shuttle ticket entitles you to free parking in the adjoining lot.

Insider's secret: Bologna makes a great base for exploring Italy—you can go to Florence on the train as a day trip and not have to worry about parking, traffic, or hotels. In fact, you are just about equidistant from Florence and Verona.

Sleeping in Bologna

Art Hotels
Hotel Orologio, Via IV Novembre 10.
Hotel Corona d'Oro, Via Oberdan 12.
Hotel Novecento, Piazza Galileo 4–3.
Hotel Commercianti, Via de'Pignattari 11.

I found this small, family-owned hotel chain through Charming Italy (www.charmingitaly.net) and was delighted with the travel site's insider tips. And the four hotels in this chain provide parking for guests, which is no small task in this city.

I stayed at the **Orologio,** the exact three-star hotel we all want to find; the only thing wrong with it was the noisy Americans one table over at breakfast. There are 50 guest rooms; mine had beams and a window with a view out to the main square. Indeed, the hotel is right off the main square and a few steps from one of the central shopping streets. There's a free e-mail station in the lobby, too. Rates are about 160€ ($208) per night, depending on the season and the kind of room. Comparison shoppers may want to note that a suite here costs less than a room at the deluxe Grand Hotel Baglioni.

If you want a fancier hotel, the four-star **Corona d'Oro** is heaven—a luxe renovated palace dating back to 1890. Its location is closer to the town's famed towers, on the other side of the square from the Orologio, and also in a key position for shopping. Some of the rooms are more modern, and junior suites are available as well.

There are two other properties in the family. A short block from Orologio, the four-star **Novocento** is a brand-new, modern, Zen-style boutique hotel with a good location. The **Commercianti** is a three-star hotel and the least charming of the bunch. ✆ **800/908-901** in Italy, or 051/745-7335. www.bolognarthotels.it.

Grand Hotel Baglioni
Via dell'Indipendenza 8.

This is the luxury hotel of the city where rock stars, celebrities, business honchos, and diplomats stay. My first time here, there was a crowd out front awaiting Bruce Springsteen.

The place is quite grand, and the location is smack-dab in the middle of the main commercial shopping street. You can walk everywhere, even to the big market on Friday and Saturday. While the Grand caters to businessmen, and is always full during fairs, the hotel is the "in" place for all who need or appreciate grand in all senses of the word.

This hotel has a very large and varied number of packages, many including food tastings and/or cooking classes. The one I plan to book next time offers a private car and driver to take you to the Ferrari factory, lunch there, 2 nights in a superior room, and many extras—this package, for two people, costs about $600. Rates include free Wi-Fi in all rooms. You can book through Leading Hotels of the World (© 800/223-6800; www.lhw.com) or contact the hotel directly. © 051/225-445. www.baglionihotels.com.

Snack & Shop

Bologna is an eaters' paradise; you will have no trouble finding cafes with tiny sandwiches, pizza, pasta, and, yes, spaghetti Bolognese.

There is also gelato literally everywhere. One of the following gelato tips comes from a famous American food writer, one of them is my personal find—and the third is the new guy in town, located right in the heart of Bologna on a pedestrian shopping street. Your job is to find the best *giandujia* (hazelnut-chocolate) gelato and then compare it with the *aceto balsamico* flavor.

GELATERIA GROM
Via d'Azeglio 13.

GELATERIA STEFINO
Via Galliera 49b.

OREFICERIA DEL GELATO
Via degli Orefici 5f.

The Shopping Scene

Take a few centuries' worth of history, add universities, toss in a large arena for business fairs, and what do you get? This town is a great place to shop, with branches of all the big Italian multiples and even a few fancy-schmancy stores. Throw into the mix the food markets and stalls, the little mom-and-pop shops, and the chance to get to nearby outlet malls, and perhaps you have the very definition of heaven.

Oops, I forgot to mention the architecture that is so astonishingly medieval that you will feel like a character in one of

Shakespeare's plays. Hmmm, did people in Shakespeare's plays carry shopping bags?

Do not underestimate the number of young people in town as a large influence for retailers. The stores that specialize in well-priced clothing are large, well stocked, and often have many branches in different parts of town.

As a final note, there is a large market—held on Fridays and Saturdays—that sells a little of everything. Because the shoe-making regions are nearby, the market has especially good deals on shoes. I bought sandals for 12€ ($16), and I have enormous American feet—so if I can get a fit, anyone can. The next trip, I found a vendor selling Frette matrimonial sets—two sheets,

Motown

I am very new to the motorcycle culture, so forgive me if I rant and rave about basics that everyone else knows. However, I find this is important reporting for guys and for women whose partners might be complaining about a few days out for shopping.

Hey, big spender, sit back and relax—many cars and even more motorcycles are made in the Bologna area. There's shopping, there's riding, there are museums, and there are things to buy and ship. You can even now take your motorcycle on the train with you throughout Italy.

If your dream is to drive a Ferrari (since you figure you'll never own one), contact Maria Teresa Berdondini at **Tuscany by Tuscans** (© **0572/704-67**; www.tuscanybytuscans.it). The tour is expensive, but less than the cost of a new car.

Motorstars (© **059/921-667**; www.motorstars.org) also offers many tours; the folks here speak English. Their most popular event is an all-day Saturday option in which you tour factories, meet drivers and experts, and shop with an employee discount.

Nearby factories include Ducati, Ferrari, Maserati, and Lamborghini.

two pillowcases in one plastic envelope—for $140 a set. I loaded up on them as wedding gifts.

The market vendors work on a rotation, so if you are not in town on market day, find out which city has a market when you are around. ***Insider's tip:*** Aim for the market in Modena if at all possible.

Foodie Tours

For a 4- to 5-hour cooking class in town, contact **Cook Italy** (**© 0349/007-8298;** www.cookitaly.com). The class takes you to the central food market to shop for ingredients; then you cook lunch. It costs 104€ ($135). If you don't want to cook but do want a guided tour of local food shops and markets, you can book a 3-hour walking tour that costs 58€ ($75).

La Vecchia Scuola Bolognese (**© 051/649-1576;** www.la vecchiascuola.com) is the other local cooking school where English is spoken. Its classes specialize in making and cooking pasta.

Shopping Neighborhoods

Main Square With a large statue of Neptune in the center, the main square (Piazza Maggiore) is not so much a shopping square as it is a directional point from which most things begin or end. The tourist office is on this square and with it an excellent shop for souvenirs.

Via Indipendenza This is the main commercial drag in terms of flagships of the big brands. The street also leads to the market, is home to the Grand Hotel Baglioni, and leads in and out of town and/or toward the train station. There are plenty of cafes, restaurants, perfumeries, gelati stands, and stores selling cheap thrills. Among some of the finds: **Armonie Naturali** (no. 58c), which sells the Perlier and Kelemata line of bath and beauty products; **Tezemis** (no. 34), for adorable and low-cost pajamas and underwear for young women; and **Oltre** (nos. 24b/d), a large-sizes brand.

Just off Indipendenza, and impossible to find if you don't know to look for it, is an enormous **Oviesse,** a branch of one of my favorite brands for low-cost Italian fashions. Ask for directions to Via dei Mille 16. For why I love Oviesse, see p. 64.

Ugo Bassi Forgive me, this is confusing and not very funny, but I keep thinking the name of this street is Hugo Boss. It intersects with Via Indipendenza, forming the two main arteries of town. Ugo Bassi changes its name to Via Rizzoli early on; this, too, is a main shopping drag.

Via Clavature This is a pedestrian-only street filled with some small branch locations of chains (**Lush**) and many mom-and-pop stores offering upscale fashion and style. It leads away from the main square and the more commercial shopping districts. This is where you'll find **Grom,** my new favorite gelato digs.

Fishermen The street of the old fishermen (Via Pescherie Vecchie) is the heart of the food district. It leads away from the main square and is nestled right alongside Via Rizzoli. Aside from the central market, there are scads of food shops and boutiques. Note that this is just the core of a neighborhood of several streets, not the only street to see or shop. You'll see many designer boutiques, including **Chanel.** Locals call this area the Mercato di Mezzo; it is truly a medieval warren of little alleys. Don't miss **Majani** (Via Carbonesi), an old-fashioned chocolate maker that is, naturally, closed in the summer.

The Ghetto Like most medieval towns, Bologna has a Jewish ghetto that is still a vibrant part of the commercial zone. While you might not find any designer boutiques, you will find olive oil and food stores. The ghetto is located near the Two Towers and Via Rizzoli.

PARMA & AREA

I was particularly drawn to Parma because of my old friend Dede Parma from high school. When I mentioned to friends that I planned to explore it, they all mentioned either Parma ham or Parmesan cheese. No fools, these friends. Parma isn't where you go if you were born to shop—it's for those who were born to eat, or born to shop for foodstuffs.

Also note that Parma has a unique location in Italy, as it stands as the crossroads to two highways: the main north-south route as well as an autostrada that leads to the sea and brings you to La Spezia (see chapter 9 for more on the Italian Riviera).

I ended up in Parma on a Sunday after a half-day at the nearby Fidenza Village outlet mall. Only the local department store was open, so it was not a day for shoppers, and frankly, it's not a city for shoppers. Rather, this is a city for dreamers, for those who worship the miracles that humans make in the name of religion, and for those who want to go to markets, to nearby villages, and to cheese houses. This is a city for those who believe in magic.

Oh, yes, once a year there is a very large antiques fair, an international dealers' affair that is worth coming to visit. Bring business cards.

Or you may want to go to spaghetti school—see below for the listing about Barilla pasta, which is located on the edge of Parma.

There are also antiques, markets, stores, and food sources in nearby Modena. I didn't get there this trip, but you don't have to make the same mistake. The closest I actually got to Modena was the gas station and Autogrill right outside of town (Nutella sold in a huge glass pitcher, for 6.75€/$8.80).

I mention Modena now for several reasons. It is not very far from Bologna and is a good market town. Modena is also the far eastern part of northwestern Italy and the easternmost anchor to the shopping one can do on a north-south access between Genoa and Milan or Turin and Como. There are plenty of outlets in the area. This is also the cradle of balsamic vinegar.

I did buy wonderful shoes from a man who not only works the Modena market but also has a shoe store there, so if you're looking for a starting point, try **Le Occasioni di Porta Portese,**

Viale della'Cittadella 57 (© **0542/147-06**; taccher@tiscali.it). His specialty is designer overstocks for men and women.

ACADEMIA BARILLA
Largo Piero Calamandrei 3a, Parma.

Foodies, please note that while Italy is crawling with designer pasta brands, good old Barilla—king of supermarket pasta—has its own cooking school, offering a range of courses that last from 1 to 10 days. © **866/772-2233** in the U.S. Local phone © 0521/264-060. www.academiabarilla.com.

AGRINASCENTE
Via San Michele Campagna 22b, Fidenza.

Forgive me, but I have nicknamed this store the Big Cheese, and I know you will always call it that once you visit and see the trade sign on the road—a giant triangular wedge of cheese. Locals know that any time they see a hexagonal store—looking much like a gunpowder magazine, for those of us who remember the tour of Williamsburg—a cheese house lies within. Note that most cheese houses sell more than cheese these days.

This particular cheese house is a virtual deli, just lacking the Zabar family and a few dill pickles and onion bagels. It has local wines, oils, vinegars, pasta, meats, and, of course, cheese. You can buy the cheese prepacked or ask them to cut it for you. The price is based on the age; the expensive stuff is the oldest and is not exported to the U.S. Speaking of which, to answer your next question: Yes, it is legal to bring cheese into the U.S. if it has been aged more than 60 days.

If you are attracted to this kind of shopping experience, I am going to assume that you are used to cheese that costs 16€ ($21) a kilo and balsamic vinegar that costs 36€ ($47) for a teeny-weeny bottle. For heaven's sake, don't shell out for the expensive stuff to give as gifts to people who have no idea what it is, how much it costs, or how to use it. Remember, with a lot of these products, a little dab will do ya.

Giandujia Alert

Giandujia is a chocolate bonbon specific to Italy that is made by many, many chocolatiers. It is invariably a triangular-shaped log wrapped in gold foil; the flavor is chocolate and hazelnut praline. I am bonkers for these candies. They vary in taste from brand to brand, and even come in dark- or white-chocolate versions. I like plain old original. Of all the gian-dujia I have tested, I think the best is actually made by the Swiss company Lindt, which has an outlet store in Fidenza Village called Chocolate Town. They are not cheap, but they are heavenly.

Final tip: Ask for a piece of the special wax paper; once you have taken the plastic off your cheese, it will keep better in the fridge if wrapped in this paper.

This store stays open on Sundays until 3pm. © **0524/522-334.** www.agrinascente.it.

FIDENZA VILLAGE
Via San Michele Campagna, Fidenza.

I know I write about stores, not food, but in this part of Italy it's hard not to think about food. So it's with pleasure that I report that the best restaurant I have ever enjoyed in an out-let mall is at Fidenza Village. **Barlumeria** bills itself as a cheese bar, but it also has restaurant service, takeout, a deli, and even some tastings. Plan your shopping trip so that you can eat lunch here. Also note that Italians tend to think about lunch around 1pm or later. If you go around 12:30pm, the crowds shouldn't be too bad.

Now then, about the mall. The second phase improved the mall enormously, although this is not the best outlet mall in Italy. Created in the style of a fake Italian village populated by Verdi's operas, the mall lacks only blaring music—say, the

"Grand March" from *Aida*—and perhaps a herd of elephants. It is small, intimate, and easy to shop.

Stores here include **Lagostina,** the Italian cookware brand; **Sapo,** the Italian copycat version of Lush; **Elena Mirò,** an Italian firm that makes large-size clothing (the poor woman's Marina Rinaldi); **Bassetti,** for linens; **Camper,** a Spanish brand of casual shoes for men and women; **Furla,** for Italian handbags; **Trussardi Jeans;** and **Samsonite,** where I found a high-quality suitcase for 52€ ($70) to take all my new clothes home.

The drive from Bologna city center takes at least an hour. Stay on the A1 until you exit for Fidenza (this is after Parma); then follow signs for FASHION VILLAGE OUTLET SHOPPING. The signs aren't huge, as you would expect in America, but you aren't in America, and for Italy, it's a miracle there are signs at all. The mall is more or less equidistant from Milan and Bologna. If you take the train, a shuttle runs between the mall and the Fidenza rail station every half-hour. The mall is open daily from 10am to 8pm. ✆ **0524/335-51.** www.fidenzavillage.com.

CASTEL GUELFO

Go south and east of Bologna and you are headed to a totally different outlet mall in Castel Guelfo. This is a tiny mall with just about 30 stores that may not be worth the trip, but it is near **Locanda Solarola,** a Michelin-rated one-star kitchen and farmhouse hotel, at Via Santa Croce 5, Castel Guelfo (✆ **0542/670-102;** www.locandasolarola.com). It serves lunch and dinner and is open on Sundays, making it the perfect accompaniment for a half-day at the outlet mall. There are also a handful of rooms at the farmhouse, so you may want to simply move in.

CASTEL GUELFO OUTLET CITY
Via del Commercio 20d, Castel Guelfo.

To get here, take the A14 from Bologna south toward Rimini and exit at Castel San Pietro Terme. You'll see the mall. I have already said that it's small—and want to reiterate that it's small. This may not be worth your time. It's open daily, including Sunday from 10am to 8:30pm. ✆ **0542/670-762.** www.outletcastelguelfo.it.

VERONA

As I have gotten into a Shakespeare thing with the discovery of my Hidden Italy, it will come as no surprise that I am smitten with Verona, home of those Two Gentlemen as well as Romeo and Juliet. Juliet's house is a major tourist attraction—right off the main shopping street, thank you very much—and is filled with graffiti and love notes. Perhaps there are shopping tips there, too.

Getting There

If you consider the boot shape of Italy as a capital letter T, then Verona lies just east of where the T crosses. This means it's just north of Bologna and between Milan and Venice on the east-west axis.

You can get here by train, car, or plane. In fact, the airport is one of the new keys to low-cost Italy—it's served by Ryanair.

Getting Around

If you are limiting your visit to beautiful downtown metro Verona, you can walk—driving is to be avoided.

If your travels include other nearby big cities—even places such as Padua—you can also visit by train. Venice is best reached on the train, too, due to the parking difficulties.

Should you want to strike out for the area rich in factories and, therefore, outlets, or the nearby wine country, you will need a car. In case you aren't that into it, far be it from me to mention that you are in the gorgeous Lake Garda district, that tons of vineyards are all around you, or that the towns stretching from Verona to Venice are filled with factories—you can

Booking It in Verona

Just like Bologna, Verona is a big fair town—hotel rooms simply don't exist when you want them, or just because you want them. If your travel agent doesn't have the fair schedule (which is set up years in advance), call your hotel of choice and ask about fairs before you begin to dream of setting head on pillow.

Fairs tend to be held March through May and September through early November; opera season begins in mid-June and runs to the end of August. When it comes to the opera season, many visitors book a year in advance.

shop your way right into Marco Polo International Airport outside Venice if you so please. The area specializes in shoes and eyeglasses, but I visited the Bottega Veneta outlet store inside the factory in Vicenza and a Giorgio Armani outlet store in the middle of nowhere but not far at all. Read on.

Please note that I drove to Verona from Venice—an easy and pleasant drive on a good highway—but was lost in Verona for a full hour because of one-way streets, Roman city planning, pedestrian-only thoroughfares, and stern, but handsome, policemen who were quite insistent that the shortest route between two places was not a straight line. "You can't get there from here unless you are on foot" should be written on every T-shirt.

Sleeping in Verona

DUE TORRI HOTEL BAGLIONI
Piazza S. Anastasia 4.

Oh my, I have died and gone to heaven. Oh my, remind me to have my next honeymoon in this hotel. Oh my, don't wake me if I am dreaming.

What can you say about a slightly hidden hotel in a slightly hidden city in the middle of heaven? Built into an ancient

Verona

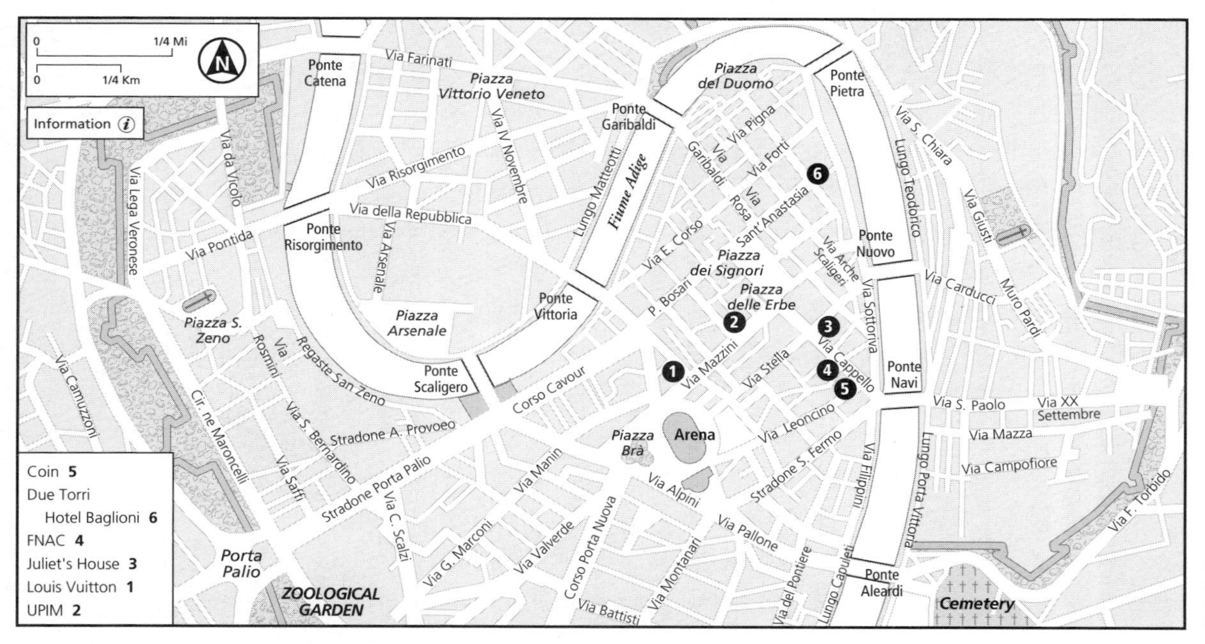

0 1/4 Mi
0 1/4 Km
N
Information
Coin 5
Due Torri
Hotel Baglioni 6
FNAC 4
Juliet's House 3
Louis Vuitton 1
UPIM 2
Piazza del Duomo
Piazza dei Signori
Piazza delle Erbe
Piazza Brà
Arena
Piazza Vittorio Veneto
Piazza Arsenale
Piazza S. Zeno
Porta Palio
Cemetery
ZOOLOGICAL GARDEN
Fiume Adige
Ponte Pietra
Ponte Nuovo
Ponte Navi
Ponte Aleardi
Ponte Garibaldi
Ponte Vittoria
Ponte Scaligero
Ponte Risorgimento
Ponte Catena
Lungo Teodorico
Lungo Porta Vittoria
Lungo Matteotti
Lungo Capuleti
Via S. Chiara
Via Giusti
Muro Pardi
Via Carducci
Via XX Settembre
Via S. Paolo
Via Mazza
Via Campofiore
Via F. Torbido
Via Sottoriva
Via Arche Scaligeri
Via Cappello
Via Filippini
Via Leoncino
Stradone S. Fermo
Via del Pontiere
Via Pallone
Via Stella
Via Mazzini
Sant'Anastasia
Via Forti
Via Pigna
Via Rosa
Via Garibaldi
Via E. Corso
P. Bosari
Via Alpini
Via Montanari
Via Battisti
Corso Porta Nuova
Corso Cavour
Via Valverde
Via Manin
Via G. Marconi
Via C. Scalzi
Via IV Novembre
Via Farinati
Via Risorgimento
Via della Repubblica
Via Arsenale
Stradone A. Provoeo
Stradone Porta Palio
Regaste San Zeno
Via S. Bernardino
Via Rosmini
Via Saffi
Via da Vicolo
Via Pontida
Cir. ne Maroncelli
Via Lega Veronese
Via Camuzzoni

palazzo, the place is furnished in grand style—my room was small but draped in velvets and silks and charm, complete with a sleigh bed and view out to, yep, the two towers. On my next visit, there were two people and one dog, and we had a very large room filled with antiques and sunshine. Bathrooms are huge and modern.

This is one of the Baglioni hotels that has a branch of Brunello, so plan to have at least one meal here. Don't forget Pam Pam pizza across the street, or Enoteca S. Anastasia, at Via Massalongo 3b (© **045/801-4448**), for wines. The hotel is located on the far side of the town center, but is within easy walking distance of all shopping. It is perched at the edge of the Via Santa Anastasia, where you can stroll in delight.

The hotel is hard to book during opera season, but fabulous in winter and off season; you can get a 2-night holiday package for about $300, which includes many extras for two. © **045/595-044.** www.baglionihotels.com.

HOTEL ACCADEMIA
Via Scala 12.

I found this hotel by accident when I was lost downtown; the Accademia is in the center of everything and is seemingly the most perfect four-star hotel in town. Alas, I didn't get to spend the night because it was sold out—friends later told me it's a well-known secret address and needs to be booked in advance.

The location is in the thick of the shopping district, a short walk from the Roman arena. This palace hotel has been modernized and now has air-conditioning as well as parking. Rates vary depending on season: A double goes for 180€ ($234) in low season, 219€ ($285) in midseason, and 260€ ($338) in high season. This rate includes tax and breakfast, making Verona look better every minute. © **045/596-222.** www.accademiavr.it.

The Shopping Scene

We're talking about a medieval town that has a moderate amount of visitors (okay, I was there out of season), the house where Shakespeare's Juliet lived, and a large **UPIM** store. While there aren't nearly as many stores as in Bologna, and the shopping may not be as great as in other towns, what's here is fun and not your average tourist trap (TT). Come to think of it, that market in the center of town is pretty touristy; but hey, the rest is great.

Some of the reasons shopping here is so much fun: The community is wealthy, it attracts well-off shoppers, and the city invests time and money in making shopping easy for others. There's even an online shopping guide at www.veronashopping.it.

Also remember that Verona is in northern Italy, not that far from Switzerland (bankers need to shop, too), and in a geopolitical area that is influenced by the nearby factories. Fashion and fur talk here. And shoes don't walk, they smile. Believe me; the shoemaker's children do not go barefoot.

Insider's tip: One reason so many locals shop here is that prices, especially on designer goods, are slightly less expensive than in nearby Venice. Venetians shop in Verona, giving you all the more reason to do so as well.

Shopping Hours

Stores in Verona are open on Sundays, making this a popular shopping destination and day out for the upper-middle classes from Venice and the Veneto district. You will love the people-watching. Basic Sunday hours are 11am to 7:30pm. Needless to say, Mondays are dead.

Assorted TTs and stores catering to real-people needs are open late during opera season.

Shopping Neighborhoods

Via Sant'Anastasia This small road leads to the Due Torri Hotel Baglioni and the main shopping districts. In its own right, it is all that makes Verona wonderful—an almost alley of a street lined with mom-and-pop stores, and not a chain to be found. There are antiques stores, food stores, bookshops, and more. Oh yes, did I mention all the gelati stands?

Piazza delle Erbe If you hadn't known the tourist era was starting by spying the first of the designer boutiques (see **Lacoste** at no. 40), the ricky-ticky-tacky street market set up in the square—selling fresh fruit, limoncello, olive oil, chianti, penis-shaped pasta, and Romeo-and-Juliet key chains—is a dead giveaway.

Via Mazzini This pedestrian walkway and main shopping thoroughfare is where you'll find most of the designer stores and fancy boutiques. If the stores aren't from major Italian brands you see everywhere, they may be branches of upmarket Venetian merchants. You will find **Max & Co., Fiorucci, UPIM, Penny Black** (a division of Max Mara), **Elena Mirò, Mandarina Duck** (made nearby), and old faithfuls such as **Gucci, Versace, Benetton, Max Mara** and **Marina Rinaldi, Tod's** and **Hogan, Geox, Loro Piana,** and more. And not to be outdone, **Louis Vuitton** has a huge and impressive store where Via Mazzini ends across from the arena.

If you think it's all for rich yuppies, you're wrong—the Fiorucci store is enormous, the UPIM is one of the largest I have ever seen, and there are branches of chains such as **Bershka, Oltre,** and **Xanaka** (the latter from the south of France) that specialize in low-cost hot styles. Oltre, by the way, is low-cost high fashion in large sizes. There are also many low-end French chains such as **Pimke** and **Promod.**

Luckily, this street is filled with banks and ATMs.

Arena Mazzini ends at the Roman theater, which is surrounded by cafes and TTs, as can be expected. Gelato? Did someone say gelato?

Cappello Quick, what was Juliet's last name? Well, that's the clue (Capulet is the answer) for finding this shopping street as well as Juliet's house. Via Cappello is narrow and can be crowded, especially when a tour group falls on Juliet's pad. Stores are mostly Italian chains for mid- to low-end fashion rather than designer brands. But wait, that's not totally true—there are branches of **Frette, Armani Jeans, Emporio Armani,**

and **Sisley.** At the far end of the street is a **FNAC** as well as **Coin** department store. Capulet, oops, Cappello leads away from Piazza Erbe and forms a junction with the beginning of Via Mazzini. ***Note:*** Juliet is, of course, spelled in Italian, making it *Giulietta.*

BEYOND VERONA

The most famous town between Verona and Venice happens to be Padua. But I didn't stop there because I was headed to Vicenza and nearby factories and outlet stores. Despite the scads of outlets in the Veneto, I chose only two simple targets, described below.

Please note that this part of Vincenza is nowhere near the historic city center.

BOTTEGA VENETA FACTORY

Viale della Scienza 15, Vicenza.

Die-hard BV fans will probably want to make this side trip—although if you bomb, don't blame me. The factory and its store are hard to find behind an industrial gate with a small, handwritten sign. The store has its own door but is attached to the real factory. It is indeed lovely and filled with gorgeous merchandise: bags, shoes, small leather goods, clothes, and gift items such as picture frames.

Here's my problem: There weren't that many handbags when I visited, there wasn't anything special that made it worth the search for this crazy place, and the prices were good for BV but too high for me if I wasn't in love. The prices are fair, considering that 320€ ($416) for a Bottega Veneta handbag is now considered a bargain—since bags are almost always over $1,000 at regular retail. ✆ **0444/396-504.** www.bottegaveneta.com.

(The Other Armani) Factory Store
Via Stazione 93, Trissino.

First off, let's not get confused. This is not the main Armani outlet store (p. 288); this is not anywhere particularly near Como. This one is in the boonies, between Verona and Venice.

Getting to this store requires a little patience, with roads and access lanes going various directions but seemingly not the way you might need them to go. This outlet is not as large as the Armani outlet near Como, nor does it have nearly as much stock. Still, it's clean, neat, and easy to shop. My son needed a sports jacket and I found one, half off of half off—or a mere $150. There were even two sleeves and a whole Armani label. ✆ 0445/492-105.

Size Conversion Chart

Women's Clothing

American	8	10	12	14	16	18
Continental	38	40	42	44	46	48
British	10	12	14	16	18	20

Women's Shoes

American	5	6	7	8	9	10
Continental	36	37	38	39	40	41
British	4	5	6	7	8	9

Children's Clothing

American	3	4	5	6	6X
Continental	98	104	110	116	122
British	18	20	22	24	26

Children's Shoes

American	8	9	10	11	12	13	1	2	3
Continental	24	25	27	28	29	30	32	33	34
British	7	8	9	10	11	12	13	1	2

Men's Suits

American	34	36	38	40	42	44	46	48
Continental	44	46	48	50	52	54	56	58
British	34	36	38	40	42	44	46	48

Men's Shirts

American	14½	15	15½	16	16½	17	17½	18
Continental	37	38	39	41	42	43	44	45
British	14½	15	15½	16	16½	17	17½	18

Men's Shoes

American	7	8	9	10	11	12	13
Continental	39½	41	42	43	44½	46	47
British	6	7	8	9	10	11	12

INDEX

A

Abercrombie & Kent, 26
Academia Barilla (Parma), 320
Access codes (area codes), 29
Accommodations
  apartment and villa rentals, 26–27
  Bologna, 313
  Capri, 112
  chains, 24–27
  Cinque Terre, 306
  Como, 284–285
  Milan, 230–233
  Monaco, 299–300
  Naples, 106
  promotions, 26
  the Riviera, 296–297
  Rome, 72–75
  Venice, 186–189
Acqua di Parma (Milan), 279
Adriano Miani (Venice), 220
A. Gargiulo & Jannuzzi (Sorrento), 118
Agrinascente (Fidenza), 320–321
Air Berlin, 16
Air France, 14
Air One, 16, 19
Airport duty-free shops, 51
Air travel, 13–17, 19
  Milan, 224–225
  the Riviera, 293–294
  Rome, 65–66
Alberta Ferretti, 92, 211, 262
Alberto & Lina (Capri), 114
Alberto Aspesi (Milan), 255
Al Covo (Venice), 189–190
Aleph (Rome), 74
Alessandro Dari (Florence), 134–135
Alitalia, 13, 14, 19
Almaplena, 56
American Airlines, 14
American Express, car insurance, 22
Amina Rubinacci, 90, 115
Angela Caputi (Florence), 157–158
Angela Pintaldi (Milan), 270
Anna Molinari, 56
Antichità e Oggetti d'Arte (Venice), 218
Antico Setificio Fiorentino (Florence), 6, 135
Antiques
  customs regulations, 53
  Florence, 146–147
  Milan, 251
  Naples, 109
  Rome, 88
  Venice, 206
Antiques Abroad Ltd., 18
Antonio Fusco (Milan), 262
Apartment and villa rentals, 26–27
Arbor (Venice), 209
Archimidi Seguso (Murano), 203
Area codes, 29

Arezzo, 147
Armandola (Milan), 268
Armani, 39. *See also* Emporio Armani; Giorgio Armani
Armani Collezioni (Milan), 262
Armani Jeans (Venice), 211
Armani Megastore (Milan), 257–258
Armonie Naturali (Perlier/Kelemata; Milan), 253–254
Art Hotels (Bologna), 313
Art Store (Florence), 148
Astolfo (Venice), 207
ATMs (automated-teller machines), 47–48
Aveda (Rome), 89
Avis, 21, 22

B

Baglioni hotels, 24
B&B Italia (Milan), 269
Barberino Designer Outlet (between Florence and Bologna), 4, 44, 165
Baroni (Florence), 155
Barovier & Toso (Murano), 203
Bars, 40
Basement (Milan), 264–265
Bassetti (Milan), 271
Beauty and bath products. *See also* Perfumes; Pharmacies and soaps
  Florence, 147–148
  Milan, 251–254
  Rome, 89
  Venice, 206–207
Beauty Planet (Rome), 89
Bellini mix, 8
Bellora (Milan), 271
Benetton, 56, 92, 153
Berdondini, Maria Teresa, 27, 28, 126, 137, 140, 316
The Best in Italy, 26
Best Western, 297
Biella, 289–290
BM Book Shop (Florence), 149
BMI, 16
Boat tours and cruises. *See also* Ship, traveling by
  Naples, 111
Boggi (Milan), 274
Bollate Antiques Market (Milan), 267
Bologna, 310–318
Bono (Florence), 171
Bookstores
  Florence, 148–149
  Milan, 254
  Rome, 89–90
Boscolo hotels, 24
Bottega Artigiana del Libro (Florence), 168
Bottega Veneta, 56, 92, 102, 153, 262, 279
Bottega Veneta Factory (Vicenza), 329
Boutique lines, 55
Boutiques. *See* Designer boutiques
Brek (Milan), 233–234
Brera Antiques Market (Mercatone dell'Antiquariato; Milan), 267–268
Brioni, 56, 92, 153, 262
British Airways, 14
Brunetto Pratesi, 160, 176–177
Bruno Magli, 221–222, 279
Bulgari, 56, 211
Burano, 204–206
Burberry, 91, 260
Bus travel, Rome, 69, 72

C

Caffarel, 8
Caffè Florian (Venice), 190
Campo dei Fiori (Rome), 86
Capri, 110–115
Cardinal's socks, 9
Carlton Hotel Baglioni (Milan), 230–231
Carpe Diem (Milan), 250
Carpisa (Rome), 95
Car rentals, 21–22
Car services, 23
  Florence, 126
  Milan, 228
Carthusia Profumi (Capri), 115
Cartier, 91, 152, 210
Cartoleria Parione (Florence), 168–169
Car travel, 21–23
Casadei (Milan), 279
Cashmere Cotton and Silk (Milan), 274

Cashmeres
Capri, 113
Florence, 135, 147, 155, 166–167
Milan, 256–257, 274
Rome, 90
Casini (Florence), 149–150
Cassina (Milan), 269
Castel Guelfo, 322–323
Castel Guelfo Outlet City (near Rome), 44, 322–323
Castel Romano Designer Outlet (Rome), 44, 99
CC I Gigli (Campi Bisenzio), 173
Celine (Milan), 260
Celine (Rome), 91
Ceramica Assunta (Positano), 121
Ceramics, 120–121, 132, 156, 178
Chanel, 91, 211, 261
Chianti Cashmere Company (Florence), 135, 147
Chocolate postcards, 8
Chocolates, 56, 57
Christian Dior, Milan, 261
Cinque Terre, 306–307
Claudio Morlacchi (Parabiago), 282
Coca-Cola Price Index, 38
Coccinelle (Milan), 56, 279
Coffee, 57
Coin, 90, 151–152, 258, 304
Coin Beauty (Venice), 206–207
Colonna Fornace (Murano), 203
Colorcasa (Venice), 218
Commercianti (Bologna), 314
Como, Lake, and environs, 283–289
Cooking classes and tours, 27, 136–137, 150–151, 317
Cook Italy, 317
Corona d'Oro (Bologna), 314
Corso Buenos Aires (Milan), 246–247
Corso Vittorio Emanuele II (Milan), 244
Courier services, 35
Cova (Milan), 234
Crime, 34–35
C.U.C.I.N.A. (Rome), 97
Cucina Toscana (Faith Heller Willinger; Florence), 150
Culinary Vacations (Florence), 151
Currency exchange, 48
Custom Italy, 26
Customs regulations, 52–53

D

D&G, Rome, 92
D&G Uomo (Milan), 262
De Herbore (Florence), 148
Delta Air Lines, 14
Department stores
best, 5–6
Florence, 151–152
Milan, 257–260
Rome, 90–91
Deruta, 2–3, 178
Design Centro Italia, 27
Designer boutiques
Florence, 149–150, 152–154
Milan, 255–256, 260–264
Rome, 78, 91–95
Venice, 209–213
Desmo (Florence), 158
Detaxe scam, 51
DF/Diffusione Tessile, 46
Diego Dalla Palma (Milan), 252
Diego Della Valle, 57
Diesel, 57, 262, 281
Diesel Outlet (near Como), 288
Diffusione Seta (Como), 286–287
Diffusione Tessile (Max Mara Outlet; Milan), 237–238, 275–276
Dior (Rome), 91
Dior Homme (Milan), 274
Discounters and stock shops, Florence, 154–155
Discount System (Rome), 94
Ditta Luca Della Robbia (Florence), 156
DMagazine (Milan), 265
Dolce & Gabbana, 57–58, 92, 211, 262
Douglas, 278
Drogheria Mascari (Venice), 215
Ducci (Florence), 139
Due Torri Hotel Baglioni (Verona), 324, 326
Duties, 52–53
Duty-free shops at airports, 51

E

EasyJet, 16
Eddy Monetti (Milan), 274–275
Elena Mirò (Rome), 101
Elysee (Venice), 209
Elysee 2 (Venice), 209
Emilio Pucci, 39, 58, 153, 211, 262
Emporio Armani, 92, 153, 211
Emporio Armani Caffè (Milan), 234
Emporio della Setta (Como), 287
Emporio Lario (near Como), 288
Emporio Le Sirenuse (Positano), 7, 121–122
Enoteca Cotti (Milan), 269
Erboristeria Palazzo Vecchio (Florence), 148
Ermenegildo Zegna, 92, 153, 211, 262, 275, 289–290
Escada, 91, 152, 261
Etro, 58, 92, 211, 263, 279
Eurailpass, 17, 20
The euro, 47
Europe Car Service (Milan), 228
Eurostar Italia, 21
Exedra (Rome), 74
Eyeglass frames, Venice, 192, 213–214

F

Fabriano, 58, 95, 278
Fabric and ribbons. *See also* Linens and lace
  Florence, 135, 156, 157, 161
  Venice, 214–215
  Factory Store (Giorgio Armani), 3, 288–289, 330
Faith Heller Willinger (website), 27
Fakes, 38–39
  Murano glass, 195
Fantasie Fiorentine (Florence), 169
Farmaceutica di Santa Maria Novella, 100
  Florence, 135–136, 171, 178
Farmacia Molteni (Florence), 171
Fashion (clothing). *See also* Designer boutiques
  boutique lines, 55
  brands, 55–62
Fashion District (Rome), 99
Feltrinelli (Rome), 89
Fendi, 5, 39, 58, 92, 153, 212, 217, 263
Fidenza Village (between Milan and Bologna), 45, 321–322
Fiera Antiquaria Napoletana (Naples), 109
Fila (Biella), 290
Flea markets, 40, 42
  Florence and environs, 146–147, 161–162
  Milan, 267–268
Florence, 123–178
  accommodations, 128–130
  antiques, 146–147
  arriving in, 124–125
  best buys in, 131–133
  comparison shopping in, 137–138
  discounters and stock shops, 154–155
  eating in, 130
  foodstuffs, 155–156
  getting around, 125–126
  hidden finds in, 134–136
  home style, 156–157
  leather goods, 158–160
  linens and lace, 160–161
  markets, 161–164
  multiples, 164–165
  outlets, 165–168
  out-of-town touring, 140
  paper goods, 132, 168–170
  perfumes, 170
  pharmacies and soaps, 170–171
  phones and addresses in, 126
  shipping purchases home, 140–141
  shoes, 154, 171–173
  shopping hours, 138–139
  shopping neighborhoods, 141–145
  Sunday shopping, 30, 139–140
  taxis, 125–126
  warnings for shoppers, 133
FNAC, 58
Fogal (Milan), 261
Fontana (Milan), 255
Foodstuffs
  Florence, 155–156
  illegal, 53
  Milan, 268–269
  Venice, 215–216

Forte dei Marmi, 139, 177–178
Forum Termini (Rome), 79, 97
Foscarini (Murano), 203
Four Seasons Hotel Milano (Milan), 231
FoxTown (Switzerland), 45, 291
Francesco Biasia (Rome), 96
Francesco Rogani (Rome), 78, 96
Franciacorta Outlet Village (near Milan), 45, 277
Fratelli Mari, 178
Fratelli Piacenza Lanificio (Biella), 290
Fratelli Rossetti, Rome, 102
Fratelli Rossetti Factory (Parabiago), 282
Free Shop (Milan), 269
Frette, 58, 97, 153, 212, 272
Frezzeria (Venice), 200
Furla, 96–97, 158

G

Gaggio (Venice), 214
Galleria Machiavelli (Florence), 156
Galleria Mazzini (Genoa), 304
Gas, 23
Gaultier (Milan), 261
Gelateria Grom (Bologna), 315
Gelateria Stefino (Bologna), 315
Genninger Studio (Venice), 208
Genoa, 297, 302–305
Gf Ferré (Rome), 92
Gherardini (Florence), 159
The Ghetto (Rome), 88
Giacomo Rizzo (Venice), 216
Gianduja, 321
Gianfranco Ferré, 58, 92, 153, 212, 263
Gieves & Hawkes (Milan), 261
Gifts, best, 8, 10
Gio Moretti (Milan), 255
Giorgio Armani, 59
  Florence, 153
  Milan, 252, 263
  Rome, 92
  Venice, 211
Giorgio Armani (Black Label; Milan), 263
Giorgio Armani (Factory Store; near Como), 3, 288–289
Giulio Giannini e Figlio (Florence), 169
Glass
  Murano, 202–204
  Venice, 192, 193–195, 216–217
Global Refund, 50
Gloves, 95, 159
Gold jewelry, Florence, 133, 144
Grande Hotel Vesuvio (Naples), 106
Grand Hotel (Portovenere), 306
Grand Hotel Ambasciatori (Sorrento), 116
Grand Hotel Baglioni (Bologna), 314–315
Grand Hotel Et de Milan (Milan), 231
Grand Hotel Miramare (Santa Margherita Ligure), 297
Grand Hotel Quisisana (Capri), 112
Grand Hotel Villa Medici (Florence), 128
Grand/Medici (Florence), 142
The Gray (Milan), 233
Grevi (Florence), 136
Gucci, 59, 92, 153, 212, 218, 263
Gucci Caffè (Milan), 235
Guida Dove Agli Spacci, 43

H

Handbags
  Florence, 132–133
  Rome, 78, 95–97
  Venice, 217–218
H&M (Milan), 281
Harry's Bar (Venice), 190
Hermès, 91, 152, 211, 261
Hertz, 21
Hibiscus (Venice), 209
High Tech (Milan), 280
Hilton Milan, 232
Hogan
  Milan, 280
  Rome, 102
  Venice, 212
Holidays, shopping on, 31
Home style
  Florence, 156–157
  Milan, 269–270
  Rome, 79, 97
  Venice, 218–219

Hotel Accademia (Verona), 326
Hotel Ala (Venice), 188–189
Hotel Bernini Palace Baglioni (Florence), 128–129
Hotel Bisanzio (Venice), 188
Hotel Excelsior (Naples), 106
Hotel Manin (Milan), 233
Hotel Manzoni (Milan), 233
Hôtel Métropole (Monte Carlo), 300
Hotel Metropole Suisse (Como), 284
Hotel Miralago (Cernobbio), 284–285
Hotel Piranesi (Rome), 75
Hotel Punta Tragara (Capri), 112
Hotels. *See* Accommodations
Hotel Villa Igea (Venice), 189
Hugo Boss (Milan), 261

I

Il Ballo del Doge (Venice), 210
Il Bussetto (Florence), 159
Il Discount Dell'Alta Moda (Rome), 94
Il Giglio, 154–155, 177
Illy coffee, 57
Il Papiro, 169, 221
Il Salvagente (Milan), 265–266
Il Salvagente Bimbi (Milan), 266
In Folio (Venice), 221
Insurance, car, 22
Inter-Continental de la Ville Roma (Rome), 72
Inter-Continental hotels, 24
Internet access, 29
I Pellettieri d'Italia (Space Outlet; Montevarchi), 167–168
Italian Government Tourist Board, 27
The Italian Riviera. *See* The Riviera

J

January shopping, 31–32
Jesurum, 219, 272
Jewelry, 10
  Capri, 113
  Florence, 157–158
  Milan, 270–271
  Venice, 207–208
Jil Sander, 59
J. K. Place (Capri), 112
J. K. Place (Florence), 129–130
Jobbers (stochistas), 45
Johnsons & Relatives (Florence), 170
Jolly Hotel Firenze (Florence), 129
Jolly Hotel La Spezia (La Spezia), 307
Jolly Hotel President (Milan), 232
Jolly hotels, 24–25
Jolly Hotel Touring (Milan), 232
Just Cavalli, 93, 212, 263

K

Kalos (Milan), 250
Kemwel, 21
Kenzo, 91, 261
Kiko (Milan), 252
Kiton, 59, 263
Krizia, 59, 263

L

Laboratorio Artigiano Maschiere (Venice), 220
La Bottega dei Mascareri (Venice), 210
La Capannina Più (Capri), 115
La Carbonara (Rome), 76
Lace. *See* Linens and lace
Lacoste, 152, 211
La Coupole (Venice), 209
La Cuchina Fiorentina (Florence), 151
Ladurée (Monte Carlo), 300
Lake Como area, 283–289
Languages. *See also* Shoes
La Perla, 93, 263
  Venice, 212
La Perla Uomo (Milan), 263
La Rinascente
  Florence, 152
  Genoa, 304
  Milan, 5–6, 258–259
  Rome, 90
La Tessitura (Como), 287
Laura Ashley (Milan), 261
Laura Biagiotti, 59, 93, 212, 263
Laurèl (Florence), 152
La Vecchia Scuola Bolognese, 317
La Venexiana (Venice), 210
Leading Hotels of the World, 25
Leather goods. *See also* Handbags; Shoes
  Florence, 133–134, 158–160
  Milan, 279–280
  Venice, 217–218

Legatoria Piazzesi (Venice), 221
Le Maschiere de Dario Ustino (Venice), 220
Leonardo da Vinci International Airport, 5
Le Perle (Venice), 208
Les Copains, 59, 93, 263
Le Streghe (Rome), 86
Le Train Bleu (Monte Carlo), 300
Libreria Edison (Florence), 149
Limoncello, 8, 113
Limoni, 164–165
Limonoro (Sorrento), 118
Linens and lace
  Burano, 205
  Florence, 160–161
  Milan, 271–273
  Venice, 219–220
Liquids in your luggage, 51–52
Lisa Corti, 7, 121, 122
Lisa Corti Home Textile Emporium
  Florence, 156–157
  Milan, 238, 270
  Rome, 79–80
L'Isola (Venice), 216
L'Occitane (Milan), 253
Lorenzi (Milan), 280
Lorenzo Villoresi (Florence), 136
Loretta Caponi (Florence), 160
Loro Piana, 60, 153, 212
Lo Scopriaoccasioni, 42
Lo Scorpione (Prato), 177
Louis Vuitton, 91, 152, 211, 261
Lucca, 178
Luciano Barbera, 60
Lufthansa, 19
Luisa Cevese (Milan), 255
Luisa Via Roma (Florence), 150
Luna & L'Altra (Rome), 80
Luna Hotel Baglioni (Venice), 188
Lush, 9, 60
  Florence, 148
  Milan, 239, 253
  Venice, 207

M

Ma Boutique (Venice), 220
MAC (Milan), 253
McDonald's (Rome), 76
Made in Italy Online, 27
Madova Gloves (Florence), 159
Maglificio della Artema (Verrone-Biella), 290
Mail Boxes Etc. (Florence), 140
Mailing purchases home, 35
The Mall (Leccio), 4, 44, 166
Malls, Rome, 97
Malo
  Florence, 166–167
  Milan, 257
  Rome, 90
  Venice, 212
Manin 56 (Murano), 203
Manrico (Milan), 257
Mantelassi (Florence), 172
Maria Mazzaron (Venice), 219
Mariano Rubinacci (Naples), 109
Mariella Burani (Milan), 263
Marina Rinaldi, 101, 153, 212, 264
Marinella (Naples), 109–110
Mario & Peola Bevilacqua (Venice), 218
Marisa (Milan), 256
Markets, 40–42. *See also* Flea markets
  Florence, 161–164
  Milan, 273
  Rome, 98–99
  Venice, 199
Marni, 60
Martinuzzi (Venice), 219–220
Masks, Venice, 192, 220
Max & Co., 93, 154, 212, 264
Max Art Shop (Venice), 210
Maxi Ho (Naples), 110
Max Mara, 46, 93, 154, 212, 264
Max Mara Outlet (Diffusione Tessile; Milan), 237–238, 275–276
MCI Direct, 28
Menswear, Milan, 274–275
Mercatino dell'Antiquariato (Venice), 206
Mercato delle Cascine (Florence), 161
Mercato delle Pulci (Florence), 161–162
Mercato di Porta Portese (Rome), 98
Mercato di Viale Papiniano (San Agostino Market; Milan), 6, 273
Mercatone dell'Antiquariato (Brera Antiques Market; Milan), 267–268
Mercato Orientale (Genoa), 305
Mercerie (Venice), 200
Meridiana, 16–17, 19

Merola (Rome), 95
Metropolitana (Metro; Rome), 68–69
Milan, 2, 54, 223–291
  accommodations, 230–233
  antiques, 251
  arriving in, 224–226
  beauty and bath products, 251–254
  best buys, 236–237
  best stores, 237–239
  department stores, 257–260
  designer boutiques, 255–256, 260–264
  eating in, 233–235
  flea markets, 267–268
  foodstuffs, 268–269
  getting around, 227–228
  home style, 269–270
  jewelry, 270–271
  linens and lace, 271–273
  market, 273
  menswear, 274–275
  outlets in and near, 275–278
  paper goods, 278
  perfumes, 278–279
  personal needs, 242
  shoes and leather goods, 279–280
  shopping hours, 241
  shopping neighborhoods, 242–250
  Sunday shopping, 30, 241–242
  tabletop and gifts, 280
  teens and tweens, 281
  "the look" in, 240
Milanese style, 239–241
Milan Rule of Supply & Demand, 37–38
Milk-frothing machine, 8
Mills, 47
Missoni, 60, 93, 212, 264
Missoni Sport (Venice), 212
Miu Miu, 61, 154, 264
Monaco, 298–302
Mondadori (Milan), 254
Monday shopping, 30
Monte Carlo, 298–302
Montecatini, 140
Moronigomma (Milan), 280
Moschino (Milan), 61, 264
Moscow Rule of Shopping, 36–37
Mostra Mercato Constantinopoli (Naples), 109
Motorcycle tours, 316
Motorstars, 316
Murano glass, 192, 193, 195, 202–204
Myself (Milan), 257

N

Naples, 103–110
Navigli Antiques Market, 268
Nazareno Gabrielli (Milan), 264
Nice (France), air travel through, 17–18
Night hours, 32
Nino (Rome), 76–77
Novocento (Bologna), 314
Nutella, 61

O

Olive oil, 9, 132, 269
Onyx (Milan), 281
Oreficeria del Gelato (Bologna), 315
Orologio (Bologna), 313–314
Osteria dell'Antiquario (Rome), 86
Ottica Carraro (Venice), 213
Ottica Urbani (Venice), 214
Outlet (Milan), 276
Outlet shops and malls, 42–47
  best, 4
  books on, 42–43
  Florence and environs, 133, 137, 165–168
  malls, 43–45
  Rome, 99
Oviesse, 7, 64–65, 164–165, 259

P

Package deals, 15, 18
Papal merchandise (Rome), 100
Paper goods
  Florence, 132, 168–170
  Milan, 278
  Venice, 220–221
Parabiago, 282
Parma and environs, 318–322
Passamaneria Toscana (Florence), 157
Passamaneria Valmar (Florence), 157
Pasta, 8
Patrizia Pepe, 61
Paul Smith (Milan), 261
Pauly & Company (Venice), 216

Peck (Milan), 235
Pegna (Florence), 155
Perfumes, 170, 278–279
Perlier/Kelemata (Armonie Naturali; Milan), 253–254
Pharmacies and soaps. *See also* Beauty and bath products
  Florence, 170–171
  Rome, 100–101
Philosophy Di Alberta Ferretti (Milan), 264
Piazza Colonna (Rome), 97
Piazza delle Erbe (Verona), 328
Piazza Fontanella Borghese (Rome), 99
Piazzale Roma (Venice), 201
Piazza Pitti Cashmere (Florence), 155
Piazza San Marco (Venice), 200
Pineider (Florence), 170
Pineider (Milan), 278
Pisa, 147
Pistoia, 147, 175–177
Plus sizes, 101, 164
Pocket Coffees, 57
Ponte Milvio Market (Rome), 98
Ponte Vecchio (Florence), 139, 144
Portrait Suites (Rome), 75
Positano, 118–122
Prada, 93, 154, 213, 264
Pratesi, 61, 154, 160, 272. *See also* Brunetto Pratesi
Prato, 177
Profumeria Inglese (Florence), 170

R

Rail Europe, 19
Rancé (Rome), 101
Rapallo, 305–306
Raspini (Florence), 150
Ratti (Cadorago), 289
Regina Hotel Baglioni (Rome), 73
Relais & Châteaux hotels, 25
Rena Lange (Milan), 261
Rental Car Group, 21
Reservations, train, 20
Restaurants
  Florence, 130
  Milan, 233–235
  Rome, 76–77
  Venice, 189–191
Rialto Bridge (Venice), 201
Rigattieri (Venice), 219
Ristorante Girarrosto Toscano (Rome), 77
The Riviera, 292–307
  accommodations, 296–297
  getting around, 295–296
  traveling to, 293–295
Rizzoli (Milan), 254
Rizzoli Roma (Rome), 90
Roberta di Camerino, 61, 213
Roberto Cavalli, 61, 93, 213, 264
Rolando Segalin (Venice), 222
Roman Holiday Rule of Shopping, 38
Rome, 63–102
  accommodations, 72–75
  antiques, 88
  arriving in, 65–67
  beauty and bath products, 89
  best buys, 78–79
  best stores in, 79–81
  bookstores, 89–90
  cashmere, 90
  department stores, 90–91
  gloves, 95
  handbags, 95–97
  home style, 97
  mall, 97
  markets, 98–99
  neighborhoods, 82–88
  outlets, 99
  papal merchandise, 100
  personal needs, 82
  pharmacies and soaps, 100–101
  plus sizes, 101
  restaurants, 76–77
  shoes, 101–102
  shopping hours, 81
  special-event retailing, 82
  Sunday shopping, 30
  taxis, 68
Rome Cavalieri Hilton, 73–74
Rubelli (Venice), 214
Ryanair, 16

S

Sales, 32
Salvatore Ferragamo, 62
  Florence, 154, 172
  Milan, 264

Rome, 93
Venice, 213
Salviati (Venice), 216
Sambonet (Vercelli), 291
San Agostino Market (Mercato di Viale Papiniano; Milan), 273
San Lorenzo (Florence), 163
San Marco Rule of Shopping, 196
San Remo, 302
Santa Croce (Florence), 145
Santa Margherita Ligure, 305–306
Santa Maria Novella (Florence), 124, 164
Sant Ambroeus (Milan), 235
Sarzana, 307
Save the Queen (Florence), 154
Scams, 32–34, 51
Scarves, Naples, 109
Scuola del Cuoio (Florence), 159
Scuola di Merletti (Burano), 205
Security procedures, 51–52
Seguso (Venice), 217
Sent (Murano), 203
Sephora, 62
Sergio Rossi (Florence), 172
Serravalle Designer Outlet (between Genoa and Milan), 4, 44–45, 277–278, 296
Seterie Martinetti (Como), 287
Ship, traveling by
the Riviera, 295
Rome, 67–68
Venice, 183
Shipping Company (Florence), 140–141
Shipping purchases home, 35
Shoes, 62
Capri, 113
Florence, 154
Milan, 279–280
Rome, 101–102
Venice, 221–222
Shopping bags, 39
Shopping hours, 29–32. *See also specific cities*
Shu Uemura (Milan), 254
Siena, 147, 174–175
Siena Market, 6–7
Silk Museum (Como), 286
Silks, 134, 161, 214, 215, 217, 286, 326
Venice, 192
Sina hotels, 25
Soap, 8–9
Sofitel hotels, 25
Sole (Rome), 80
Solimene (Positano), 120
Sonia Rykiel (Milan), 261
Sonnenblume (Venice), 222
Sorrento, 115–118
Spaccio Etro (Milan), 238, 276
Space Outlet (I Pellettieri d'Italia; Montevarchi), 167–168
Spanish Steps/Via Condotti (Rome), 82–83
Sprint, 28
Standa, 91, 305
Starwood hotels, 25–26
Stochistas (jobbers), 45
Straw Market (Florence), 163–164
Street markets, best, 6
Summer hours, 31
Sunday shopping, 30
Rome, 81
Venice, 198
Switzerland, 291

T

Tad (Rome), 80–81
Tanino Crisci (Florence), 173
Taxis
Rome, 68
tipping drivers, 49
Tax refunds, 49–51
Telephones, 28–29
10 Corso Como (Milan), 1–2, 238, 256
10 Corso Como Caffè (Milan), 235
10 Corso Como Outlet (Milan), 276–277
Terrazza Danieli (Venice), 191
Tezemis (Milan), 272–273
Thrifty By Car, 21
Through the Looking Glass, 18
Ties, Rome, 79
Tincati (Milan), 275
Tipping, 48–49

Tod's, 39, 102, 213, 264
Tornabuoni area (Florence), 141
Toscanamia (Florence), 155–156
Tours, shopping, 18, 27–28
Train travel, 19–20
  Florence, 124
  from London and continental Europe, 14, 16
  Milan, 226
  the Riviera, 294
  Rome, 66–67
  Venice, 181
Traveling to Italy, 13–18
Trenitalia, 16
Trevi and Tritone fountains (Rome), 84
Trussardi
  Florence, 154
  Rome, 93
  Venice, 213
Tuscany by Tuscans, 27, 28, 126, 316

U

United Airlines, 14
UPIM, 90–91, 110, 259–260, 305
USA Direct (AT&T), 28
US Airways, 14

V

Valentino, 62, 93, 213
Valextra (Milan), 280
Valli (Venice), 214–215
VAT (value-added tax) refunds, 49–51
The Vatican, 27
Venetia Studium (Venice), 2, 215
Venice, 3, 179–222
  accommodations, 186–189
  addresses in, 186
  antiques, 206
  arriving in, 181–183
  beauty and bath products, 206–207
  best buys, 191–192
  designer boutiques, 209–213
  eating in, 189–191
  eyeglass frames, 192, 213–214
  fairs and markets, 199
  foodstuffs, 215–216
  getting around, 183–184
  glass, 193–195, 202–204, 216–217
  gondoliers, 196–197
  handbags and leather goods, 217–218
  home style, 218
  jewelry, 207–208
  linens and lace, 219–220
  masks, 192, 220
  paper goods, 220–221
  porters, 185–186
  shipping purchases home, 199
  shoes, 221–222
  shopping history, 180
  shopping hours, 197–198
  shopping neighborhoods, 199–201
  silks, 192
  street vendors, 198–199
  Sunday shopping, 30, 198
Venice Card, 184
Venini (Venice), 217
Ventilo (Milan), 261
Vercelli, 290–291
Verona, 323–329
Versace, Florence, 154
Vestistock (Milan), 266–267
Vetreria Foscari (Murano), 204
Vetreria Gritti (Murano), 204
Via dei Cestari (Rome), 85
Via dei Coronari (Rome), 85–86
Via dei Tornabuoni (Florence), 141
Via del Babuino (Rome), 83–84
Via del Corso (Rome), 85
Via del Governo Vecchio (Rome), 86, 88
Via del Tritone (Rome), 84–85
Via Durini (Milan), 245
Via Fontanella Borghese (Rome), 83
Via Montenapoleone (Milan), 243
Via Nazionale (Rome), 84
Via Roma (Florence), 143–144
Via Sannio (Rome), 98
Via Sant'Anastasia (Verona), 327
Via Veneto (Rome), 84
Victoria (Sarzana), 307
Vietri (Positano), 120
Viktor & Rolf (Milan), 262
Villa d'Este (near Como), 7–8, 285
Villa Laetitia (Rome), 75
Villa San Michele School of Cookery (Florence), 151
Villas International, 26

Vintage clothing, 62
Viterbo, 146–147
Volare, 16
Vueling, 16

W

Websites, 27
Westin hotels, 25–26
Willinger, Faith Heller, 150–151
Wines and wineries, 296
Wolford, 153, 211, 262

Y

You & Me, 208, 239, 271
Yves Saint Laurent (Florence), 152
Yves Saint Laurent Rive Gauche (Rome), 91

Z

Zara, 165, 281
Zora (Venice), 217

Notes

Notes